M000121821

Pass it on...

A Cookbook published by Delta Delta Delta National Fraternity

Additional copies may be obtained at the cost of $17.95,
plus $3 postage and handling, each book.
Texas residents add $1.40 sales tax, each book.
Send To:
Delta Delta Delta
P.O. Box 5987
Arlington, TX 76005-5987

ISBN: 0-9639957-0-7

LCCN: 93-74842

Copyright ©1994, Delta Delta Delta, Arlington, TX

First Printing   10,000   June, 1994

Artwork - Bob Haydon
Consulting - Sheryn Jones and Josie Ware

Printed in the USA by

WIMMER
The Wimmer Companies, Inc.
Memphis • Dallas

INTRODUCTION

"It only takes a spark to get a fire going, and soon all those around will warm up to its glowing."

These opening lines of Kurt Kaiser's song "Pass It On", which is loved by Tri Deltas everywhere, helped inspire and title this project, *Pass It On...A Treasury of Tastes and Traditions.*

The recipes and traditions collected in *Pass It On...*serve as our "sparks." Once shared with another, a recipe or tradition lives on beyond the originator. Each cook can add a personal touch or variation, and a recipe can actually become better the more it is passed on. By sharing a recipe or tradition, we can give a part of ourselves and touch lives far beyond a single location or circle of family and friends. When we have something special, it's only natural we want to share it with others.

As we live by Tri Delta's open motto, "Let us steadfastly love one another," we reach out to each other. From a sisterhood based on sharing, we take pleasure in giving you some of our best recipes and richest traditions to enjoy with your own family and friends. We hope that you too will want to *Pass It On...*

Eve Woods Riley
Delta Delta Delta National President
1992-1994

DELTA DELTA DELTA

Delta Delta Delta is an international collegiate women's fraternity which was established at Boston University in 1888. It has a diverse membership of over 175,000, with 129 collegiate and 350 alumnae chapters.

Like all fraternities and sororities, Tri Delta primarily is a friendship group, but its purpose also includes encouraging members to assume "the highest responsibilities of college women." The Delta Delta Delta Foundation and its philanthropic program perhaps best illustrates the scope of such efforts. The Crescent Fund assists members in need, but Tri Delta's foremost charitable efforts always have been in the field of education for women, and numerous scholarships and fellowships are available for both undergraduate and graduate members. A major Centennial gift of more than three quarters of a million dollars was presented in 1988 to the National Humanities Center in Research Triangle Park, North Carolina, where research scholars receive grants annually.

Tri Delta's other major philanthropy is Children's Cancer Charities, wherein philanthropic efforts of both collegiate and alumnae chapters are directed to oncologic centers for children in all areas of the country. More than $500,000 is raised annually for these clinics and hospitals, and countless volunteer hours and special equipment items are donated as well. In some places, special recognition of these contributions has taken the form of names of wings, rooms or entire units.

Friendship, philanthropies, sharing and caring is what Tri Delta is all about.

Margaret Paddock Haller
Past National President 1958-62

TABLE OF CONTENTS

Cookbook Committee

Martha Toler Williams, Cookbook Chairman
Mary Estelle Kanning Amberg, Alumnae Vice President
Kathy Robinson Hillman, Lifestyles and College Intern Coordinator
Deborah Green Shotwell, Production and Marketing Coordinator
June Rickard Aldridge, Area Coordinator
Carol Sibley Garner, Area Coordinator
Betty Joyce Bevis Hand, Area Coordinator
Sherry Hildreth Jorgenson, Area Coordinator
Sara Burwash Soracco, Area Coordinator
Anne Booth, Proofreader
Carole Hauge Carpenter, Proofreader
Angela Hackett Driver, Proofreader
Karen Terhune Francisco, Proofreader
Susan Hakes, Proofreader

Acknowledgements

Mary Steinmetz Ward, 1993 Cookbook Chairman
Linda Trojan Juba, 1992 Cookbook Chairman
Carrie Bradley Crudup, Past Lifestyles Chairman
Pat Stansfield Norris, Past Area Coordinator
Marsha Beck Sparks, Past Editor
Janet Veerman Harvey, Past Design/Graphics
LuLu Peal Grace, Past Nutrition Analysis Chairman
Sally Byrd Jilek, Past Marketing Chairman
Bonnie McLean Peterson, Past Administrative Assistant
Elizabeth Hunter Peabody, Past Consultant
Connie Armstrong, College Intern
1990-1992 Executive Board of Delta Delta Delta
1992-1994 Executive Board of Delta Delta Delta
Delta Delta Delta Executive Office Staff
Members and friends of Delta Delta Delta Fraternity

In loving memory of:
Peg Hart Harrison
Area Coordinator

Appetizers & Beverages

The prettiest ever ice ring was floating in the punch bowl - real pansies and small ivy leaves had been frozen in the ice. Mary said it was easy to a What a great idea to pa on to you. much love, mom

ANNIVERSARY PUNCH

Makes 6 quarts

Note: Requires freezing period.

6 bananas
1 can frozen lemonade, undiluted
1 can frozen orange juice,
   undiluted
2 (12-ounce) cans peach nectar

1 (46-ounce) can pineapple juice
3 cups water
2 cups sugar
2 (64-ounce) bottles of lemon-lime
   carbonated soda

▲ Combine the bananas, lemonade and orange juice in a blender. Mix well. Pour into a large container and add peach nectar, pineapple juice, water and sugar. Freeze. To serve, thaw until slightly slushy (just enough to get out of container). Add two bottles lemon-lime carbonated beverage. Stir just enough to mix. Garnish with orange and lemon slices.

Pass It On...My sister, Janet, and her husband have taken a picture using the same pose every anniversary. My nieces enjoy the special album to see how funny their mom and dad looked when "they were young." Preparing a similar holiday or birthday album would be a great tradition, too.

APPLECOT PUNCH

16 servings

3 sticks cinnamon
1 teaspoon whole cloves
6 whole allspice
1 (46-ounce) bottle apple juice

1 (12-ounce) bottle apricot nectar
1 (6-ounce) can lemonade
   concentrate

▲ Pour all ingredients into large kettle. Simmer 10 minutes and serve warm.

Pass It On...One summer at my grandfather's farm in central Ohio, my older brother (then about 14 or 15) decided we should make fresh cider. He dug out the old cider press from back in the corner of the barn and washed it thoroughly. My assignment was to wash the apples. We cut out the bad spots and then pressed. Boy, was it good! No commercial cider ever tasted quite like it.

ALMOND TEA

Makes 4 quarts

1½ cups sugar
2 cups boiling water
3 tablespoons instant lemon tea
1 (12-ounce) can frozen lemonade

3 teaspoons almond extract
3 teaspoons vanilla extract
2½ quarts cold water

▲ Mix all ingredients together and serve over ice or chilled in a punchbowl.

Pass It On...*Always read through every recipe first before beginning preparation.*

ICE CREAM BRANDY ALEXANDERS

4 servings

1 quart coffee ice cream, slightly softened
5 tablespoons brandy
5 tablespoons crème de cacao

¼-½ cup half-and-half (depending on desired consistency)
whipped cream
grated nutmeg

▲ Place the ice cream, brandy, crème de cacao and half-and-half in blender. Blend on medium speed until smooth. Pour into 4 glasses. Garnish with whipped cream and grated nutmeg. Serve immediately.

Pass It On...*A great way to combine dessert and an after dinner drink. This may also be made ahead and frozen (allow to thaw as guests complete the main course).*

CAFE MEXICANO

A spicy, rich mocha...a great pick-me-up for a cold, rainy afternoon

4 servings

4 teaspoons chocolate syrup
½ cup whipping cream
¾ teaspoon cinnamon
¼ teaspoon nutmeg

1 tablespoon sugar
1½ cups hot, strong coffee, preferably Mexican

▲ Put one teaspoon chocolate syrup into each of 4 (4-ounce) warm cups. Combine whipping cream, ¼ teaspoon cinnamon, nutmeg and sugar. Whip into soft peaks. Stir remaining ½ teaspoon cinnamon into hot coffee and pour into cups. Stir to blend with syrup. Top with spiced whipped cream.

Pass It On...*Coffee and unpopped popcorn will stay fresh longer if stored in the freezer.*

CAFE AU VIN

A great dinner coffee

2 servings

1 cup cold strong French roast
coffee, regular or
decaffeinated
2 tablespoons granulated sugar

dash of cinnamon
2 ounces tawny port
½ teaspoon orange peel, grated

▲ Combine ingredients in blender and mix at high speed. Pour into chilled wine glasses.

Pass It On...To honor some friends who were moving out of town, we turned our house into the "Love Boat" and invited 12 couples to join us for a "dinner cruise." The "passengers" walked up a gang plank to reach the entry. Inside, we had draped the stair railing with thick ropes and hung a huge life preserver inscribed "Bon Voyage, Don and Sue!". The rest of the house was dotted with construction paper portholes. Everyone dressed for glitz. Those who didn't own anything glamorous enough had visited the local thrift shop earlier in the week. As each couple arrived, the ship's photographer took their picture in front of the life preserver. Copies of the photos were given to Don and Sue as well as to each couple as a party favor. Appetizers were passed until dinner time. We needed three tables to seat all the guests. At each table we left two extra seats reserved for the guests of honor. They joined one table for salad, another during the main course and the last for dessert. After dessert, we distributed a "Don and Sue Trivia Quiz" to each table, and they competed to answer the most questions. To close the evening, we moved to the ship's lounge (living room) for flavored coffee, and everyone shared a Don and Sue story, toast or blessing.

CELEBRATION CHAMPAGNE PUNCH

20 servings

1 fifth Chablis or other dry white wine
1 fifth Champagne

1 quart ginger ale
orange peel

For Decorating Ice Ring:
slices of lemon, lime, orange
piece of holly

cherries, strawberries, cranberries, pansies

▲ Pour chilled wines and ginger ale over the decorative ring of ice in a punch bowl. Stir to mix and add a few spirals of orange peel (with white pith removed). For decorative ice ring: Fill a plastic container or ring mold with water to cover bottom and freeze to slush. Add slices of lemon, lime, orange, piece of holly, pansies, cherries, strawberries and cranberries in a design. Add a bit more water and freeze; continue adding fruit and water until filled. Freeze, then unmold and place in punch bowl.

Pass It On...These days more and more of my party guests either cut back on their alcohol intake or abstain altogether. To make non-drinking friends feel at home and to move the party emphasis away from alcohol, I offer an H$_2$O Bar. I buy a wide assortment of interesting bottled waters - Australian, Mendocino, raspberry or kiwi-flavored sodas and geyser waters. I make a creative sign with the letters "H$_2$O" and highlight it with glitter or balloons. I then display the waters by flavor, even putting some in a cooler like wine. I always serve the waters and non-alcoholic beverages in wine glasses. This makes an acceptable alternative for friends who aren't drinking or for the occasional guests who may have already had just a little more than their share.

SOFIA'S COCKTAIL DESSERT

A great summer cooler

4 servings

1 pint vanilla ice cream
6 ounces Kahlua
6 ounces Amaretto

1 cup half-and-half
handful of ice

▲ Blend all ingredients in blender and serve in chilled glasses.

COFFEE PUNCH

8-12 servings

¼ cup sugar
2 tablespoons instant coffee
crystals
½ teaspoon cinnamon
¼ teaspoon ground cloves
1 teaspoon vanilla extract

6 cups milk
¼ teaspoon orange extract
1 quart coffee ice cream
½ cup whipping cream, whipped
ground nutmeg
dash of salt

▲ Combine sugar, cinnamon, cloves, coffee crystals, vanilla and a dash of salt. Add milk and extracts. Stir until sugar dissolves. Chill. Spoon ice cream into punch bowl. Pour coffee mixture over ice cream. Top with whipped cream and sprinkle with nutmeg.

Pass It On...If coffee ice cream isn't available, use vanilla ice cream and double coffee crystals.

HOT CRANBERRY PUNCH

Reheats nicely in microwave

36 (¾) cup servings

2 (32-ounce) bottles cranberry
juice cocktail
20 cups water
2-4 cups white sugar (less can be
used)

½ cup fresh lemon juice
2 whole cinnamon sticks
1 tablespoon whole cloves
2 cups orange juice

▲ In large kettle combine all ingredients except orange juice. Simmer 10 minutes. Add 2 cups orange juice. Serve hot. Drain off spices before refrigerating leftovers.

Pass It On...If desired, transfer to a slow cooker to keep hot.

MRS. WRIGHT'S EGG NOG

10-12 servings

1 quart whipping cream
6 egg yolks, lightly beaten by hand

sugar to taste
whiskey

▲ Add sugar to egg yolks. Add 8-10 tablespoons whiskey or to taste. Beat cream in mixer (not too stiff). Gently fold egg mixture into whipped cream.

Pass It On...Each Christmas season at the family farm, Martlesham Heath, we enjoyed salted and sugared pecans with Mrs. Wright's Egg Nog.

FANTASY PUNCH

25-30 servings

2 (6-ounce) packages peach or apricot gelatin
1 cup boiling water
3 cups warm water
1 (12-ounce) can frozen lemonade, undiluted

1 (46-ounce) can peach or apricot nectar
1 (46-ounce) can pineapple juice
½ gallon cold water
4 quarts chilled ginger ale

▲ Dissolve flavored gelatin in boiling water. Add all liquids except ginger ale. Freeze in one-quart containers or 4 containers of equal size. Remove from freezer one hour before serving and allow to thaw. To serve, scoop mixture into chilled glasses, filling each glass half full. Pour white wine, champagne or ginger ale over mixture to fill the glass.

FRUIT PUNCH

20 servings

5 cups water
1 cup sugar
16 individual tea bags
12 two-inch sprigs of mint

1 large frozen orange juice
1 large frozen lemonade
4½ cans water, measured using orange juice/lemonade can

▲ Bring 5 cups of water to a hard boil. Add tea bags and crushed mint. Let sit for 10 minutes. Add 1 cup sugar and mix until sugar is thoroughly dissolved. Add orange juice, lemonade and cold water. Serve in iced tea glasses with a sprig of fresh mint, a strawberry, or with a slice of fresh peach in season.
Pass It On...Equally good served hot.

SPARKLING GRAPE PUNCH

Servings vary

white grape juice
ginger ale

grapes
mint leaves

▲ Mix equal parts of white grape juice and ginger ale in a punch bowl. Float an ice ring containing grapes and mint leaves in the punch bowl.
Pass It On...The number one cause of fatigue is dehydration. Drink water. Nothing else reverses dehydration faster, and cool water works better than cold. The body first heats anything cold to body temperature before using it. Try one or two glasses of water during an afternoon low for a perk up!

13

FRESH PEACH PUNCH

A perfect recipe for a ladies' event

40-50 servings

4 cups ripe peaches, pureed in blender
1 (12-ounce) can frozen orange juice concentrate, thawed

1 (12-ounce) can frozen lemonade concentrate, thawed
2 (1-liter) bottles club soda
2 bottles champagne

For Ice Ring:
1 cup fruit juice mixture   **¾ cup water**

▲ Peel, pit, and puree ripe peaches in blender. Add orange juice and lemonade concentrates. Refrigerate. Add club soda and champagne just before serving. For ice ring: Combine ice ring ingredients and freeze in ring or cubes.

PUNCH FOR A BUNCH

25-30 servings

1-1¼-ounce package flavored drink mix
1 cup sugar
1 quart warm water
1 (6-ounce) can frozen lemonade

1 (12-ounce) can unsweetened pineapple juice
1 (6-ounce) can frozen orange juice
2 (28-ounce) bottles ginger ale

▲ Dissolve drink mix in warm water. Add sugar. Stir until dissolved. Add juices and freeze well. Thaw several hours before use. Pour into punch bowl and add ginger ale.

Pass It On...We celebrated my daughter's 16th birthday and her brand new driver's license with a traffic theme. Red octagonal signs reading, "Stop and Wish Shelley a Happy Birthday," lined the sidewalk, and red, yellow and green streamers decorated the room. The serving table featured a red checked cloth, miniature traffic signs, and red, yellow and green paper goods. A stuffed bear held red, yellow and green balloons and a stop sign (I wasn't successful locating a stop light). Refreshments carried out the color scheme, including yellow punch and cookies made with red, yellow and green chocolate covered candies (we saved the orange and black for Halloween).

CHURCH CROWD'S PERCOLATOR PUNCH

Especially good in cool or cold weather

30 servings

*9 cups unsweetened pineapple
    juice
9 cups cranberry juice cocktail
4½ cups water
1 cup brown sugar*

*3-4 whole cloves
4 cinnamon sticks, broken into
    pieces
¼ teaspoon salt*

▲ Remove any residual coffee oils in the pot by washing the coffee pot with soap and hot water followed with a vinegar and water rinse and then rinse again with clean water before using. Repeat this procedure after use. Put juices and water in a 30-cup percolator. Place sugar, spices and salt in percolator basket. Assemble, plug and perk.

ORANGE COFFEE

1 serving

*1 orange slice
4-ounces strong, hot coffee,
    regular or decaffeinated*

*4 ounces hot chocolate
¼ cup sweetened whipped cream
⅛ teaspoon cinnamon*

▲ Place orange slice into a warm 8-ounce mug. Pour coffee and hot chocolate over orange. Top with sweetened whipped cream and sprinkle with cinnamon.

Pass It On...Baking soda absorbs odors in the refrigerator or freezer and removes stains from coffee pots.

TANGY TEA

5 servings

2 family size tea bags
3 cups boiling water
1 cup sugar (less if desired)
1 (6-ounce) can cranberry juice,
    undiluted

1 (6-ounce) can lemonade,
    undiluted
2 cups water

▲ Pour boiling water over tea bags and steep about 5 minutes, discard bags. Add sugar and stir well to dissolve. Combine tea with juice, lemonade and water. Chill and serve over ice garnished with lemon.

Pass It On... "Let us remember that our freedom allows us to believe, to belong, to accept responsibility, to be involved, to lead, to do something about that for which we care." - Mary Kay Paup Baker, Delta Delta Delta National President 1972-76

SANGRIA

24-30 servings

3 (1.5-liters) red zinfandel wine
2 cans concentrated frozen orange
    juice
½ cup sugar

½ cup water
2 bottles ginger ale
2 each of lemons, limes and
    oranges, sliced

▲ Make simple syrup by boiling sugar and water until sugar dissolves, then cool. Combine wine, orange juice and ginger ale. Sweeten to taste with sugar syrup. Place in punch bowl and float fruit slices on top.

Pass It On ...This is especially attractive when served from a limonada or large glass barrel shaped jar sometimes found in Mexican markets.

ARTICHOKE FRITTATA

8 servings

3 (6½-ounce) jars marinated
    artichokes (substitute non-
    marinated artichokes for fewer
    calories)
½ pound medium Cheddar cheese,
    grated

1 small onion, finely chopped
4 large eggs, lightly beaten
6 single soda crackers, crushed
dash of hot pepper sauce
salt and pepper
Parmesan cheese

▲ Preheat oven to 325°. Drain artichokes and chop into small pieces. Mix with the remaining ingredients and pour into a buttered 8 to 9-inch quiche or pie pan. Bake in 325° oven for 35-40 minutes or until a knife inserted in the side comes out clean. Center should be loose, as it will continue to cook after removing from oven. Top with additional Parmesan cheese, if desired. Let set 10-15 minutes before cutting. Cut into 1-inch squares and serve warm.

Pass It On...Can be made a day ahead, then reheated at 350° for about 10-15 minutes before serving.

STUFFED BELGIAN ENDIVE

18-20 servings

3 Belgian endives
3 ounces cream cheese
3 ounces blue cheese (any variety)
2 tablespoons parsley, chopped

¼ teaspoons garlic powder
2½ ounces alfalfa sprouts for
    garnish

▲ Trim bottom from endive and separate leaves. Blend softened cheeses, parsley and garlic powder with fork. Spread 1 tablespoon mixture on bottom of each endive leaf. Garnish with sprouts. Cover with damp towel and plastic wrap and refrigerate until ready to serve.

Pass It On...Substitute drained yogurt for cream cheese for a light touch.

PANSY BRIE

A beautiful, festive appetizer

30-40 servings

fresh pansies
1 envelope unflavored gelatin
2 cups dry white or blush wine

2 pound wheel of Brie cheese, well
 chilled
crackers or baguettes

▲ Cut a paper pattern the size and shape of the cheese to plan the arrangement of the pansies on the top of the cheese. Sprinkle gelatin over wine in a small saucepan. Let stand 3 minutes. Stir constantly over low heat until mixture almost boils, looks clear, and gelatin is completely dissolved. Chill in refrigerator about 1 hour, stirring 3 or 4 times until mixture thickens to consistency of unbeaten egg white (to speed up, set pan in bowl of ice water, stirring often, about 15 minutes). If mixture gets too stiff, reheat and chill again.

Put cheese on a rack over waxed paper in a large, shallow pan. Spoon a thin coating of the gelatin mixture over top and sides of cheese. Let stand about 3 minutes until almost set. Press in decorations. Refrigerate, uncovered, 10 to 15 minutes, until gelatin is completely set. Add another layer of gelatin mixture; chill until set. Repeat procedure, adding one or two more layers as necessary to thoroughly cover cheese and decorations. When last layer is completely set, slide cheese onto plate or board. Cover with an inverted bowl large enough to cover cheese without touching it. Refrigerate up to 8 to 12 hours. Serve with crackers or baguettes. Garnish with pansies or other edible flowers and/or fresh herbs.

Pass It On... *"We must recognize the fact that the quest for self-knowledge is an ongoing one. It will never be completed because we are constantly changing." - Sara Vaughn Gabbard, Delta Delta Delta National President 1980-84*

STUFFED BAKED BRIE

A guaranteed hit at your next cocktail party

12-16 servings

1 jar pesto sauce (or make your own)
1 (8-ounce) piece Brie cheese

1 egg white, beaten with a fork
1 package of puff pastry sheets (not shells)

▲ Drain oil from pesto. Cut Brie in half horizontally. Spread pesto on top side of bottom layer. Place other layer of Brie on top of pesto, cut side down. Slightly roll out thawed dough. Place entire Brie on top of pastry sheet. Brush corners and edges with egg white wash. Fold up edges, completely enclosing cheese. Brush top with egg white wash. Bake in 375° oven for 25 minutes. Let stand 25 minutes before serving.

Pass It On...*Use Havarti instead of Brie; substitute pepper jelly, chutney, champagne mustard or dill for pesto sauce.*

BRUSCETTA

8 servings

1 loaf (3"- 4" diameter) Italian bread (or any other crusty bread)
4-6 tomatoes, peeled and chopped
2 cloves garlic, finely chopped

1 medium onion, finely chopped
1 tablespoon olive oil
2 sprigs fresh basil, chopped
dash of salt and pepper

▲ Mix all ingredients, except bread. Refrigerate. When ready to serve, cut bread into ½-inch slices. Place on baking sheet and drizzle with olive oil. Place pan under 500° broiler until just brown. Remove, top with tomato mixture and serve (napkins necessary). Serve with soup for a delicious light supper.

CINDY'S HOT CRABMEAT APPETIZER

6-8 servings

8 ounces cream cheese, softened
1 teaspoon half-and-half
½ teaspoon Worcestershire sauce
½ pound backfin crabmeat
½ small onion, minced

½ teaspoon horseradish
½ teaspoon salt
1 teaspoon butter
¼ cup almonds, toasted and sliced

▲ Preheat oven to 350°. Blend cream cheese with half-and-half and Worcestershire sauce in small bowl. Blend in crab, onion and horseradish. Mix well and add salt. Butter a small oven-proof dish and fill with crab mixture. Sprinkle almonds on top and bake for 15 minutes. Finish by broiling to brown the top for 3-4 minutes. Serve with assorted crackers.

Pass It On...Christmas Eve we always served a buffet of appetizers instead of a sit-down dinner. As we helped ourselves to the food, we sat by the roaring fire to share fun and family time. Pickled herring always found its way to the buffet. I can almost smell the fresh fish as I remember the trips to the fish markets where we scooped out pickled herring from huge wooden barrels.

SMOKED SALMON DEVILED EGGS

A colorful dish to serve to guests

12 deviled eggs

12 hard cooked eggs
¼ pound smoked salmon
6 tablespoons cream cheese
2 tablespoons sour cream
2 tablespoons lemon juice
2 teaspoons fresh dill, chopped

2 teaspoons snipped chives or
green part of onions
salt and freshly ground pepper
salmon caviar to garnish
dill sprigs to garnish

▲ Carefully cut cooked eggs in half and reserve the egg white halves. Puree the yolks, salmon, cream cheese, sour cream and lemon juice in a food processor or blender. Stir in dill and chives or scallions. Season with salt and pepper to taste. Refrigerate until needed to fill hard boiled egg white halves. Garnish with salmon caviar, dill sprigs or both.

Pass It On...To remove shells from hard boiled eggs, rinse immediately in cold water. Shells come off of eggs more easily if eggs aren't fresh.

AUNT EVELYN'S CHEESE BALL

30-35 servings

2 (3-ounce) wedges bleu cheese
2 (5-ounce) jars Old English
cheese spread
4 (3-ounce) packages cream
cheese

1 teaspoon Worcestershire sauce
1 teaspoon onion, grated
½ cup pecans, finely chopped
½ cup parsley, finely chopped

▲ Let cheese soften to room temperature. Combine cheeses, onion, Worcestershire sauce, half the nuts and parsley. Spoon into round bottom bowl lined with plastic wrap and chill overnight. About half an hour before serving, remove from bowl, roll in remaining nuts and parsley. Serve with unpeeled tart and sweet apples and fancy crackers.

CURRIED CHUTNEY COCKTAIL CHEESE

Makes 1½ cups

1 (8-ounce) package cream cheese
1 (9-ounce) jar chutney (Major
Grey's)
¼ teaspoon dry mustard

½ cup ground pecans
½ teaspoon curry powder (or more
to taste)

▲ Blend all ingredients into softened cream cheese. Serve in a bowl as a spread or divide into two patties and chill. Decorate patties with pecan halves and wrap in plastic wrap. Freeze or refrigerate before serving.

Pass It On...Make into one large patty for a more dramatic presentation.

SMOKED TURKEY CHEESE BALL

18-20 servings

1 cup finely ground smoked turkey
1 (8-ounce) package cream cheese
3 tablespoons mayonnaise

½ cup pecans, chopped
2 tablespoons parsley, chopped

▲ Combine first three ingredients well and chill for several hours. Shape into one or two balls and roll in pecans and parsley. Wrap well, freeze or refrigerate. If you are freezing, omit the mayonnaise.

Pass It On...To keep prepared ahead carrot and celery sticks fresh, place in jars, cover with water, and put on the refrigerator shelf.

PESTO CHEESECAKE

A savory appetizer to go with crackers

8-10 servings

Crust:

1 tablespoon butter at room temperature
¼ cup dry breadcrumbs

2 teaspoons Parmesan cheese, freshly grated

Cheesecake:

2 (8-ounce) packages cream cheese
1 cup ricotta cheese
½ cup Parmesan cheese, freshly grated
¼ teaspoon salt

⅛ teaspoon cayenne pepper
3 large eggs
½ cup purchased pesto sauce
¼ cup pine nuts or pecans, sliced and roasted

▲ Preheat oven to 325°. Butter bottom and side of 9-inch spring form pan. Mix breadcrumbs with 2 teapoons Parmesan cheese. Coat pan with mixture. With electric mixer, beat cream cheese, ricotta, remaining ½ cup Parmesan, salt and cayenne until light. Add eggs, one at a time, beating well after each addition. Transfer ½ of the mixture into medium bowl. Mix pesto with remaining half of mixture. Pour pesto mixture into prepared pan. Smooth top. Carefully spoon reserved mixture over top and smooth gently. Sprinkle with nuts. Bake about 45 minutes (center should not move when pan is shaken). Cover tightly and refrigerate overnight. Loosen around edges with knife and transfer to serving platter. Serve with crackers.

Pass It On...*Pour a good grade of olive oil in a dish and sprinkle with Italian herbs, minced garlic and freshly grated Parmesan cheese. Serve with warm French bread slices for dipping.*

RICOTTA-STUFFED CHARD LEAVES

6 servings

6 chard leaves (wash well - remove
*   but save white stems)*
1 cup ricotta cheese
4 green onions, chopped, including
*   green tops*
1 sprig parsley, chopped

2 tablespoons pine nuts, lightly
*   toasted*
2 tablespoons Monterey Jack
*   cheese, grated (or Parmesan*
*   cheese, grated)*
1 (17-ounce) can tomato sauce

▲ To prepare leaves: Have ready two large pans, one filled with boiling water, the other filled with cold water. Dip leaves into boiling water, one at a time, for 1-2 minutes. With fork or spatula, remove leaf and plunge it into cold water. Place on clean, dry towel. Dry carefully with another towel; they will be very fragile. For filling: Wash and chop the chard stems very finely. Boil 8-10 minutes, drain, and let cool. Mix ricotta cheese, green onions, parsley, pine nuts and chard stems. To assemble: Place a spoonful of filling in center of each leaf. Fold in the sides and roll up. Place folded side down in flat 9x13-inch baking dish. Top with tomato sauce and a sprinkling of cheese. Bake uncovered 25 minutes in a 350° oven.

TEX-MEX CORN DIP

3-4 cups

Note: Requires a four hour waiting period.

1 (11-ounce) can yellow corn, no
*   salt or sugar added*
1 green bell pepper, chopped
2 medium tomatoes, chopped
1 small red onion, chopped

½ bunch cilantro, chopped
⅓ cup hot salsa
salt and pepper to taste
2 tablespoons balsamic vinegar
2 small avocados, chopped

▲ Mix all ingredients together. Let stand at least four hours before serving with tortilla chips.

Pass It On...When I don't seem to have just the right serving dish, I look around. Something else is usually more attractive than what I had in mind. I've been know to serve dip in a carved out bell pepper or bread loaf, fresh fruit in a scooped out watermelon, and almost anything in a basket.

CARAMEL FRUIT DIP

1¼ cups

¼ cup white sugar
¾ cup light brown sugar, packed
1 teaspoon vanilla
8 ounces cream cheese, softened

assorted fruits: sliced apples,
strawberries, pineapple sticks
and banana chunks

▲ Place first four ingredients in food processor or blender. Mix until smooth. Serve with in-season fruit such as apples, pears, and strawberries.

Pass It On...*Serve over apple pie. Also good on muffins and toast.*

ROASTED GARLIC

A healthful substitute for mayonnaise or butter

8-12 servings

4-6 heads of garlic
2-3 tablespoons virgin olive oil

¼ cup chicken broth (or water)

▲ Peel some of the papery wrap off garlic, but leave head intact. Place heads in baking dish and pour oil and broth over them. Bake at 350° for one hour, or until soft.

Pass It On...*Serve as an appetizer with crusty French bread, dishes of virgin olive oil, sun dried tomatoes and niçoise olives; squeeze the soft pulp out of the cloves and spread on the bread. Equally good on mashed potatoes, roasted chicken or eggplant.*

BAKED HAVARTI

12 servings

1 pound Havarti cheese
Champagne mustard (example:
  Cherchies)

dried dill
frozen puff pastry sheet
plain water or wafer crackers

▲ Defrost frozen puff pastry sheet. Preheat oven to 350°. Unfold puff pastry sheet carefully. If sheet splits, dampen with water and roll together with rolling pin. Spread champagne mustard generously over sheet. Sprinkle with dried dill. Wrap sheet around the chunk of Havarti. Use only enough pastry to fully enclose the cheese. Seal seams. Place in oven-proof casserole dish, uncovered. Bake 20 minutes.

Pass It On...*Serve warm with simple wafer crackers, unsalted.*

BURGUNDY MEATBALLS

10-12 servings

Note: Requires two hours chilling.

For meatballs:

1 pound ground beef
½ cup fine bread crumbs
½ cup milk

2 tablespoons onion, grated
1 teaspoon salt and pepper

For sauce:

1 cup Burgundy (dry red wine)
½ cup ketchup
¼ cup fresh lemon juice
2 beef bouillon cubes

¼ cup fresh parsley (optional)
1 teaspoon lemon peel, grated
3 tablespoons sugar

▲ Mix all meatball ingredients; using a teaspoon, make into meatballs and chill for about 2 hours. After meatballs are chilled, brown them in a frying pan with butter and serve them with the sauce. For sauce: Combine sauce ingredients and heat. Pour over meatballs and cook gently for 30 minutes. Serve in a chafing dish.

"LIGHT" MEXICAN DIP

20 servings

1 pound ground turkey
½ cup onion, chopped
2-3 cloves garlic, minced
1 (12-ounce) jar green chili salsa
1 (15-ounce) can spicy refried beans

1 teaspoon salt
½ cup longhorn or Cheddar cheese, grated
¼ cup black olives, sliced

▲ Brown turkey until crumbly. Add ¼ cup onion and garlic. Cook until onion is soft. Add salsa, beans and salt. Cook until bubbly. Spoon into chafing dish and garnish with cheese, olives and remaining onion. Serve with tortilla chips.

Pass It On...For a quick salsa dip, use half low-fat sour cream and half plain yogurt. Add salsa and serve with unsalted chips. Even those on a low-fat, no-salt diet can enjoy.

BACON STUFFED MUSHROOMS

20-25 servings

Note: Can be made ahead and refrigerated up to two days.

1 pound small mushrooms (about 50)
1 medium onion, diced
1 teaspoon salt
1 (3-ounce) package cream cheese, softened

½ cup buttered breadcrumbs
4-6 slices bacon, diced
2 tablespoons green pepper, minced
dash of pepper

▲ Preheat oven to 375°. Butter a 9x13-inch baking dish. Wash and dry mushrooms. Remove stems, chop, and reserve for stuffing. Sauté diced bacon, onion, green pepper, stems, salt and pepper. Remove from heat when cooked, but not browned. Combine cream cheese with bacon mixture. Press firmly into mushroom caps, mounding slightly. Put buttered breadcrumbs into small bowl - lightly press filling side of mushrooms into crumbs to coat. Can be covered and refrigerated for 1 or 2 days and bake uncovered for 15 to 20 minutes.

Pass It On...*This is a great side dish to any roast, beef, pork, chicken or turkey.*

GRILLED QUESADILLAS

1 appetizer

¼ cup jalapeño Monterey Jack, grated
1 tablespoon tomato, diced

1 tablespoon cilantro, chopped
1 flour tortilla
1 tablespoon fresh salsa

Pico de Gallo:
3 fresh tomatoes, chopped
1 onion, chopped
2 garlic cloves, crushed
¼ bunch cilantro leaves
juice of fresh lime

3 fresh jalapeños, seeded and chopped
1 tablespoon oil
salt
pepper

▲ Sprinkle cheese, tomato, cilantro and salsa on half a flour tortilla. Fold tortilla over filling and grill until slightly browned, turning once. Cut into thirds and serve. For Pico de Gallo: mix all ingredients and serve with quesadillas.

GREEK TRIANGLES

13-15 servings

¼ cup raisins
¼ cup olive oil
2 cups onion, finely chopped
1 tablespoons garlic, minced
1 pound ground lamb
2 teaspoons salt
1½ teaspoons pepper

½ teaspoon cinnamon
⅛ teaspoon cayenne pepper
¼ cup tomato paste
1 cup fresh tomato, chopped
⅓ cup honey
1 package phyllo
melted butter

▲ Cover raisins with hot water, let sit 10 minutes, then drain and set aside. Heat olive oil in a skillet. Add onion, garlic, and sauté over medium heat until tender and golden; transfer to a bowl and set aside. Add the lamb to the skillet and cook until no longer pink. Drain off any excess oil. Add the next seven ingredients, sautéed onions, and the reserved raisins. Sauté 5-7 minutes over medium-high heat to blend flavors and evaporate any liquid. Cool to room temperature. Proceed with making the phyllo packets, using about 2 teaspoons filling for each.

Follow directions on the package for thawing and working with phyllo sheets. Remove 15 sheets and, with a very sharp knife, cut in half lengthwise. Cover with plastic wrap and damp towel. For each packet, lay out one strip of phyllo with short end toward you and brush very lightly with melted butter. Fold in half lengthwise and butter again.

Place filling at bottom of strip off to one corner. Fold up strip as you would a flag, so you end up with a neat triangular packet. Set on buttered baking sheet and brush once with butter. Repeat with all strips of phyllo, laying out two or three at a time and keeping the rest covered. Bake 20-25 minutes at 350° until crisp and golden. Serve hot.

Pass It On...Blend ¼ pound Feta cheese and 1 pound ricotta cheese, 2 beaten eggs, and 1 crushed garlic clove. Brush one sheet of phyllo with butter. Place another sheet on top and butter. Cut lengthwise into six strips. Place 1 teaspoon filling near the end of each strip. Fold corner over the filling and continue to fold triangles (like folding a flag). Place on baking sheet and brush tops with butter. Repeat with remaining phyllo and filling. These may be frozen at this point; freeze on baking sheet and transfer to plastic freezer bags when frozen solid. May be baked frozen. Bake about 45 minutes at 350° or until browned and heated through.

SZCHEUAN PEANUT DIPPING SAUCE

4 cups

⅓ cup fresh ginger, minced
⅓ cup fresh garlic, minced
⅓ cup green onions, sliced
1 cup rice vinegar or wine
2 tablespoons sesame oil

¼ cup peanut oil
1 tablespoon Dijon mustard
2 teaspoons hot pepper sauce
1 (18-ounce) jar peanut butter
  (crunchy or smooth)

▲ Combine all ingredients in a food processor. Refrigerate. Serve with pita bread triangles, vegetables, apples, egg rolls or Chinese steamed dumplings.

Pass It On...I found out at 4:00 p.m. that my husband had invited a client and his wife over for drinks and hors d'oeuvres that evening. But what hor d'oeuvres? These were not people impressed with cheese and crackers! I didn't have time to pick up from a deli or even run to the grocery store, so I checked the kitchen drawer where I keep restaurant take-out flyers and came up with the perfect solution. Chinese food offers a wealth of appetizer-sized finger food. I ordered potstickers, fried prawns, egg rolls, scallops and my favorite, steamed dumplings. And I asked them to throw in lettuce or orange rind to garnish the trays. They delivered in 30 minutes, just in time for me to arrange the food nicely. And best of all, the bill came to only $15. My husband thought I was a miracle-worker. But I told him that, in the future, all miracles should be requested at least 24 hours in advance.

SMOKED OYSTER PATE

20 servings

Note: Requires 2-3 hours chilling.

1 can beef consommé, heated
1 (8-ounce) package cream cheese
1 package plain gelatin
¼ cup cold water

1 (4-ounce) can smoked oysters,
  chopped
½ teaspoon curry powder
½ cup toasted pecans, chopped

▲ Dissolve cream cheese in consommé. Soak gelatin in cold water, add to hot consommé. Add smoked oysters, curry powder and chopped pecans. Put in mold and refrigerate for a few hours before turning out to serve.

Pass It On...Allow ingredients to thicken, then stir to distribute oysters and pecans before pouring into the mold to set.

SKEWERED SCALLOPS

32 appetizers

Note: Requires 2-3 hours for marinade.

*12 strips bacon, partially cooked
  and cut into same size as
  scallops*
*16 sea scallops, washed, patted dry
  and halved horizontally*
*16 water chestnuts, halved
  horizontally*

32 long wooden skewers
⅓ cup soy sauce
2 tablespoons white wine vinegar
1½ tablespoons sugar
1 tablespoon dry sherry
1 clove garlic, minced
1 teaspoon fresh ginger, minced

▲ Soak wooden skewers in water so they won't burn. Alternate bacon between scallops and water chestnut slices on long wooden skewers. Arrange in shallow dish. Combine remaining ingredients in processor or blender and mix well. Pour over skewered scallops. Cover and marinate in refrigerator 2 to 3 hours. Turn frequently. Drain marinade and pat scallops dry with paper towels. Broil until scallops are barely firm, about 6 minutes per side.

Note: *Keep a close eye on them and decrease temperature slightly if skewers begin to burn.*

SHRIMP PROVENCAL

8 servings

2 pounds jumbo shrimp
1 tomato, chunked
⅓ cup olive oil
2-4 cloves garlic, minced

*2 tablespoons fresh parsley,
  chopped*
1 tablespoon soy sauce
1 lemon, cut in wedges, for garnish

▲ Clean and peel shrimp. Mix other ingredients and toss together with shrimp. Place in large iron skillet. Bake at 450° for 10-15 minutes. Serve right from skillet with toothpicks and lemon wedges.

Pass It On...*For my birthday one year, my husband decided to take me visiting before dinner. He called six of our closest couples and asked if we could drop in for hors d'oeuvres and a drink. By the time we finished at the sixth home, we decided to skip dinner. I enjoyed a delightful evening, and my husband didn't have to do anything — except make six telephone calls and buy a gift!*

NITA'S PICKLED SHRIMP

12-15 servings

Note: Requires at least one day refrigeration.

2½ pounds big shrimp (21-25 per
pound), unshelled
2 cups onions, thinly sliced
7-8 bay leaves
1 cup oil

1 cup white vinegar
1½ teaspoons salt
2½ teaspoons celery seed
2½ tablespoons capers and juice
dash hot pepper sauce (to taste)

▲ Boil or steam shrimp for a few minutes just until pink. Do not overcook or they will be tough. Shell and devein. Put shrimp, onions and bay leaves in a shallow two-quart glass dish. Mix remaining ingredients and cover shrimp and onions. Cover with plastic wrap and refrigerate for at least 24 hours. Count 4 shrimp per person.

Pass It On...To make a holiday shrimp tree, wrap a styrofoam cone with leaf lettuce, curly edge down. Overlap the lettuce to resemble a pine tree. Anchor with regular toothpicks slanted into cone. Attach shrimp in a spiral with decorative toothpicks, but leave curly lettuce edges showing through. Set cone on a plate covered with lettuce. Place a star or other decoration on top of a cone. Use as a single centerpiece or place two smaller ones at each end of the table. The "tree" can be put together several hours ahead, wrapped tightly in plastic wrap, and refrigerated.

SPINACH BALLS

20-24 servings

A great make ahead appetizer.

2 packages chopped spinach,
cooked and drained
2 cups herb seasoned stuffing mix
½ cup Parmesan cheese
1 large onion, chopped

4 eggs
½ cup margarine or butter, melted
½ teaspoon garlic salt
½ teaspoon Accent
black pepper

▲ Combine all ingredients and chill for about 30 minutes. Roll into small balls and place on cookie sheet. Bake at 350° for 20 minutes. Remove from cookie sheet immediately and serve warm.

Pass It On...May be made ahead and frozen on cookie sheet, then transferred to plastic bag and stored until needed. Thaw before baking.

SHRIMP REMOULADE

10-12 servings

Note: Requires at least 12 hours refrigeration.

**3 pounds medium shrimp, boiled
and peeled**
2 eggs, hard boiled
1 cup finely chopped celery
**¼ cup fresh parsley, finely
chopped**

**2 tablespoons green onions,
chopped**
**1 tablespoon green pepper,
chopped**

Marinade:
1½ cups olive oil
½ cup prepared mustard
⅓ cup white wine vinegar

**2 teaspoons each of salt and
paprika**

▲ Chop hard boiled eggs. Toss shrimp, eggs, celery, parsley, onion and pepper together. Beat all marinade ingredients until well blended. Pour marinade mixture over shrimp mixture. Cover and refrigerate at least 12 hours. Stir several times. Drain off any extra marinade at serving time.

BAKED SOUTHWEST DIP

10 servings

1 (16-ounce) loaf round bread
**1 (8-ounce) package cream cheese,
softened**
½ cup sour cream
¼ cup hot salsa
**1½ cups (6 ounces) Cheddar
cheese, shredded**

**¼ cup Monterey Jack cheese with
jalapeño peppers, shredded**
**1-2 fresh plum tomatoes, diced
(optional)**
black olives to garnish (optional)

▲ Preheat oven to 400°. Cut ¼-inch slice from top of bread; set aside. Remove center from bread, leaving ½-inch thick shell. Cut center into one-inch cubes. Bake until toasted, about 5 minutes. With an electric mixer, beat cream cheese, sour cream and salsa until smooth. Stir in Cheddar cheese and Monterey Jack cheese. Spoon into bread shell. Place reserved top slice on top; wrap in foil. Bake until hot, about 1½ hours. Serve with sliced fresh vegetables, toasted bread cubes and tortilla chips.

Pass It On*...Present in a bread shell or bake and serve in a shallow one-quart baking dish.*

ONION MOUSSE

20 servings

1 tablespoon unflavored gelatin
¼ cup water
12 ounces sour cream
¼ cup chives

8 ounces cream cheese, room
*   temperature*
1 cup small curd cottage cheese
¼ cup onion, grated
jalapeño pepper jelly

▲ Soften gelatin 2 minutes in water. Heat in microwave 45 seconds. Allow to cool. Fold in remaining ingredients and pour in mold. Refrigerate until firm. Garnish by covering with jalapeño jelly. Serve with corn tortilla chips.

Pass It On…Use non-fat sour cream and cottage cheese and crackers.

PICKLED OKRA SANDWICHES

4-6 servings

1 jar pickled okra
1 (8-ounce) package cream cheese,
*   softened*

soft white bread slices

▲ Drain okra well and pat dry on paper towel. Trim crusts from bread; roll each piece flat with rolling pin. Spread slice with softened cream cheese. Place okra pod on each slice and roll. Secure with toothpick if necessary and refrigerate until firm, tightly covered with plastic wrap. Slice each roll in half and serve. May be made the day before.

Pass It On…Use other pickled vegetables such as green beans or asparagus.

Brunch

Hint: to roast garlic
4-6 heads of ga...
2-3 Tablespoons of o...
or ch...

Peel some...
garli... add:
S... in...
in...
fo...

Dissolve: 2 pkg
1 cup
1 tsp...
t cup

Crab Muff...

3 cans crab mea...
1 lb. grated che...
8 hard boiled eg...
Hellman's mayon...
to make smooth...

Serve on toasted
Muffins (warm t...
bubbly) open face...

You may throw...
the egg yolks away...
you are health cons...

FAX T...

TO: Bob
M: Cindy
E: 1-10-93

TES: Be

choice on the...
for the accounting de...
at lunch luncheon. I...

BAKED GRAPEFRUIT ALASKA

6 servings

3 medium grapefruit
1 (10 or 12-ounce) jar orange
  marmalade

4 egg whites, room temperature
¼ cup granulated sugar
confectioners' sugar

▲ Cut each grapefruit in half. Section each grapefruit half; remove core and membranes with a grapefruit knife. Core, leaving flesh in grapefruit shell. Place on a baking sheet. Place marmalade in a small saucepan. Heat until warm. In a medium bowl, beat egg whites until soft peaks form. Slowly beat in granulated sugar, 1 tablespoon at a time. Continue beating until stiff. Carefully fold in warm marmalade. Cover grapefruit in shells with meringue, bringing meringue to the edge of the shells. Filled shells may stand at room temperature 2 to 3 hours until ready to serve. Just before serving, preheat oven to 425°. Bake grapefruit 8 to 9 minutes or until nicely browned. Sprinkle with powdered sugar and serve immediately.

Pass It On...We have lots of fun entertaining informally on April Fool's Day. We invite guests for dinner, but greet them in sleepwear and bathrobes. We set the table using old kitchen cloths or the colored newspaper comics as covering, paper napkins from various other holidays, mismatched plates and glasses, and silverware from the utility drawer such as wooden spoons, carving fork, scoops, etc. Of course, we have real silverware handy for actual dining. The centerpiece consists of fresh broccoli, radish roses and turnip daisies with eye centers. And instead of dinner, the guests enjoy breakfast with us.

CHEESE SANDWICH FRENCH BREAD

28 slices

2 loaves French bread
Swiss cheese slices
2 cups butter
2 tablespoons poppy seed

2 tablespoons prepared mustard
¼ cup onion, chopped
4 strips bacon

▲ Slice bread diagonally (do not cut through the bottom). Put each loaf on large piece aluminum foil, placing slices of Swiss cheese between bread slices. Melt butter, add poppy seed and mustard, mixing well. Sprinkle chopped onion on top of loaf. Pour butter mixture over all, making sure some gets down into the slices. Place two strips of bacon on top of each loaf. Seal foil and bake at 400° about 20 minutes. Broil to crisp bacon, if necessary.

BABY DUTCH BABIES

A wonderful brunch item

24 small muffins

2 tablespoons butter
2 large eggs
½ cup flour, sifted
½ cup milk

1 (3-ounce) package cream cheese,
divided into 24 cubes
¼ cup chopped chutney

▲ Divide the 2 tablespoons of butter among 24 greased mini muffin tins. Set pans in 425° oven to melt butter. In a blender, combine eggs, flour, and milk. Blend. Spoon batter evenly into muffin tins with melted butter. Bake 2 minutes or until bottoms are firm, then add cream cheese cubes and chutney. Continue to bake 10 minutes until browned and puffed. Cool and remove from tins. Serve warm or cold.

Pass It On...My mom always told us and lived by it, too: "Always look for the good in every person and any situation. It makes life so much happier."

MACARONI AND CHEESE

6 servings

Sauce:
3 tablespoons margarine
3 tablespoons flour
1¼ cups milk
1 egg, beaten
1 teaspoon dry mustard

1 teaspoon salt
1 teaspoon white pepper
3 cups sharp Cheddar cheese,
grated

Pasta:
8 ounces macaroni

▲ Melt margarine over low heat. Blend in flour and cook until bubbly. Blend in milk, stir until smooth. Add small amount to beaten egg. Blend egg into margarine/flour mixture. Add seasonings. Add cheese and stir until smooth and thickened. Remove from heat. Cook macaroni according to package directions. Drain. Combine sauce and pasta and serve immediately.

Pass It On...Great for brunch served with ham and fruit salad.

BREAKFAST CASSEROLE

12-16 servings

2 dozen eggs
1½ tablespoons parsley, chopped
3 tablespoons butter

¼ cup of milk
salt and pepper

Vegetable mixture:
1 (12-ounce) package chopped
* broccoli or spinach*
1 can shoe peg corn

1 medium jar chopped pimentos,
* drained*

Topping:
1½ cans cream of mushroom soup
1 pint sour cream
8-10 ounces sharp Cheddar
* cheese, grated*

4 ounces Monterey Jack cheese
* with jalapeño peppers, grated*
16 slices bacon, fried and
* crumbled*
1½ cups sliced mushrooms

▲ Whip eggs with milk and seasonings. Melt butter in skillet and scramble egg mixture until set, but still soft. Pour into greased 9x13-inch casserole dish. Mix the vegetables and add to eggs. Mix mushroom soup and sour cream together and spread on top of egg and vegetable mixture. Top with sharp cheese and Monterey Jack cheese. Sprinkle mushrooms and crumbled bacon over top of cheese and bake 30-40 minutes at 325°.

Pass It On...*Most casseroles can be made ahead and refrigerated - just be sure to take out of refrigerator 30 minutes before baking.*

CHILI CHEESE CASSEROLE

10 servings

1 pound Monterey Jack cheese,
* grated*
1 pound Cheddar cheese, grated
3 (10-ounce) cans chopped green
* chilies*

4 eggs, beaten
3 tablespoons flour
⅔ cup milk
8-ounce can tomato sauce

▲ Line buttered 9x13-inch glass casserole dish with green chilies. Combine grated cheeses and sprinkle over chilies. Beat eggs, flour and milk. Pour over chilie/cheese mixture. Bake uncovered for 35 minutes, pour tomato sauce over and return to oven, continue baking for 15 minutes or until set. Serve cut into squares.

Pass It On...*Serve with Spinach and Strawberry Salad.*

PEACH FRENCH TOAST

12-14 servings

Note: Requires overnight refrigeration.

1 cup dark brown sugar
½ cup butter or margarine
2 tablespoons water
1 (29-ounce) can peaches or fresh
  peaches, sliced

5 eggs
1½ cups milk
1 tablespoon vanilla
1 loaf French bread (12-14 slices)

▲ In a saucepan, heat butter and sugar on medium-low heat; add water and continue cooking until sauce comes to a full boil. Cook 10 minutes, then pour into a 9x13-inch baking dish and cool 10 minutes. Place drained peaches on top of cooled sauce and cover with slices of bread placed close together. Blend together eggs, milk, vanilla and pour over bread. Cover pan, and refrigerate overnight. To bake, place in a 350° oven for 40 minutes. Loosely cover with foil the last 10-15 minutes if mixture is browning too quickly. Serve with bread on the bottom and peaches on top.

SPINACH MOZZARELLA LOAF

Good served with soup for supper or lunch

12-20 servings

1 loaf frozen bread dough
1 pound hot Italian sausage
1 (10-ounce) package frozen,
  chopped spinach

8 ounces mozzarella, shredded
1 tablespoon water
1 egg white
1 tablespoon caraway seed

▲ Cook and drain sausage. Drain spinach. Thaw bread dough in greased glass baking dish in microwave for 4 minutes on medium/low setting. Roll out to 10x14-inch rectangle on greased cookie sheet. Spread with drained sausage. Sprinkle spinach and then cheese evenly over sausage. Roll dough lengthwise and seal edges. Place seam side down on baking sheet. Brush with egg white mixed with water. Sprinkle caraway seed on top and bake at 350° for 30-35 minutes, uncovered.

SCOTCH EGGS

Great for tailgates and picnics

6 servings

1 pound sausage
2 tablespoons parsley, finely
  chopped
6 hard cooked eggs, peeled

seasoned flour
2 eggs, lightly beaten
bread crumbs

▲ Mix sausage and parsley, then divide into six equal patties. Completely cover each egg with a sausage patty. Roll balls in seasoned flour, then beaten eggs, then in breadcrumbs. Fry in one-inch hot oil turning until sausage is cooked through and is nicely browned. Serve hot, cold, or at room temperature with mustard for extra spice.

CHEESE MUFFETS

A quick, easy brunch item

4 servings

1 cup Cheddar cheese, shredded
1 cup fresh mushrooms, sliced
2 tablespoons butter

1 teaspoon Worcestershire sauce
  or sherry
4 slices buttered toast or English
  muffins

▲ Sauté mushrooms in butter. Add Worcestershire sauce or sherry. Spread on toast or muffins and top with cheese. Broil until cheese melts.

Pass It On...For added flavor, scramble a slightly beaten egg with cooked seasoned mushrooms. For canapes, cut toast slices in quarters.

CRAB MUFFINS

20-24 muffins

3 cans crab meat or 1 pound fresh
  crab
1 pound Cheddar cheese, grated

8 hard boiled eggs, grated
mayonnaise to make smooth

▲ Mix all and warm until bubbly. Mound on toasted English muffins and serve open faced.

GIANT OVEN PANCAKE

A unique, delectable pancake

4 servings

½ cup butter
4 eggs
1 cup milk
1 cup all-purpose flour, sifted

¼ teaspoon ground nutmeg
confectioners' sugar
lemon wedges
maple syrup

▲ Preheat oven to 425°. Place butter in 3 or 4-quart round or oval shallow baking dish or casserole and set in a 425° oven to melt. Whirl eggs and nutmeg in a blender or food processor at high speed for 1 minute. With motor running, gradually pour in milk, then slowly add flour and continue to whirl for 30 more seconds. (Or, in a bowl, beat eggs until well-blended, gradually beat in milk, then flour.) When butter is melted, remove pan from oven and quickly pour in batter. Return pan to oven and bake for 20-25 minutes, or until pancake is puffy and well-browned. Cut into wedges and serve immediately with maple syrup, confectioners' sugar and lemon wedges.

Pass It On...On each family member's birthday, the rest of us treat the birthday person to a warm wake-up washcloth followed by breakfast in bed with all their presents. Mom and dad included looked forward to this special celebration every year.

GRANDMA'S BUTTERMILK PANCAKES

2 servings

2 tablespoons butter
1 cup all-purpose flour, sifted
½ teaspoon salt
1 teaspoon soda

1 large egg
1 cup plus 2 tablespoons
  buttermilk

▲ Melt butter. Sift flour with salt and soda into a medium bowl. Drop in 1 large egg (unbeaten) Add buttermilk and butter. Stir slightly, just until flour is moistened. Batter will still be lumpy. Wipe hot griddle with greased paper towel and drop onto hot griddle by tablespoons and spread to 4-inch cakes. Turn just before bubbles break.

Pass It On...I gave a recipe box to each of my three sons with their favorite family recipes when they left home.

PANCAKES

4-6 servings

Note: Excellent when mixed the night before.

1 cup sour cream
1 cup sour milk or buttermilk
2 eggs
1 teaspoon soda dissolved in 1
   tablespoon hot water

2 teaspoons salt
1¾ cups flour, sifted
2 teaspoons baking powder

▲ Beat all ingredients thoroughly and refrigerate until ready to make pancakes. Pour onto griddle and spread with spoon for a thin pancake.

Pass It On...This pancake recipe was my mother's from approximately 1923. Always a favorite as I was growing up, it became a favorite of my family as I introduced them to pheasant and pancakes. My father was a hunter; it was a sad year if the pheasant population was down and no pheasant made it to the freezer. You cannot imagine how good pheasant (lightly sautéed breast pieces) and pancakes tastes on a cold, snowy night. And then to look forward to pancakes, again, the following morning is an added delight. To this day, my children always ask for Grandma's pancakes, even though we no longer have a source for pheasant.

OAT AND BLUE CORNMEAL WAFFLES

4 servings

1 large egg
2⅔ cups buttermilk
1⅓ cups all-purpose flour
⅔ cup each regular rolled oats and
   blue cornmeal

1¼ teaspoons baking soda
¼ teaspoon salt
3 tablespoons sugar
⅓ cup melted butter or margarine

▲ In a bowl, beat egg until blended; stir in buttermilk. In another bowl, stir together flour, oats, cornmeal, soda, salt and sugar. Add oat mixture and ⅓ cup of butter to the buttermilk mixture and stir until batter is evenly mixed. Heat waffle iron. Brush grids with melted butter, then half fill with mixture. Bake until waffle is well-browned and crisp (time depends on each waffle iron). Serve hot and accompany with syrup, fruit or sour cream.

Pass It On...New Mexico blue corn products are sometimes hard to find. If not at the regular grocery store, try gourmet or food specialty shops. It's a little expensive, but well worth it!

SPINACH QUICHE

8-10 servings

1 package frozen spinach soufflé
2 eggs
3 tablespoons milk
¼ cup onion, chopped

½ cup mushrooms, sliced
¾ cup hot Italian sausage
¾ cup Swiss or Cheddar cheese,
  grated

▲ Thaw spinach soufflé. Sauté onions. Sauté mushrooms. Cook and crumble sausage. Combine all ingredients and pour into a 9-inch, unbaked quiche pie shell. Bake at 350° for 45 minutes to 1 hour. Test with knife at edge. If knife comes out rather clean, quiche is done. The center should be quivering, but it will set after removing from oven.

***Pass It On**...Eggs will beat better if brought to room temperature first.*

ZUCCHINI QUICHE

A great way to enjoy the summer vegetable

16-20 servings

3 cups zucchini, sliced
1 cup light biscuit baking mix
½ cup light oil
1 medium onion, chopped

4 eggs, well beaten or 2 cartons
  egg substitute
¾ cup Parmesan cheese, grated
salt and pepper to taste

▲ Mix all the ingredients in a large bowl. Bake at 350° for 40-45 minutes in two pie pans. Cut and serve in wedges.

CRESCENT MOON STRATA

6-9 croissants (cut in half)
6 eggs, beaten
1½ cups milk
½ teaspoon salt
¼ teaspoon pepper
3-4 drops Tabasco

¼ teaspoon nutmeg
10 ounces frozen spinach, thawed
  and drained dry
1½ cups Monterey Jack cheese,
  shredded
½ cup Feta cheese

▲ Grease a 9x13-inch casserole. Place croissant halves cut side down in casserole. Beat eggs, milk, seasonings and spinach. Pour over croissants. Sprinkle Monterey Jack cheese, cover with Feta cheese. Refrigerate 6-8 hours or overnight. Bake at 350°, uncovered, for 35-40 minutes. Watch that cheese does not overbrown.

***Pass It On**...Ideals are like stars. You will not succeed in touching them with your hands, but following them will guide you to your destiny.*

EASY SAUSAGE, EGG AND CHEESE STRATA

A make ahead dish perfect for Christmas morning

8-10 servings

1 pound bulk sausage
⅓ cup onion, chopped
1 cup Cheddar or Swiss cheese,
*   shredded*
2 cups milk

1 cup biscuit baking mix
4 eggs
⅛ teaspoon pepper
¼ teaspoon salt

▲ Preheat oven to 400°. Fry sausage and drain well. Spread in a 10-inch quiche dish or casserole. Sprinkle onion over sausage; then cheese. Blend remaining ingredients in blender or food processor. Pour over sausage mixture. Cool in refrigerator several hours or overnight. Bake 35-40 minutes. Cool 5 minutes. Test for doneness by inserting a knife in the center. If it comes out clean, then the strata is done.

Pass It On...*Substitute bacon or ham for the sausage.*

STRATA SURPRISE

8 servings

Note: An overnight recipe.

1 loaf sandwich bread
1 dozen eggs
3½ cups milk

½ cup Grand Marnier
8 empty grapefruit shells

▲ Use a glass that will fit inside grapefruit shell to cut bread rounds, allowing three per shell. Mix eggs, milk and Grand Marnier. Place shells in greased or sprayed baking dish and slowly layer bread rounds and egg mixture - this is a gradual process as each bread round needs to absorb as much egg mixture as possible before the next round is in place. Reserve any remaining egg mixture. Cover with plastic or foil and refrigerate overnight. If there is room for more egg when ready for baking, add reserved mixture to each shell. Bake at 300° for 45 minutes or until set. Strata will puff up like a top hat.

VEGETABLE PIE

6-8 servings

Crust:

1½ cups flour
1½ teaspoons sugar
1 teaspoon salt

½ cup vegetable oil
2 tablespoons cold milk
½ cup Parmesan cheese, grated

Filling:

½ pound broccoli tips
2 cups Monterey Jack cheese,
*   grated*
½ cup Parmesan cheese, grated
2 tablespoons flour
¼ teaspoon pepper
1 teaspoon dried basil (3 teaspoons
*   chopped fresh)*

½ teaspoon dried thyme (1½
*   teaspoon chopped fresh)*
1 bunch chopped green onion (¼ -
*   ½ cup)*
2 tomatoes, thinly sliced
¼ cup unsalted butter, melted

▲ Preheat oven to 350°. Combine crust ingredients, shape into a ball, then press into pie pan. Boil broccoli for 3 minutes in salted water. Drain and rinse in cold water and drain again. Combine cheeses, flour, seasonings and onion. Put half of mixture in pie shell. Layer broccoli, then tomatoes. Add remaining cheese mixture. Pour melted butter over pie. Bake 30 minutes before slicing. Serve warm or at room temperature.

Pass It On...For perfect hard cooked eggs, put eggs in pan and cover with cold water and bring to a boil. Remove from heat, cover and let stand for 20 minutes.

PINEAPPLE CASSEROLE

8-10 servings

Casserole:
2 cans chunk pineapple, drained
6 tablespoons pineapple juice
6 tablespoons self rising flour

1 cup sugar
1½ cups Cheddar cheese, grated

Topping:
1 cup crushed crackers
1 cup pecans, chopped

¼ cup margarine, melted

▲ Mix all casserole ingredients together. Spread all topping ingredients over pineapple mixture. Bake at 350° in a 1 to 2-quart glass baking dish for approximately 30 minutes or until cheese melts and topping is slightly browned and crunchy.

Pass It On...Recipe may be doubled and put in a 3-quart baking dish.

ITALIAN SPINACH FRITTATA

4-6 servings

2 tablespoons olive oil
¾ cup thinly sliced onion
6 eggs
1½ cups coarsely chopped parsley
½ teaspoon salt
pepper

¼ teaspoon dried basil
2 tablespoons minced parsley
⅓ cup grated Parmesan cheese
2 firm tomatoes
small can sliced black olives

▲ Heat oil in 12-inch omelet pan and cook onion until soft and transparent. Beat eggs, add spinach, seasonings and cheese. Pour over onions in pan and cook over low heat, gently lifting edges as egg sets and tilting to allow soft egg to run underneath. While still slightly soft on top, arrange tomato slices and olives on frittata. Run under broiler about 3 inches from heat and cook about 5 minutes or until set and slightly browned. Cut into wedges and serve hot.

Breads & Rolls

BREAKFAST
3 cans
1 1/2 CUPS BUTTER
1 CUP pecans
1 cinnamon
sugar in sugar
it was MY SELF

Pam dear

Your orange bread was wonderful.
We finished it this morning and
enjoyed every bite. If you would
part with it, I would love to have
the recipe. Jack hopes you will
pass it on as he was most enthusiastic
about it!

As ever,
Sara

TABL

Inst

IRISH BROWN BREAD

Especially good for restricted diets

2 small loaves

4 cups whole wheat flour
½ cup oats
¼ cup dark brown sugar
¼ cup caraway seed, optional
2 teaspoons baking powder

1 teaspoon soda
½ teaspoon salt or salt substitute
1¾ cups buttermilk or sour milk
1 egg
¼ cup margarine, melted

▲ Mix dry ingredients and work in wet ingredients. Knead on a floured surface until it holds together. The dough should be slightly damp, not wet. Divide into two rounded loaves. Cut an "X" on top with a floured knife if desired. Put both on a cookie sheet and bake at 375° for forty minutes.

Pass It On...*"I received this recipe while in Ireland researching the third book in my juvenile Cinderella series." - Shirley Beistle Climo, children's literature writer.*

CHOCOLATE CHIP BANANA BREAD

8-10 servings

⅓ cup shortening
⅔ cup sugar
2 eggs
1 cup very ripe bananas (about 3), mashed
½ cup nuts, optional

1¾ cups flour
2 teaspoons baking powder
¼ teaspoon baking soda
½ teaspoon vanilla
½ cup mini semi-sweet chocolate chips

▲ Cream sugar and shortening. Add all other ingredients and mix just until all dry ingredients are moist. Pour into one large loaf pan (9x5x3-inch) or 2 small loaf pans that have been sprayed with non stick aerosol and bake at 300° for 45-50 minutes, cool 2 hours.

Pass It On...*My Grandma Steinberg made this for us on Sunday mornings after church. It makes a wonderful gift anytime.*

BUTTERMILK BISCUITS

14 servings

1½ cups flour
2 teaspoons baking powder
¼ teaspoon baking soda

½ teaspoon salt
1 teaspoon sugar
¾ cup buttermilk

▲ Sift flour, baking powder, baking soda, salt and sugar together. Cut in shortening. Add buttermilk. Mix quickly and lightly. Knead slightly on floured surface and cut into biscuit rounds with biscuit cutter. Bake at 450° for about 15 minutes.

Pass It On...Serve leftovers split, buttered, toasted and served with marmalade or jam. Delicious!

YEAST BISCUITS

2 dozen

¼ cup shortening, melted
¾ cup milk
¼ cup sugar

1 package yeast, dissolved in ¼ cup milk
¼ teaspoon salt
3 cups flour, sifted

▲ Mix shortening, milk, sugar and dissolved yeast. Add salt and flour. Mix together and pour on a well-floured board. Work dough, adding flour until dough is no longer sticky. Place in greased bowl and cover with foil, refrigerate for 2 hours or up to 1 week. Roll out on floured board and cut into 2x½-inch squares. Dip in melted butter and let rise 2 hours. Bake at 325° for 15-20 minutes.

Pass It On...Happiness adds and multiplies as we divide it with others.

CHILI CORNBREAD

Excellent to accompany barbecued meat, poultry and fish

8 servings

1 cup yellow corn meal
½ teaspoon baking soda
¾ teaspoon salt
1 (16-ounce) can cream-style corn
1 (4-ounce) can diced chilies

¼ cup oil
2 eggs
1 cup milk
1½ cups Cheddar cheese, grated

▲ Preheat oven to 350°. Grease a 9x9-inch baking dish. Combine all ingredients, reserving ½ cup cheese for top. Turn into greased baking dish and top with reserved cheese and bake 45 minutes.

MOM'S CORNBREAD

8 servings

1 cup white cornmeal
½ teaspoon salt
½ teaspoon soda
2 teaspoons baking powder

1 cup buttermilk
2 eggs
2 tablespoons liquid oil

▲ Preheat oven to 450°. Mix dry ingredients together. Add oil, eggs and buttermilk, blending well. Pour into greased 8-inch round pan and bake at 450° for 20 minutes.

Pass It On...*My mother, in her attempts to prepare her children for the ups and downs of married life, recited this little poem: To keep your marriage brimming with love in the loving cup, whenever you're wrong admit it, whenever you're right...shut up!*

HERB BREAD

Makes a great gift

1 loaf

2 cups flour, sifted	¼ teaspoon oregano
⅓ cup sugar	½ teaspoon basil
½ teaspoon salt	pinch of thyme
1½ teaspoons baking powder	1 egg, lightly beaten
½ teaspoon soda	¼-⅔ cup buttermilk
¼ teaspoon marjoram	1 tablespoon butter, melted

▲ Sift flour, sugar, salt, baking powder and soda into a bowl. Add herbs and mix thoroughly. In a separate bowl, beat the egg; add buttermilk and butter. Stir into dry ingredients; mix until moistened throughout. Add more milk, if needed, to make the dough cling together. Turn onto a floured board and knead until it handles well. Form into a round ball then place in a well-buttered cake pan and bake at 375° for 40 minutes. Serve warm with sweet butter.

Pass It On...Add floured raisins, dried cranberries, dried blueberries or nuts instead of herbs; or use 1 tablespoon of dill seed and a sprinkling of dill weed.

MEXICAN SURPRISE BREAD

8-10 servings

1 loaf French bread	2 cups Monterey Jack cheese,
½ cup margarine, melted	shredded
1 (4-ounce) can green chilies,	1 cup mayonnaise
chopped	

▲ Split a loaf of French bread lengthwise. Drain green chilies and add to melted margarine. Spread mixture over both halves of bread. Mix grated cheese with enough mayonnaise to spreading consistency, and spread over both pieces of bread. Place on a foil-covered baking sheet. Bake in a 350° oven for 25-30 minutes, or until light brown. Cut into serving-sized pieces.

ORANGE BREAD

1 loaf

2 cups flour, sifted
1 cup sugar
2 teaspoons baking powder
¼ teaspoon salt

1 cup milk
1 cup candied orange peel (see
  recipe below)
1 egg

Candied Orange Peel:
3 orange skins cut into thin strips
water

½ cup sugar

▲ To candy orange peel: Peel oranges with a potato peeler to keep free of the bitter white pith. Cut peels into match stick-like pieces. Cover the peel with water in a sauce pan, and boil for 10-15 minutes. Drain water from peel, add sugar, and simmer for 15-20 minutes, stirring occasionally. To make bread: Sift all dry ingredients together. Add 1 cup candied orange peel. Add milk and egg and stir well. Place in a greased 4½x8½-inch loaf pan. Sprinkle lightly with sugar. Let stand 10-20 minutes. Bake at 350° for about 1 hour.

PARMESAN BREAD

6-8 servings

1 loaf French bread
½ cup butter, softened
¼ cup green onions, chopped

¼ cup Parmesan cheese, grated
½ cup mayonnaise

▲ Cut loaf of bread in half lengthwise. Spread each half with butter, onions, mayonnaise and cheese. Wrap in foil and bake at 350° for 20 minutes. Open foil and place under broiler to brown.

POPPY SEED BREAD

A great gift

2 large or 4 mini loaves

1½ cups milk
1⅛ cups oil
2¼ cups sugar
1½ tablespoons poppy seed
3 eggs
3 cups flour, sifted

1½ teaspoons salt
1½ teaspoons baking powder
1½ teaspoons vanilla
1½ teaspoons almond flavoring
1½ teaspoons butter flavoring

Glaze:
½ cup any type orange juice
1 cup granulated sugar
1 teaspoon vanilla

1 teaspoon almond flavoring
1 teaspoon butter flavoring

▲ Combine all ingredients in a large bowl and mix thoroughly until smooth. Bake at 350° for 1 hour if baking in 2 large loaf pans. Bake 45-50 minutes if baking in 4 small loaf pans. Cool loaves 5 minutes before glazing. For glaze: Shake or blend glaze ingredients and pour over warm bread.

Pass It On...To add nutritional value and cut down on fat, replace ¾ cup of oil with applesauce in sweet bread recipes.

SPOON BREAD

A traditional Southern bread

10-12 servings

¾ cup cornmeal (do not use country or home ground)
1 teaspoon salt
3 tablespoon butter, melted

1 cup boiling water
1 cup scalded milk
2 eggs, well-beaten
2 teaspoons baking powder

▲ Combine cornmeal, salt and melted butter. Stir in boiling water slowly and beat until smooth. Scald milk. Add milk, baking powder and eggs, mix well. Pour into 8x8x2-inch casserole or a 9-inch iron skillet and bake at 350° for 40-50 minutes.

Pass It On...To prevent scalding milk from sticking to pan, first rinse the pan in cold water.

STRAWBERRY BREAD

2 loaves

2 cups flour
1 teaspoon baking soda
1 teaspoon salt
1 tablespoon cinnamon
4 eggs

1¼ cups oil
2 cups sugar
2 (10-ounce) packages frozen
strawberries with juice/sugar,
thawed

▲ In medium bowl sift together flour, soda, salt and cinnamon. In large bowl beat eggs; add oil, then beat in sugar. Gradually beat in flour mixture and strawberries. Pour into two greased and floured 5x9-inch loaf pans and bake for 1 hour at 350°. Cool for 10 minutes in pan. Remove and finish cooling on rack. Very moist.

Pass It On...*Serve with sweet butter for breakfast, brunch, tea or as a lunch salad accompaniment.*

HONEY WHOLE WHEAT BREAD

2 loaves

1 cup milk
¾ cup shortening
½ cup honey
2 teaspoon salt
1 teaspoon soft butter

¾ cup warm water
2 packages yeast
3 eggs, slightly beaten
4½ cups all-purpose flour
1½ cups whole wheat flour

▲ Heat milk; add shortening, honey, salt and butter. Stir until melted. Pour yeast over warm water in a large bowl. Stir until yeast is dissolved. Stir milk mixture into the eggs, then add to yeast and mix well. Combine both flours and add ⅔ of flour mixture to yeast mixture. Beat at low speed for 1 minute. With wooden spoon, beat in rest of flour. Knead 10 to 15 minutes; place dough in greased bowl. Cover. Let rise in a warm draft-free area for one hour, then punch down. Shape into loaves and place in two large (9x5x3-inch) greased bread pans and bake at 375° for 45-50 minutes. To test doneness, thump underside of loaf with hand, it should sound hollow.

OLD FASHIONED WHITE BREAD

4 large loaves

Note: Overnight recipe.

1 envelope yeast
½ cup warm water
1 teaspoon plus 6 tablespoons
  sugar
2 tablespoons vegetable shortening
1 quart milk (whole or 2%)

2 tablespoons salt
15 cups bread flour, sifted
additional shortening for greasing
  pans
butter

▲ Mix one envelope yeast in lukewarm water with 1 teaspoon sugar. Mix vegetable shortening with sugar in large bowl. Add yeast mixture and milk to sugar mixture. Add salt to 15 cups bread flour and incorporate well into the above mixture. Turn onto floured surface and knead for 5 minutes. Transfer dough to large greased bowl. Grease top of dough with shortening. Cover with clean towel and let rise in a warm, draft-free area overnight. Grease 4 (9x5x3-inch) baking pans. Divide dough into 4 pieces. On a lightly floured surface, roll each piece into a large rectangle. Starting at one long side, roll up, jelly roll style. Pinch long edge to seal. Place loaf seam side down in prepared pan. Repeat with three remaining pieces. Heat oven to 425°. Bake loaves, uncovered, for ½ hour. Remove pans from oven. Brush butter over crust of just baked loaves. Cool 2 hours before cutting.

Pass It On...When making sandwiches for a party, use one slice of dark bread and one slice white to make a checkerboard pattern on the serving tray. Cover the sandwiches with a damp cloth or paper towel under plastic wrap to keep them from drying out.

BREAKFAST BUNDT

10-12 servings

3 cans refrigerator biscuits
1½ cups butter, melted
1 cup pecans, chopped

cinnamon, sugar, brown sugar and
  milk to taste

▲ Tear biscuits into thirds and put into the Bundt pan layering with ½ cup butter per can. Sprinkle each layer with pecans, cinnamon, sugar and milk. Bake for 425° for 10-13 minutes. Unmold like a cake, serve hot, tear apart.

Pass It On...Frozen yeast rolls may be substituted for refrigerator biscuits.

CARAMEL PECAN BUNS

18 rolls

Note: An overnight recipe.

1 cup boiling water
½ cup sugar
½ cup butter
1 teaspoon salt
1 package yeast

2 tablespoons lukewarm water
½ teaspoon sugar
2 beaten eggs
4 to 4½ cups flour, sifted

Caramel:
2 teaspoons cinnamon (optional)
6 tablespoons butter
1 cup brown sugar

4 tablespoons dark corn syrup
1 cup pecan halves

▲ Pour boiling water over sugar, butter and salt. Stir and set aside until the mix is lukewarm. Dissolve yeast in lukewarm water to which you have added ½ teaspoon sugar. Add the yeast and 2 beaten eggs to the first mixture. Stir in flour until soft dough is formed, then beat well. Cover and refrigerate overnight, if desired. If you do not refrigerate, allow dough to rise until doubled in bulk.

When ready to use, prepare topping. Melt butter and stir in brown sugar and dark corn syrup. Divide evenly among 2 (8x8x2-inch) baking pans and scatter pecan halves over mixture. Roll dough out into a rectangle about ⅜-inch thick and 12-inches wide. Brush with a little melted butter and then roll up the long way, jelly roll style. Cut into slices that are about ½-inch thick (use string or thread) and set these on brown sugar mixture. Place pans in warm place covered with a towel. Let rise until doubled in bulk, about 40 minutes and bake in 375° oven about 20 minutes, uncovered. Turn out of pan immediately when removed from oven.

Pass It On...*To make even cuts without mashing dough which has been rolled into a log, use a long piece of dental floss. Place under one end of the log, bring over the top, criss-cross floss and pull tightly.*

CRANBERRY COFFEE CAKE

Especially festive for the holidays

12-14 servings

½ cup butter, softened
1 cup sugar
2 eggs, unbeaten
2 cups flour, sifted
1 teaspoon baking soda
1 tablespoon baking powder

½ teaspoon salt
½ cup sour cream
1 teaspoon almond extract
1 (16-ounce) can whole berry
   cranberry sauce
½ cup walnuts, finely chopped

Glaze:
¾ cup confectioners' sugar
2 tablespoons hot water

½ teaspoon almond extract

▲ Cream butter and sugar together. Add the unbeaten eggs. Sift dry ingredients and add to mixture. Add sour cream and almond extract and blend well. Spread ⅓ of batter into greased 9x3-inch Bundt pan. Spread ⅓ can of cranberry sauce over batter. Alternate layers. Sprinkle walnuts on top of layers of batter and cranberries. Bake at 350° for 50 minutes. Cool 5 minutes or more in pan, then turn coffee cake onto plate. For glaze: Mix above ingredients until smooth and pour carefully over coffee cake. Glaze should soak into coffee cake.

Pass It On...When doubling a recipe be sure to double everything. The same applies to halving. Seasonings may be adjusted to taste, but the proportions of flour, shortening, baking powder and liquid must not vary from the original recipe.

HEAVENLY COFFEE CAKE

18-20 servings

Dough:

1 package yeast
¼ cup warm milk
1 tablespoon sugar
1 cup margarine

2½ cups flour
½ teaspoon salt
4 egg yolks, slightly beaten

Filling:

2 (8-ounce) packages cream cheese
1 egg yolk (reserve white)

1 cup sugar
1 teaspoon almond or vanilla extract

Topping:

1 egg white

1 cup chopped pecans or sliced almonds

▲ Dissolve yeast in warm milk with sugar. Let stand 5 minutes. Cut margarine into dry ingredients. Combine yeast mixture with beaten egg yolks, then add to flour mixture. Mix lightly just until all ingredients are combined. Handle as little as possible. Divide dough into two parts. Roll each piece on a floured surface to fit a 9x13-inch pan. Put one piece of dough in the pan. Blend cream cheese, egg yolk, sugar and flavoring. Pour over dough. Cover with second piece of dough. Brush with beaten egg white and sprinkle with nuts. Cover, let rise two hours in a warm place (mixture will not rise like bread - but needs this time prior to baking). Bake at 350° for 30 minutes. Sprinkle with powdered sugar.

Pass It On...*With tree trimming, shopping, Santa Claus, package wrapping and all the other activities, my husband and I worried that our children might lose the real meaning of Christmas. So one year on Christmas morning, we all gathered around the tree before the mad scramble to unwrap packages and sang "Happy Birthday" to Jesus. We continued the tradition every year. Now I enjoy seeing all my grandchildren gathered around the tree on Christmas morning, singing "Happy Birthday" to Jesus and carrying on a very special family tradition.*

STREUSEL FILLED COFFEE CAKE

A sure hit coffee cake

9-12 servings

1½ cups flour, sifted
¾ cup sugar
2½ teaspoons baking powder
¾ teaspoon salt

¼ cup shortening
¾ cup milk
1 egg

Topping:
½ cup brown sugar, packed
2 teaspoons cinnamon

½ cup nuts, finely chopped
2 tablespoons butter, melted

▲ Mix topping ingredients and set aside. Grease baking pan (round 9x1½-inch, square 8x8x2-inch or 9x9x2-inch). Blend all ingredients except topping. Beat vigorously ½ minute. Spread ½ batter mixture in pan and sprinkle ½ topping mixture over batter in pan. Top with remaining batter, then remaining topping mixture. Bake 25-30 minutes at 375°. Serve warm.

Pass It On...On Christmas morning we always opened our gifts first thing. Then mom brought out hot coffee cake, fresh from the oven. It always smelled yummy and tasted delicious. This year, my husband and I couldn't go home, so I decided to make the cake myself. It was just as good as I remembered as my husband and I shared our first Christmas morning eating homemade Streusel Filled Coffee Cake. I even passed this tradition and some cake on to the rest of the flight crew when I arrived for work later Christmas morning.

APPLE MUFFINS

20-24 muffins

3½ cups flour
2 cups sugar
1 teaspoon salt
1 teaspoon baking soda
1 teaspoon cinnamon

1 (21-ounce) can apple pie filling,
*   chopped*
1½ cups salad oil
½ cup chopped pecans (toasted)
1 teaspoon vanilla

▲ Combine all ingredients. Mix until well blended. Pour into muffin cups and bake at 350° for 20 minutes.

BLUEBERRY MUFFINS

12 large muffins

½ cup butter
2 cups flour
1¼ cups sugar
2 eggs
½ cup milk

2 teaspoons baking powder
½ teaspoon salt
2½ cups blueberries
2 teaspoons sugar (topping)

▲ On low speed, cream butter and sugar until creamy. Add eggs one at a time and mix until blended. Sift dry ingredients, add to egg mixture alternating with milk. Remove bowl from mixer. Stir in berries by hand. Grease and flour muffin tins well. Pour batter in tins, sprinkle sugar on top of each one. Bake in a pre-heated oven at 375° for 25 to 30 minutes. Cool 5-10 minutes before removing from pans.

Pass It On*...I buy fruit in season for use on cereal later. I wash blueberries, strawberries, raspberries or blackberries, and turn them out on paper towels to dry. I freeze the berries in a single layer on a baking sheet but package them in freezer bags when frozen. Added to cereal, the fruit thaws while the family dresses.*

REFRIGERATOR BRAN MUFFINS

36 muffins

Note: Will keep about one month in the refrigerator.

1½ cups sugar
½ cup shortening
2 eggs
2 cups buttermilk
½ cup boiling water

3 cups 100% bran, divided use
2½ cups flour
2½ teaspoons soda
½ teaspoon salt

▲ Beat sugar, shortening and eggs together until fluffy. Add buttermilk. Pour boiling water over 1 cup bran to soften, then add to egg mixture. Sift flour, soda and salt together, then slowly add to mixture. Last, fold in 2 cups dry bran. Line muffin tin with fluted paper cups and fill ¾ full of muffin mix. Bake at 400° for 30 minutes.

FUDGE MUFFINS

Good for brunch, picnics, and tailgate parties

26 large muffins

Note: No leavening, no problem!

2 squares unsweetened chocolate
1 cup butter
1¾ cups sugar

4 eggs
2 teaspoons vanilla
1½ cups flour, sifted

▲ Melt chocolate and butter in a saucepan. Add sugar, eggs and vanilla. Mix gently. Add flour and mix (do not overbeat). Pour into greased muffin tins. Bake at 350° for 20-25 minutes. Store in air-tight container.

Pass It On...In my family, the women all love tea. So when my three-year-old daughter acquired the taste, we had cause for celebration and an excuse for a party. The Mad Hatters Tea Party. We invited three other little girls and their moms. In the invitations, we also asked them to invite a favorite neighborhood grandma to accompany them. And we were clear that all in attendance must wear hats. In our entry, we set my daughter's tiny table with her Minnie Mouse china tea set, a gift from my grandmother, of course. The smallest guests wasted no time finding their seats and serving one another. From the dining room, I poured tea for the adults and served mini-muffins and tea sandwiches. When the little girls tired of their tea party manners, we moved into the living room where a craft table was set for them to make hats out of paper plates, fabric, ribbon, glitter, markers, construction paper, scissors and glue. We then had each model her creation in a hat parade. The grandmas judged each hat a winner and presented each girl with her party favor, a little china teacup and saucer.

CARAMEL ROLLS

36 rolls

Note: An overnight recipe.

1 package yeast
½ cup warm water
4 cups boiling water
1½ tablespoons oil
½ cup sugar

3 teaspoons salt
3 eggs, well-beaten
11 cups flour, half white and half
    whole wheat, sifted

Caramel:
3 cups brown sugar

1 cup cream or sour cream

▲ Dissolve yeast in ½ cup warm water; set aside. Heat water to boiling; add oil, sugar and salt. Cool. Add eggs and yeast to water mixture. Mix in flour. Knead until elastic and doesn't stick to bowl. Form into a ball. Grease top and sides, cover and place in warm draft-free area, let rise 2 to 3 hours. Punch down. Let rise 3 to 4 hours.

Divide dough in half and roll out to about ½-inch thick. Spread with butter and sprinkle with brown sugar and cinnamon. Roll up and cut into rolls about ¾-inch thick. Lay in pans and pour caramel over top. Let rise overnight. Bake at 350° for 25 minutes. Turn upside down while still hot. Caramel for rolls: Mix brown sugar and cream together and pour over rolls when in the pans.

DROP ROLLS

A very easy, good dinner roll

24 small rolls

½ cup butter, softened
1 cup self-rising flour

½ cup sour cream
½-1 teaspoon dill weed

▲ Add the butter, sour cream and dill weed to the flour. Mix with a spoon and drop by the spoon in a mini muffin tin. Bake 15-20 minutes at 375°.

Pass It On...*For quick bread ideas, use one loaf French bread, 1 package brown and serve rolls or freezer yeast rolls and roll in melted butter and your favorite seasoning (Parmesan cheese, fresh herbs, poppy seeds, sesame seeds, etc.). Bake according to package directions.*

OUT OF THIS WORLD ROLLS

3 dozen

2 packages yeast
¼ cup warm water
3 eggs, well-beaten
½ cup shortening

½ cup sugar
1 cup warm water
4½ cups flour, sifted
2 teaspoons salt

▲ Soften yeast in the ¼ cup warm water. Combine eggs, shortening, sugar, softened yeast, 1 cup warm water, salt and 1½ cups flour; beat until smooth. Add remaining flour to make a soft dough. Cover and allow to rise until double. Punch down and place in refrigerator overnight. Three hours before baking, roll out as desired:

For dinner rolls: Divide dough in half. Flour board or pastry cloth and roll each half into a ½-inch thick rectangle. Spread with butter, roll up jelly-roll style and cut into 1-inch slices. Place in greased muffin tins, cut-side down. Cover and allow to rise 3 hours. Bake in 400° oven for 12-15 minutes. (Makes 2 dozen).

For orange rolls: frost while hot with icing of ¼ cup undiluted frozen orange juice mixed into 1⅓ sticks butter and one box powdered sugar (Makes 2 dozen).

For garlic Parmesan sticks: pinch small pieces of dough off and roll between hands to make slender sticks. Place on greased baking sheet, brush with melted butter, and shake lightly with garlic salt and heavily with Parmesan cheese. Allow to rise and bake as above.

Pass It On...For a crisp crust, place a small pan of hot water in the oven when baking bread.

SWEDISH TEA RING

10-12 servings

*2 packages yeast, dissolved
  according to package
  instructions*
1 cup milk
1 teaspoon salt
2 eggs, beaten
½ cup shortening
½ cup sugar

5 cups flour, sifted
*1 cup candied fruit mix, reserving
  cherries*
⅓ cup pecans or walnuts, chopped
1 cup confectioners' sugar
*2-3 tablespoons milk or lemon
  juice*

▲ In a large bowl, combine first six ingredients and 3 cups of flour. Dredge fruit mix with ½ cup of flour. Add remaining flour to yeast mixture to make a soft dough, then add flour-dredged fruit, mixing or kneading in well. Place in greased bowl. Cover and let rise until doubled in bulk. Punch down, transfer to floured pastry cloth and roll out to rectangle about 10x20-inches. Divide into 3 strands and braid them together. Place braid in a circle on greased cookie sheet and let rise again. Bake at 375° for 20-25 minutes. Cool before frosting with mixture of confectioners' sugar and milk (or lemon juice); decorate with reserved cherries cut in half and chopped nuts. Dough may be divided into two loaves, changing oven temperature to 350° and baking 30 minutes.

Pass It On...*When my first son married, I'd get a phone call nearly every week from his new wife. She'd say, "John keeps talking about your spaghetti and how much he used to love it. Can I have the recipe?" or "Can you tell me how to make the Swedish Tea Ring that John's grandmother made every Christmas?" After about five of those calls, I sat down, rifled through my old recipe box, and pulled out all the recipes my son loved. I copied each on a card, bought a special recipe box, and sent it to my daughter-in-law. She was thrilled! After that, when each of my sons married, I presented my new daughter-in-law with a recipe box full of my son's old favorites.*

ORANGE ROLLS

12 rolls

Rolls:

2 packages yeast
1 cup lukewarm water
1 teaspoon salt
⅓ cup sugar

⅓ cup salad oil
2 eggs, well beaten
4 cups flour

Butter:

¼ cup frozen orange juice, undiluted

1⅓ sticks butter
1 box confectioners' sugar

▲ Dissolve yeast in water. Add salt, sugar, salad oil and eggs. Add flour in two parts. Beat until elastic. Let rise until it has more than doubled in bulk. Make dough into rolls and let it rise again. Bake at 375° until brown. For butter: mix and put in covered container. Spread on warm rolls.

BLUEBERRY COFFEE CAKE

6-12 servings

Cake:

2 cups sifted flour
⅓ cup sugar
1 teaspoon baking powder

⅓ cup butter, very soft
3 large eggs
pinch of salt

Filling:

1 pint fresh blueberries (or 16 ounce package frozen)

⅓ cup sugar
¼ cup flour

Topping:

⅓ cup sugar
¼ teaspoon cinnamon

⅔ cup sifted flour
½ cup cold butter

▲ For cake: in a large mixing bowl, sift together flour, sugar and baking powder. Add salt, butter and eggs. Work mixture until it forms a dough. Press dough against bottom and sides of a buttered or non-stick sprayed 13x9x2-inch pan. For filling: combine all ingredients, stir to blend and spoon evenly over cake dough. For topping: sift sugar, cinnamon and flour. Cut in butter until particles are the size of small peas. Sprinkle over filling. Bake coffee cake in preheated 350° oven for 30-45 minutes, or until crust is nicely browned.

CINNAMON ROLLS

48 rolls or 4 pans of twelve rolls

Dough:

2 cups scalded milk
½ cup shortening
1 cup potatoes, mashed
2 packages yeast
½ cup warm water
2 eggs, slightly beaten

1 cup sugar
2 teaspoons salt
½ cup walnuts, chopped
1 cup raisins
7 cups flour, sifted
cinnamon and sugar, as required

Icing glaze:

1 cup confectioners' sugar

2-3 tablespoons lemon juice or
*   milk*

▲ Pour milk over shortening and allow to cool to lukewarm. Soften yeast in the ½ cup warm water. Add eggs, sugar, salt, mashed potatoes, 4 cups of the flour and yeast mixture to milk mixture. Beat until smooth. Flour nuts and raisins with part of the remaining flour and add to dough. Slowly add remaining flour to make a soft dough. Cover and allow to rise until doubled. Divide dough in fourths and roll in rectangle ¼-inch thick. Spread with butter and sprinkle with cinnamon and sugar. Roll up and cut into ½-inch slices. Nestle in round pans and cover. Let rise until doubled. Bake at 350° for 20 minutes. When cool, drizzle icing glaze over rolls. To make icing: stir lemon juice or milk into confectioners' sugar to a smooth, runny consistency.

SWEDISH BREAD

4 loaves

1 package rapid rise yeast
4 cups lukewarm water
4 cups flour
¾ cup brown sugar
¾ cup white sugar

¾ cup liquid oil
1 (12-ounce) bottle molasses
2 teaspoons salt
½ teaspoon baking soda

▲ Mix all ingredients with mixer, then begin adding 5 to 6 cups additional flour one cup at a time until dough is very stiff. Use a large wooden spoon to mix as dough will be too stiff for mixer. Divide dough into four sections. Place one section at a time on a lightly floured surface and knead briefly into a loaf shape. Place in loaf pan which has been sprayed with butter flavored cooking spray. Repeat with other sections. Allow to rise 4-5 hours in oven with the oven light on. Remove pans. Heat oven to 325° and bake bread 40-45 minutes. Brush top of bread with melted butter and turn out on cooling rack.

Soups & Salads

Carol, enclosed
is the Recipe for
Tortilla Soup
that we had last
Thursday. Please
copy and pass it
on to June.
Thanks

MEXICAN CORN CHOWDER

10-12 servings

½ cup butter
2 medium onions, chopped
1½ cups celery, chopped
1½ cups carrots, chopped
1 red bell pepper, chopped
2 quarts strong chicken broth
6 tablespoons flour

2 (16½-ounce) cans cream style corn
1 teaspoon ground cumin
2 tablespoons chili powder (to taste)
4 shakes hot pepper sauce or cayenne to taste
½-1 cup milk

▲ Melt butter and sauté vegetables until cooked but not limp. Add flour and stir until bubbly. Add chicken broth and mix well. Add remaining ingredients and simmer, uncovered, 10 minutes. Add milk until desired consistency.

Pass It On...It's easy to make rich brown soup stock at home. Simply preheat the oven to 450° and roast 4 or 5 pounds beef or veal bones for 30 to 40 minutes or until well browned. Add 2 quartered onions, 2 carrots cut in pieces and 2 stalks celery cut in pieces and roast about 20 minutes more. Then transfer everything to a stock pot or Dutch oven. Tie 1 clove garlic, 1 teaspoon peppercorns, a bay leaf and a few sprigs of thyme and parsley together in a square of cooking cheesecloth and add it to the stock pot. Add 4 quarts water and simmer about 5 hours. Cool and strain.

CHICKEN AND SAUSAGE GUMBO

8-10 servings

Note: Good to make ahead.

⅔ cup oil
⅔ cup flour
2 cups onions, chopped
1 cup celery, chopped
½ cup green bell pepper, diced
4 cloves garlic, minced
¼ cup parsley, chopped
3 pounds favorite pieces of chicken

4 cups hot water
3 cups chicken stock
2-3 teaspoons salt
1 teaspoon pepper
1 pound Andouille sausage or
  spicy garlic sausage, cut in
  1-inch slices

▲ Brown sausage in skillet and drain off fat. Mix oil and flour in a 4-cup glass measuring cup. Microwave on high 6-7 minutes, stir after 6 minutes, then microwave 30 seconds more until roux reaches a dark brown. Add onions, celery and green bell pepper and return to microwave. Cook on high 3 minutes. Add garlic and parsley to roux, stir and return to microwave. Cook on high 2 minutes. Slowly add enough hot tap water to bring roux to the 4-cup mark. Stir until roux is smooth and dark (about 12 minutes). In a large pot, brown chicken in a very small amount of oil. Add roux mixture and 4 cups hot water plus chicken stock. Add salt, pepper and sausage. Simmer for at least 1½ hours. Serve over rice.

Pass It On...Buy chicken backs to use in making chicken stock. Place in a large pot with several slices onion, green onion tops, celery leaves, a carrot and salt and pepper. Cover with water and simmer about an hour, then cover and cool. Strain and discard skin, bones and vegetables. When cooked chicken is to be used in a recipe, buy the necessary pieces and proceed as above being sure water does not boil. Cooking chicken in water at too high a temperature not only makes it tough, but causes the fat to be incorporated into the broth making the broth cloudy.

BEST SEAFOOD GUMBO

8-10 servings

4 tablespoons light oil
3 tablespoons flour
2 cups onions, chopped
1 clove garlic, minced
3 cups chicken broth
1 pound shrimp, raw and peeled
½ pound crabmeat
1 pint oysters

1 package crab claws (if available)
3 tablespoons parsley, chopped
½ pound okra, chopped
1 (16-ounce) can stewed tomatoes
1 teaspoon salt
1 teaspoon pepper
2 tablespoons gumbo filé

▲ Make brown roux of oil and flour. Stir until brown and thick. Add onion, garlic, broth, tomatoes, salt, pepper and parsley; simmer for 10 minutes. Add seafood and cook another 20-30 minutes. Remove from heat and add filé powder. Serve in bowl over hot cooked rice.

Pass It On*...Filé is gumbo's secret. It will become stringy if heated. If desired, add the filé to each individual bowl so that the large pot can be reheated. This creole dish has been a favorite along the Gulf coast of the South for years, and most large grocery stores everywhere now sell the ingredients.*

SHRIMP GUMBO

6 servings

10-ounce soup bone
2 quarts water
2 tablespoons salt

gumbo filé
rice

Roux:
5 tablespoons hot bacon grease
3 tablespoons flour
1 garlic clove, mashed
1 onion, chopped

2 bay leaves
small sprig of thyme
1 (16-ounce) can tomatoes
2 pounds shrimp

Seasoning:
¾ teaspoon black pepper
⅓ teaspoon cayenne pepper
1 teaspoon salt

1 tablespoon Worcestershire sauce
6 drops hot sauce

▲ Boil soup bone in water and salt. Brown bacon grease and flour; add garlic, onion, bay leaves and thyme. Cook together. Add soup bone stock, tomatoes and shrimp. Season with peppers, salt, Worcestershire and hot sauce. Cook an additional 30 minutes or more. Add ½ teaspoon gumbo filé one minute before serving over rice.

QUICK POSOLE

6-10 servings

2 (15-ounce) cans white hominy
2 pounds pork steak in bite size
*   pieces*
1 medium white onion, finely
*   chopped*

½ teaspoon oregano
1 clove garlic, minced
2 dried red chilies
salt to taste

▲ Soak chilies a few hours in water; then puree. Pour hominy into large kettle. Add one 15-ounce can of water and meat. Add remaining ingredients. Simmer approximately 3 hours (if using pork bones, leave in during simmering to add good flavor).

HEARTY BLACK BEAN SOUP

6-8 servings

Note: Requires a few hours to simmer.

2 cups dried black beans
water
2 cups red onion, chopped
4 cloves garlic, minced
¼ cup olive oil
1 tablespoon ground cumin
1 tablespoon oregano
2 bay leaves
¼ cup fresh parsley, chopped
1½ teaspoons salt

1 teaspoon pepper
1 pound hot Italian sausage
1 sweet red pepper, cut in ½ to
*   1-inch cubes*
⅓ cup dry sherry
sour cream and chopped green
*   onions for garnish*
freshly ground black pepper
cayenne pepper (optional)

▲ Pick over beans, carefully removing stones. Place beans in a large, heavy saucepan with enough water to cover by 2 inches. Bring to a boil and boil 2 minutes. Remove from heat, cover and let stand 1 hour. Drain. Sauté onions and garlic in oil until onions are limp. Place in pan with beans. Add seasonings and 7 cups water. Simmer, covered, 2½ hours or until beans are tender. Meanwhile, cook Italian sausage in skillet. When cooked, slice into ¼-inch slices. Remove 2 cups of the beans and some liquid and puree until smooth. Return puree to pan, stirring to combine. Add sausage slices and red pepper. Cook 30 minutes, stirring to prevent sticking. Adjust seasoning and add a pinch of cayenne pepper if desired. Add sherry and cook about 5 minutes. Garnish each serving with sour cream and onions. Pass pepper grinder.

Pass It On...Add ½ pound shrimp, if desired.

KATHY'S BEEF BARLEY SOUP

10 cups

Note: Make a day ahead for flavors to combine nicely.

½ pound ground round or ground sirloin
5 cups water
1 (14½-ounce) can tomatoes
1 (6-ounce) can cocktail vegetable juice
⅓ cup barley
1 bay leaf

¾ cup celery, chopped
½ cup carrots, sliced
⅓ cup dried split peas
½ cup onion, chopped
½ cup undiluted, canned bouillon
¼ teaspoon each pepper, basil and oregano

▲ Coat Dutch oven with cooking spray. Brown meat, drain well. Add all ingredients, bring to a boil. Simmer 1½ hours or longer. Remove bay leaf and serve.

Pass It On*...I remember when we were ill, mother would always serve soup or fix a soft boiled egg with torn up pieces of toast in it.*

BROCCOLI CHEESE SOUP

6 servings

3 tablespoons butter or margarine
1 cup sliced leeks (or green onions, thinly sliced)
1 cup mushrooms, sliced
3 tablespoons flour

3 cups chicken broth
1 cup broccoli florets (fresh or frozen)
1 cup light cream
1 cup Jarlsberg cheese, shredded

▲ Melt butter and sauté onions and mushrooms until tender (do not brown). Add flour and stir just until it boils. Remove from heat and gradually add chicken broth stirring constantly until it thickens. Return to the heat and add broccoli. Simmer until the broccoli is tender. Stir in cream and cheese and serve when the cheese melts.

Pass It On*...Spoon over baked potatoes for a deliciously different topping.*

BRIE SOUP

6 servings

2 tablespoons butter
4 large onions, thinly sliced
½ teaspoon salt
4 cups beef broth or consommé

⅓ cup dry Madeira
¼ pound Brie cheese at room
temperature

▲ Melt butter in heavy saucepan. Add onions and salt and cover tightly. Cook over low heat until tender, steaming about 15 minutes. Do not brown. Add broth and simmer for 20 minutes. Correct seasonings. Add Madeira. Strain, or not. Dice Brie in bottom of soup cups or tureen, pour soup over. Stir and serve.

FESTIVE FALL SOUP

6-8 servings

1¼ pound butternut squash
2 Granny Smith apples
1 medium onion
6 cups chicken broth
2 slices dry white bread

¼ teaspoon marjoram
¼ teaspoon rosemary
1 teaspoon salt
¼ teaspoon pepper
¼ cup heavy cream

▲ Peel, seed and chop the squash and apples. Thinly slice the onion. Place all in a large kettle with the chicken broth, dry bread and seasonings. Simmer, covered, for 45 minutes. Puree in blender or processor and return to heat. Heat to just below boiling. Add ¼ cup heavy cream. Ladle soup into bowls and garnish with sprig of fresh rosemary. For microwave: Place in 8-cup glass measure (using only 3-4 cups broth at this state, reserve the rest). Cover tightly with plastic wrap and microwave on high for 12-15 minutes. Puree, return to heat with reserved broth. Microwave, covered, for 8-10 minutes. Continue as above. Time will depend on microwave power and bulk of ingredients.

Pass It On...For a light touch, substitute evaporated skimmed milk for half-and-half or heavy cream.

LEEK AND POTATO SOUP

A perfect microwave soup

4 servings

*¾ pound potatoes, peeled and
    diced*
*1 cup leeks, white part and 1-inch
    of green, diced*
2 cups chicken broth

1 cup heavy cream
2 tablespoons butter
*salt and freshly ground black
    pepper to taste*

▲ Place potatoes, leeks and 1 cup of broth in 8-cup glass measure. Cover tightly with microwave plastic wrap. Place in microwave. Cook at 100 percent for 12 minutes. Remove from oven, uncover and use processor or blender to puree. Stir in cream, butter and remaining 1 cup broth. Season with salt and pepper. Heat in a two-quart glass measure or soufflé dish covered tightly for 5 minutes. Serve hot.

ROASTED RED PEPPER SOUP

8 servings

8 red bell peppers, roasted
3-4 garlic cloves, minced
2-3 shallots, diced
½ cup onion, diced
2 tablespoons olive oil
½ cup vermouth
6 cups chicken stock

½ cup heavy cream (optional)
1 tablespoon fresh chives
1 tablespoon fresh oregano
1 tablespoon fresh parsley
1 tablespoon fresh basil
2 tablespoons lemon juice
salt and pepper to taste

▲ To roast red peppers, make a slit in the pepper and roast in one of the following ways: spear with a long-handled fork and roast directly over the burner of the gas or electric range; or place on a broiler rack and set under a pre-heated broiler 4-6 inches from the heat source; or roast over charcoal grill. Peppers are roasted when the skins are blistered and charred. Immediately place the roasted peppers in a paper bag or a plastic bag for about 10 minutes to steam off the skins. The charred skin should slip off, but some may adhere and will need to be peeled. Slice peppers and remove seeds and veins. Mince garlic, dice shallots and onions. Sauté in 2 tablespoons olive oil over low heat for 1 minute. Add vermouth, cook for 2 minutes, then cover and sweat for 5 minutes over low heat. Add sliced pepper and herbs. Simmer for 15 minutes. Puree in blender until smooth. Return to heat, add chicken stock and lemon juice. Salt and pepper to taste. Add cream for extra thickness and body and garnish with croutons and fresh chives.

SAUSAGE MINESTRONE SOUP

15 servings

Note: Best made the day before to blend flavors. Freezes well.

1 pound Italian sausage (half hot and half sweet)
1 tablespoon olive oil
1 cup onions, chopped
1 clove garlic
1 cup carrots, diced
1 teaspoon dried basil
2 cups cabbage, shredded
2 small zucchini, diced

1 (28-ounce) can plum tomatoes, (chopped and use juice)
4 cans beef bouillon, not diluted
2 cups water
1 (19-ounce) can white kidney beans with juice
½ cup uncooked rice
¾ cup hearty Burgundy
fresh Parmesan cheese to garnish

▲ Crumble and brown sausage in oil in large soup pot. Add onion, carrot, garlic and basil; cook 5 minutes. Skim fat. Add zucchini, tomatoes, bouillon, water and cabbage. Simmer for 1 hour. Add beans with liquid, rice and wine. Cook 20 minutes more. If too thick, thin with bouillon or water. Serve in soup bowls topped with cheese.

Pass It On...Substitute uncooked pasta for rice.

LINDA'S SAUSAGE SOUP

A cool weather favorite

6-8 for dinner

2 pounds pork sausage
1 cup onion, chopped
2 (15-ounce) cans pinto beans
1 (16-ounce) can tomatoes, diced
1 bay leaf

2 teaspoons garlic powder (or 2 garlic cloves, minced)
½ teaspoon black pepper
1½ teaspoons seasoned salt
1 quart water
2 cups raw potato, diced

▲ Brown and drain sausage well. Add all ingredients except potato and cook slowly for 2 hours. Add potato and cook until soft.

Pass It On...I love to invite guests to enjoy this hearty soup at a Winter Mitten Party. I scour thrift stores for inexpensive mittens and gloves then mail the invitations tucked inside, one per person. Upon arrival, each guest finds his or her match. The pairs become dinner partners. Sometimes I use socks or almost anything that comes in pairs.

SUMMER SHRIMP SOUP

3 quarts

Note: A two-day recipe.

2 (32-ounce) bottles Clamato juice
3-4 cloves garlic
¼ cup olive oil
½ cup vinegar
1 (14-ounce) jar fresh salsa
1 (14-ounce) jar spiced apple
*   rings, including liquid*
½ cup green onions, chopped

1 cup celery, chopped
2 fresh tomatoes, chopped
1 tablespoon sweet fresh basil
salt and pepper to taste
1 pound small bay shrimp
2 avocados, cubed
1 (8-ounce) package cream cheese,
*   cubed*

▲ At least 24 hours ahead, put first 6 ingredients in blender and process until smooth. Mix in the chopped green onion, chopped celery, chopped tomato and seasonings. Add shrimp, cubed avocado and cream cheese on the day served.

Pass It On*...My accountant husband's favorite piece of advice: "It doesn't cost you anything to be nice."*

CURRIED SQUASH SOUP

4 appetizer portions

1 medium butternut squash, cubed
*   and boiled until soft enough to*
*   mash*
2½ cups chicken broth
1 teaspoon curry
¼ teaspoon each cinnamon,
*   nutmeg and coriander*

½ teaspoon salt
½ teaspoon white pepper
¼ cup heavy cream to thicken
sour cream
1-2 green onion tops, diagonally
*   sliced, to garnish*

▲ Combine mashed squash with broth and heat to boil. Add spices and simmer 10-15 minutes. Add cream to thicken. Pour into bowls and top with dollop of sour cream. Sprinkle slivers of green onion on top.

TORTILLA SOUP

6-8 servings

2 tablespoons oil
1 small onion, chopped
1 can chopped green chilies
2 cloves garlic
1 (8-ounce) can chopped tomato
1 (10½-ounce) can beef bouillon
1 (10½-ounce) can chicken broth
1½ cups water

1½ cups tomato juice
1 teaspoon cumin
1 teaspoon chili powder
1 teaspoon salt
⅛ teaspoon pepper
2 teaspoons Worcestershire sauce
1 tablespoon steak sauce
1 tablespoon lime juice

▲ Sauté onion, chilies and garlic in oil. Add remaining ingredients and simmer for 1 hour. Serve hot with various condiments such as fried tortilla chips, grated Monterey Jack cheese, shredded chicken, chopped fresh tomatoes, onions and cilantro.

BRUNSWICK STEW

1+ gallons

Note: Freezes well.

1 medium fryer
3 pounds Boston Butt
2 medium onions, chopped
2 (16-ounce) cans stewed tomatoes
2 (16-ounce) cans corn
2 (16-ounce) cans butter beans

4 medium potatoes, cubed
1 teaspoon lemon pepper
¼ cup Worcestershire sauce
juice of 2 lemons
salt to taste

▲ Cook meats in salted water until meat is tender and falls from the bone. This takes several hours and the meats may be cooked together if pot is large enough. Allow for plenty of water for broth. Remove meat and let cool. Shred into bite-size pieces, removing all fat. Skim fat from liquid. Return meat to liquid. Add vegetables and remaining seasonings. Cook slowly over low heat several hours until well blended. Stir often.

KENTUCKY BURGOO

Sometimes a ragout, sometimes a stew, but in Kentucky it's called a burgoo!

6-8 servings

2 pounds soup meat: beef, pork and/or veal
2 quarts boiling water
2 medium potatoes, peeled and diced
1 cup tomatoes

1 (12-ounce) can whole kernel corn, undrained
1 teaspoon parsley flakes
1¼ teaspoons salt
⅛ teaspoon pepper
1¼ teaspoons Worcestershire sauce

▲ Add meat to boiling water in large kettle. Reduce heat and simmer until meat is tender, about 1-2 hours. Remove meat from bones and dice. Add meat, vegetables and seasonings to stock. Continue to cook over low heat until mixture has thickened. Stir occasionally. Spoon into soup bowls and serve with crusty bread, and salad.

Pass It On…Try with Swedish Cream and Strawberries for dessert at a Derby Day dinner party.

CREAM OF ARTICHOKE SOUP

4 servings

1 (6-ounce) jar marinated arti-choke hearts
1 cup thinly sliced celery
¼ cup chopped onion
½ cup water
1 tablespoon chicken bouillon granules

2 teaspoons cornstarch
¾ teaspoon salt
2 cups half-and-half
1 teaspoon fresh lemon juice
fresh, chopped parsley
grated lemon zest

▲ Drain and reserve marinade from artichokes. Remove 2 tablespoons oil, then heat marinade in a saucepan with celery and onion until vegetables are tender and crisp. Add water and chicken bouillon granules. Cover and simmer about 10 minutes. Stir salt and cornstarch into half-and-half. Add to hot mixture. Cook, stirring until mixture boils and thickens slightly. Chop artichoke hearts and add to soup. Add lemon juice and keep hot until served. Garnish with chopped parsley and sprinkle with lemon zest.

Pass It On…For a smoother soup, puree sautéed celery, onion and artichoke hearts; then combine with salt, cornstarch and half-and-half.

CHICKEN SOUP CHAPULTEPEC

6-8 servings

3 pounds chicken, cut up
2 pounds tomatillos, halved
1 green bell pepper, chopped
1 onion, chopped
1 bunch fresh cilantro, chopped

2 cups cooked white rice
1 tablespoon cumin
1 tablespoon salt (or to taste)
½ tablespoon pepper

▲ Cook chicken in 8 cups water for 30-40 minutes or until completely cooked. Remove chicken from water and set aside until cool enough to separate from bones and skin, then shred. Add tomatillos, bell pepper, onion and cilantro to broth. Simmer about 30 minutes, then remove from heat and cool to room temperature. Remove vegetables from broth and puree in blender or food processor. Strain broth, then return puree to broth and bring to a boil. Reduce heat to simmer and add rice, shredded chicken, cumin, salt and pepper. Serve hot with warm flour or corn tortillas and butter.

Pass It On…You may wish to add more chicken broth when reheated the next day.

BAKED POTATO SOUP

8-10 servings

4 large potatoes
⅔ cup butter
⅔ cup flour
1½ quarts milk (6 cups)
salt and pepper to taste
4 green onions, chopped

1 cup sour cream
2 cups crisp-cooked, crumbled
*   bacon, well drained*
5 ounces Cheddar cheese, grated
chives

▲ Scrub potatoes and bake in 350° oven until tender. Melt butter in medium saucepan and slowly blend in flour with a wire whisk. Gradually add milk, whisking constantly. Add salt and pepper and simmer over low heat taking care that it does not burn. Cut potatoes in half, scoop out meat and set aside. Chop half the potato peels and discard the rest. Mash potato meat, then add to hot milk mixture, blending well. Add onions, peels, sour cream and bacon. Heat thoroughly then add cheese and melt it in. Add additional milk if soup is too thick. Serve garnished with chives.

CHICKEN SALAD

6-8 servings

4 cups white chicken, cooked and chopped
2 cups celery, chopped
1 cup onion, grated
1 teaspoon salt
½ teaspoon white pepper

2½ cups hard boiled eggs, chopped
1 teaspoon lemon juice
2 cups mayonnaise
8 tomatoes
paprika
8 stuffed green olives

▲ Mix first eight ingredients together in a large mixing bowl. Add more mayonnaise, salt and pepper to taste as desired. Add 2 packages of slivered almonds if desired. Peel, salt and cut in quarters 8 tomatoes and place on lettuce leaves. Fill tomatoes with chicken salad mixture, top with paprika and a green stuffed olive.

Pass It On... *"The year we moved from the farm that had been in the family for a hundred years, we compiled a small book of recipes and sent them as Christmas cards. We included the above Chicken Salad traditionally served for summer lunch at Willow Plunge, the swimming pool." - Ruth McDowell Kinnard, National President Delta Delta Delta (1952-56) and the first woman federal judge in Tennessee as well as the only woman (1973) federal referee on bankruptcy in the U.S.*

SUMMER TOMATOES

6-8 servings

6-8 tomatoes

Dressing:
½ teaspoon dried oregano
2 teaspoons dried basil or 2 tablespoons shredded fresh basil
½ teaspoon garlic, minced

½ teaspoon salt
1 teaspoon sugar
2 green onions, finely diced
2 tablespoons finely diced red onions

▲ Blend ingredients. Blanch tomatoes and peel skins. Pour dressing over whole tomatoes and marinate overnight. Serve in a large bowl garnished with fresh parsley and basil. No further dressing is necessary.

Pass It On… *Slice and drizzle with balsamic vinegar and olive oil and sprinkle with bits of mozzarella cheese.*

ASPEN VILLAGE SALAD

A traditional chef salad with a Tex-Mex flavor

2 servings

Salad:

1 head Romaine lettuce
2 chicken breasts, cooked, skinned
   and boned
6 slices Monterey Jack cheese,
   julienned

6 slices salami, julienned
6-8 slices orange
6 slices avocado
6-8 black olives, pitted

Dressing:

¼ cup sour cream
¼ cup mayonnaise
1 tablespoon fresh lemon juice
⅛ teaspoon dry mustard

¼ teaspoon cumin
2 tablespoons salsa or chili sauce
⅛ teaspoon garlic salt
8-10 tortilla chips for garnish

▲ For each salad, arrange outer Romaine leaves on plate. Finely chop a few inner leaves and arrange on top. Cut chicken breasts into strips and place on lettuce. Add cheese, salami, orange slices, avocado and olives. Cover and chill. For dressing, blend sour cream and mayonnaise. Add remaining dressing ingredients and chill. At serving time, add dressing and garnish with tortilla chips.

BROCCOLI SALAD

6-8 servings

1 envelope gelatin
1 can beef consommé
¾ cup mayonnaise
4 tablespoons Worcestershire
   sauce

2 tablespoons lemon juice
2 small packages chopped
   broccoli, slightly cooked
4 hard boiled eggs, chopped

▲ Dissolve gelatin in a little cold water and add to heated consommé. Add other ingredients. Add broccoli and chopped eggs last. Mix well and pour into greased 9x13-inch casserole to mold. Refrigerate, cut and serve on lettuce with a dollop of mayonnaise and a strip of pimiento to top.

Pass It On...Fresh, slightly cooked vegetables enhance a recipe that calls for frozen vegetables. Also, to center a gelatin mold on a plate, wet the plate before unmolding.

FRESH BROCCOLI-MANDARIN SALAD

12 servings

Dressing:

*1 egg plus 1 egg yolk, lightly
    beaten*
½ cup sugar
1½ teaspoons cornstarch
1 teaspoon dry mustard

¼ cup balsamic vinegar
¼ cup water
*3 tablespoons soft butter or
    margarine*
½ cup mayonnaise

Salad:

*4 cups broccoli florets, fresh or
    frozen*
*6 slices bacon, cooked and
    crumbled*
2 cups fresh mushrooms, sliced

*½ cup almonds, slivered and
    toasted*
*1 (11-ounce) can mandarin
    oranges, drained*
½ large red onion, sliced

▲ In top of double boiler, whisk egg, yolk, sugar, cornstarch and mustard. Combine vinegar and water and slowly add to egg mixture, whisking constantly. Place over hot water and cook, stirring until thick. Remove from heat, stir in butter and mayonnaise. Chill. Toss dressing with salad ingredients in large bowl.

Pass It On...Even better the second day when ingredients soak up the dressing!

Pass It On...My mother served a wonderful salad made by putting a few cinnimon red hot candies and a squeeze of lemon juice in the center of a canned peach half. She made it early in the day so the candies would melt spreading a tasty red stain deep into the peach half. Sometimes she would just mix the candies and lemon juice with drained peach slices stirring until the candies dissolved. Several sprigs of fresh mint were often added for summer meals.

A '90s CAESAR SALAD

4 servings

Dressing:

1½ teaspoons garlic, minced
½ teaspoon salt
⅓ cup Parmesan cheese, freshly
    grated
2 tablespoons Dijon mustard
2 teaspoons Worcestershire sauce

1½ teaspoons sugar
⅓ cup lemon juice
⅔ cup olive oil (extra virgin
    preferred)
1 tablespoon fresh parsley, minced
    (optional)

Salad:

1 head Romaine lettuce
½ bag garlic and butter flavor
    croutons

⅓ cup Parmesan cheese, grated or
    shredded

▲ To mix dressing, place all ingredients in food processor and blend. Refrigerate if possible. In large bowl, place Romaine lettuce (torn into bite-size pieces), croutons and Parmesan cheese; add dressing. Toss salad until leaves are evenly coated with dressing.

Pass It On...Grate Parmesan cheese upon purchase. It will refrigerate in a tight jar in refrigerator for several days. Also you may keep it in a tight jar in the freezer for quite a while.

BROOKHOLLOW CHICKEN SALAD

A very light and crunchy salad — perfect for a hot summer day

4 servings

2 whole chicken breasts, cooked
    and shredded
¾ head iceberg lettuce, finely
    shredded with a knife
3 or more green onions, chopped

1 small package slivered almonds,
    toasted
1 (3-ounce) can Chinese rice
    noodles, lightly toasted to
    warm

Dressing:

4 tablespoons sugar
1 teaspoon salt
½ teaspoon seasoned salt
½ teaspoon pepper

4 tablespoons vinegar
½ cup salad oil
⅛ cup poppy seeds

▲ Mix chicken, lettuce and onion. Make the dressing by combining the sugar, salt, seasoned salt, pepper and vinegar. Whisk in the oil a little at a time. Add the poppy seeds. Combine the chicken mixture with the dressing. At the last minute, add the almonds and the noodles.

CHINESE CHICKEN SALAD

6 servings

*2 whole chicken breasts, skinned
   and boned*
¼ cup cornstarch
½ cup oil
*1 medium head iceberg lettuce,
   thinly shredded*
4 green onions

¼ cup chunky peanut butter
¼ cup sugar
3 tablespoons white vinegar
2 tablespoons sesame seeds
1 teaspoon salt
⅛ teaspoon pepper

▲ Cut chicken into 2½-inch strips. Coat with cornstarch. Heat ¼ cup oil and cook chicken 3-4 minutes until golden brown. Drain, cover and refrigerate. Cut onions into 2-inch strips and toss with lettuce. In a small bowl with wire whisk, beat peanut butter, ¼ cup oil and sugar until smooth. Beat in remaining ingredients. Cover and refrigerate. Just before serving, toss chicken and lettuce mixture with dressing.

Pass It On...To remove the core from lettuce easily, sharply hit the core against a counter top.

CHICKEN PASTA SALAD

6-8 servings

1 (8-ounce) package rotini
½ cup mayonnaise
½ cup bottled Italian dressing
1 tablespoon lemon juice
1 tablespoon prepared mustard
1 teaspoon pepper
½ teaspoon salt

3 cups chopped, cooked chicken
1 cup sliced cucumber
1 cup chopped celery
¾ cup ripe olives, sliced
1 medium onion
*1 can quartered artichoke hearts,
   drained*

▲ Cook pasta according to directions and let cool. Combine next 6 ingredients and stir until blended. Add to pasta and mix well. Stir in rest of ingredients. Cover and chill at least 2 hours (best chilled overnight).

Pass It On...For crispier cucumbers, seed slices or sticks and keep in ice water until ready for use.

GOURMET CHICKEN SALAD

6 cups

3 cups chicken breast , cooked and cubed
2 cups new potatoes, cooked and cubed
1½ cups artichoke hearts, cut into bite size wedges
½ cup red pepper strips
½ cup yellow pepper strips

2 tablespoons fresh chives, chopped
2 tablespoons fresh parsley, chopped
just under ½ teaspoon pepper
just under ½ teaspoon salt
⅓ cup mayonnaise
⅓ cup sour cream

▲ Mix all but the last 2 ingredients in a very large bowl. Gently stir, but don't break up potatoes. In a small bowl mix mayonnaise and sour cream. Gently fold into salad. Chill several hours before serving.

HOT CHICKEN SALAD

10-12 servings

4 cups chicken, chopped
2 cups celery, chopped
1 cup slivered almonds
1 teaspoon salt
⅓ cup onion, grated

4 tablespoons lemon juice
1-2 cups mayonnaise
1 cup sharp Cheddar cheese, grated
1 cup broken potato chips

▲ Mix all ingredients except cheese and potato chips in a large bowl. Turn into a shallow, buttered casserole dish. Combine potato chips and cheese; spread over top of casserole. Bake at 375° for 20 minutes.

WILD RICE AND CHICKEN SALAD

10 servings

2 (6-ounce) packages long grain, wild rice
3½ cups cooked and chopped chicken breast
1 (4¼-ounce) can ripe chopped olives, drained

½ cup green onions with tops, chopped
1 cup chopped celery
1½ cups mayonnaise
salt and lemon pepper to taste

▲ Cook rice according to instructions. Combine chicken, olives, onions, celery and mayonnaise and mix with rice. Season with salt and lemon pepper. Refrigerate. Serve on lettuce leaf and top each serving with slivered almonds and paprika.

BEST CRANBERRY SALAD

A tradition at holiday dinners with friends and family

6-8 servings

2 cups fresh cranberries
1¼ cups water
¾ cup sugar
1 small package cherry gelatin
¾ cup celery

¼ teaspoon salt
½ cup English walnuts, chopped
1 small can crushed pineapple,
*   drained (optional)*

▲ Cook cranberries in water until soft. Add sugar and cook 5 minutes. Add gelatin and stir until dissolved. Chill until partially congealed. Add celery, salt, walnuts and pineapple (if desired). Pour into a ring mold and chill until set.

Pass It On...Friends call long distance for this recipe. It has now become a tradition at our holiday dinners and theirs, too.

MINTED CUCUMBER SALAD

6-8 servings

4 medium-sized cucumbers
½ teaspoon salt
2 cups plain non-fat yogurt
3 cloves garlic, minced
2 tablespoons lemon juice

1 tablespoon fresh dill (1½
*   teaspoons dry), minced*
1 tablespoon fresh mint (1½
*   teaspoons dry), minced*
8 butter lettuce leaves

▲ Peel cucumbers, remove seeds and coarsely chop. Mix with salt and let drain in colander 30 minutes. Pat dry with paper towels. Combine all ingredients except lettuce and chill at least 3 hours or overnight. Serve on butter lettuce leaves.

Pass It On...Garnish the salad with various edible flowers such as pansies, or a sprig of mint or dill.

FIREWORKS SALAD

6-8 servings

Note: Perfect for preparing early in the day.

¾ pound snow peas, trimmed
1 large red bell pepper, julienned
1 large yellow bell pepper, julienned
1 cup large radishes, sliced and julienned

2 tablespoons fresh lemon juice
2 teaspoons fresh ginger root, peeled and grated
⅓ cup olive oil
salt and pepper to taste

▲ In a saucepan of boiling water, blanch the snow peas for 15 seconds. Drain. Put into a bowl of ice water for 2 minutes. Drain again and cut peas diagonally into thin strips. Toss with peppers and radishes. In a small bowl, whisk together lemon juice, ginger root, salt and pepper. While whisking, add oil in slow stream and continue to whisk until dressing is emulsified. Pour dressing over salad and toss well. Can be refrigerated overnight or prepared early in the day.

JADE TREE SALAD

A delicious luncheon salad

6-8 servings

2 heads butter lettuce
5-8 chicken breasts, cooked and shredded

2 cans water chestnuts, sliced
¼ cup sesame seeds, toasted
½ cup Parmesan cheese, grated

Dressing:
1⅓ cups salad oil
⅔ cup tarragon vinegar
2 teaspoons salt
1 teaspoon dry mustard

½ teaspoon garlic powder
½ teaspoon black pepper
¼ cup sugar

▲ Combine oil, vinegar, sugar and seasonings in jar and shake well. Break up lettuce and toss with dressing, chicken and chestnuts. Add sesame seeds and cheese. Toss again.

Pass It On...*Garnish with avocado slices, orange slices or grapes.*

HOT AND COOL MANGO SALAD

8 servings

Note: Requires at least 2 hours to chill.

4 to 6 firm, ripe mangos
1 sweet onion (such as Vidalia or
Texas 1015), thinly sliced

4 fresh jalapeños, seeded and
slivered

Dressing:
¼ cup light salad oil
¾ cup cider vinegar

salt and pepper to taste
dash of sugar

▲ Peel mangos, remove meat from seed and cut in chunks. Combine mango, onion slices and jalapeños. Combine last 4 ingredients and mix well. Pour dressing over salad and gently mix all ingredients. Refrigerate 2 hours or more before serving.

Pass It On...*Remember that winners do what losers don't want to do.*

WINTER ORANGE-ONION SALAD

8 servings

1¼ cups cranberries, fresh or
frozen
⅓ cup sugar
4 medium oranges
2 tablespoons salad oil
2 tablespoons red wine vinegar

12 cups mixed greens, torn and
crisped
½ cup red onion rings, thinly
sliced and separated into rings
salt and pepper

▲ In a 1½- or 2-quart pan, combine and stir cranberries and sugar. Cover and cook over low heat, shaking pan occasionally, just until a few cranberries begin to burst (about 8 minutes for fresh, 15 minutes for frozen). Let cool. Grate enough orange peel to make 1 teaspoon. Ream one of the oranges to make 3 tablespoons of juice. Mix orange peel, orange juice, oil and vinegar; gently stir into cranberry mixture. (At this point mixture may be covered and refrigerated for up to 2 days.) Remove peel and white membrane from remaining oranges; thinly slice. In salad bowl, combine orange slice, greens and onion. Pour cranberry dressing over salad. Toss well.

Pass It On...*If I take the time to soak the oranges in hot water for 10 minutes, the peel and pith come off instantly. The same with tomatoes (10 seconds) and peaches (10-20 seconds).*

SALAD NIÇOISE AND DRESSING

5-6 servings

Dressing:

1 egg
1 cup corn oil
¼ cup wine vinegar
1 teaspoon garlic, minced
1 teaspoon sugar
2 tablespoons each dill and
    parsley, minced (optional)

1 teaspoon dried basil
½ teaspoon salt
1½ teaspoons pepper
1 (2-ounce) can anchovies in oil,
    drained and finely chopped

Salad:

½ pound green beans
6-8 small red skin potatoes,
    quartered
2 tablespoons olive oil
2 (7-ounce) cans white meat tuna
1 red pepper, julienned

1½ cups cherry tomatoes, halved
    or tomatoes in season,
    quartered
½ cup pitted Kalamata olives
½ cup scallions, julienned
3 hard-cooked eggs, halved
Romaine leaves

▲ For dressing: Whisk egg in food processor or blender, or whisk by hand until light-colored. Gradually add corn oil until well homogenized. Add remaining ingredients except for anchovies and whisk until smooth. Stir in anchovies and refrigerate. For salad: Cut beans into 2-inch long pieces and blanch in boiling salted water until crisp-tender (about 2 minutes). Plunge into ice water to crisp. Drain well, and chill until ready to use. Cook unpeeled potatoes in boiling, salted water until tender. Drain and when cool enough to handle, slice or quarter. Toss potatoes in olive oil. Chill until ready to use. Drain tuna and chunk or flake. Combine all (except hard-boiled eggs) with the dressing several hours before serving. Serve on Romaine leaves and garnish with hard cooked egg halves. Serve at room temperature.

Pass It On...*Substitute ½ to 1 tablespoon cream for a raw egg in salad dressing recipes — or use egg substitute according to package directions in almost all recipes.*

HOT POTATO SALAD

8 servings

8 medium potatoes
1 pound Colby longhorn cheese,
   diced
1 large onion, diced

1 cup green olives, sliced
1 cup mayonnaise
6-8 slices bacon, partially cooked

▲ Boil potatoes in jackets. Cool, peel and dice. Add cheese, onion, green olives and mayonnaise. Mix together thoroughly and pour into 9x13-inch pan. Arrange partially cooked bacon on top. Bake at 350° for 30-40 minutes.

Pass It On...*Sweet potatoes make great French fries or baked potatoes.*

GREEK SHRIMP AND PASTA SALAD

10-12 servings

Salad:
½ pound small pasta shells, cooked
   according to directions
1 pound bay shrimp, cooked,
   peeled and deveined
1 cup crumbled Feta cheese, and a
   little extra for topping

1 pound frozen or canned
   artichoke hearts, cooked and
   quartered
2 large tomatoes
¼ cup parsley, minced
1 small red onion, thinly sliced and
   separated into rings

Dressing:
½ cup olive oil
2 tablespoons white wine vinegar
1 teaspoon Dijon mustard
2 tablespoons fresh lemon juice

1 teaspoon oregano
1 clove garlic, pressed
salt and pepper to taste

▲ In large bowl, combine pasta, shrimp, Feta cheese, artichoke hearts, tomatoes, parsley and red onion. In separate bowl, combine the remaining ingredients to make dressing. Toss dressing with pasta and sprinkle with crumbled remaining Feta cheese.

Pass It On...*Some fish departments can quickly steam cook the shrimp for you, making it easy to peel.*

INDIAN SHRIMP SALAD

10-12 servings

6 cups rice, cooked
3 pounds shrimp, cooked and
* cleaned*
3 cups celery, chopped
1½ cups green pepper, diced

1 cup Major Grey's mango
* chutney*
seasoned salt to taste (optional)
1 cup oil and vinegar base salad
* dressing*
1½ teaspoons curry powder

▲ Cut shrimp in half lengthwise. Toss all ingredients in non-metal bowl and marinate overnight.

SPINACH AND STRAWBERRY SALAD

6 servings

½ bag fresh spinach, washed and
* dried*

1 pint strawberries, washed and
* sliced lengthwise*

Dressing:
½ cup sugar
2 teaspoons sesame seeds
1 teaspoon poppy seeds
1½ teaspoons onion, minced

½ teaspoon Worcestershire sauce
¼ teaspoon paprika
½ cup salad oil
¼ cup cider vinegar

▲ Prepare spinach and strawberries in bowl. Mix dressing ingredients in blender except for seeds. Add seeds at the last minute. Toss spinach and strawberries and dressing just before serving.

***Pass It On**...In place of the strawberries, add fresh bean sprouts, mandarin orange slices, water chestnuts, hard cooked eggs, bacon, onions, cheese or mushrooms for different versions.*

RED AND GREEN BEAN SALAD

A very different twist to salad

4-6 servings

¾-1 pound green beans
½ small red onion, sliced
½ cup walnuts, chopped
½ cup Feta cheese, crumbled

4 tablespoons olive oil
1 tablespoon wine vinegar
½ teaspoon Dijon mustard
pinch each salt, pepper and sugar

▲ Wash and break green beans into bite-size pieces. Lightly steam green beans. Run under cold water. Combine beans with onions, walnuts and cheese. Combine oil, vinegar, mustard and seasonings to make dressing. Toss bean mixture with dressing.

TOMATO ASPIC SALAD

12-15 servings

Note: Requires 5 hours to chill.

2 (46-ounce) cans tomato juice
1 tablespoon dry mustard
1 bay leaf
2 whole cloves
1 tablespoon sugar
dash of Accent
1 teaspoon celery seed

1 teaspoon orange juice
1 cup finely chopped celery
1 medium onion, finely chopped
1 lemon, juiced and strained
1 (3-ounce) package lemon gelatin
3 tablespoons unflavored gelatin
2 cups water

▲ Combine first 5 ingredients in large saucepan and simmer (do not boil) for 1 hour. Combine remaining ingredients in large bowl. Strain hot mixture into cold mixture and stir making sure the gelatin has completely melted. Pour into 9x13x2-inch pan and refrigerate at least 5 hours or overnight. Slice into squares and serve on lettuce leaves and garnish with sliced ripe olives.

VEGETABLE SALAD

6-8 servings

Note: Requires 4 hours refrigeration.

1 can white shoepeg corn
1 can tiny green peas
1 can French green beans
½ cup onion, thinly sliced
½ cup green pepper, sliced

1 cup sugar
1 cup cider vinegar
½ cup salad oil
1 tablespoon water
lettuce

▲ Drain and wash the corn, peas and beans. Put in bowl with onions and green peppers. Boil sugar, cider vinegar, salad oil and water until sugar is dissolved. Pour mixture over vegetables. Refrigerate for at least 4 hours. Drain and serve with lettuce.

***Pass It On**...Seen on a friend's refrigerator door: "Home is where I hang my heart."*

BLACK BEANS AND RICE SALAD

Good served warmed or chilled

6-8 servings

2 cans black beans (washed and drained)
2 cups rice
1 bunch green onions

2-3 tomatoes
1 green bell pepper
¼ cup cilantro, minced
⅓ cup Parmesan cheese, grated

Dressing:
2 tablespoons fresh lime juice
2 tablespoons olive oil
2 cloves garlic, minced

¼ teaspoon cumin
salt and pepper to taste

▲ Wash and drain black beans. Cook rice according to directions. Thinly slice green onions, dice bell pepper and tomatoes. Prepare dressing. Toss warm rice and beans with Parmesan cheese, add fresh condiments and toss with dressing.

HERB DRESSING

2½ cups

½ cup parsley leaves
½ cup watercress leaves (or use all
    parsley)
8 peeled shallots or scallions
2 teaspoons dry mustard
1 teaspoon horseradish

1 teaspoon Worcestershire sauce
2 egg yolks
1 cup salad oil
⅓ cup tarragon vinegar
1 teaspoon mixed dried herbs

▲ Put all ingredients in a blender and whip until thickened. Thin with cold water.

Pass It On...When Rich and I announced our engagement with the wedding date set months ahead, my mom started preparing. Each week, she gave me a gift: a typed family recipe along with a jar of a spice or herb used in the dish. Eleven months later, we began married life with a full recipe box, a full array of herbs and spices, and hearts full of love.

LEMON GARLIC DRESSING

1 cup

1 clove garlic, finely crushed
1 teaspoon salt
½ teaspoon pepper

6 tablespoons salad oil
2 tablespoons vinegar, any flavor
1 lemon, juiced and strained

▲ Mix well and let stand about an hour.

CHILI DRESSING

2 cups

¾ cup rice wine vinegar
½ cup soy sauce
3 tablespoons sugar
2 tablespoons sesame oil

2 tablespoons fresh ginger, minced
2 tablespoons crushed dried red
    pepper flakes
2 cloves garlic, minced

▲ Combine all ingredients.

Pass It On...Great with grilled chicken that has been shredded. Serve on lettuce with cucumber, fresh cilantro, roasted peanuts and a freshly sliced green onion.

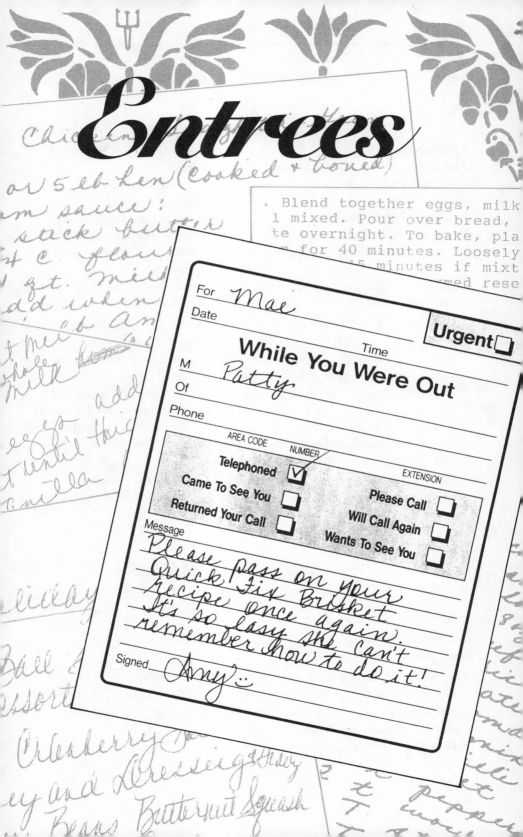

Entrees

chicken... Ho...
or 5 lb hen (cooked & boned)
m sauce:
stick butter
4 c. flour
1 qt. milk
dd when
+ milk Am...
whole h...
milk h...
eggs add
t until thic...
nilla

. Blend together eggs, milk
l mixed. Pour over bread,
te overnight. To bake, pla
n for 40 minutes. Loosely
15 minutes if mixt
med rese

While You Were Out

For **Mae**

Date _____ Time _____

Urgent ☐

M **Patty**

Of _____

Phone _____

AREA CODE ___ NUMBER ___ EXTENSION ___

Telephoned ☑

Came To See You ☐

Returned Your Call ☐

Please Call ☐

Will Call Again ☐

Wants To See You ☐

Message

Please pass on your
Quick Fix Brisket
recipe once again.
It's so easy she can't
remember how to do it!

Signed **Amy** ☺

liday

Ball...
assort...

Cranberry...
y and Dressing & Gravy...
Beans Butternut Squash

BEEF BOURGUIGNON

A make ahead party dish

10-12 servings

6 slices bacon, diced
4 pounds beef, cut from the round
into 4-inch strips
2 tablespoons brandy
2 cloves garlic, crushed
2 pounds mushrooms, sliced
14 small white onions (more if
pearl onions are used)
3 tablespoons butter
½ cup flour

2 (10½-ounce) cans beef
consommé
1½ cups burgundy
2 bay leaves
2 tablespoons parsley, chopped
1 teaspoon each salt and thyme
⅛ teaspoon freshly ground black
pepper
1 bag baby carrots (or large, cut in
2-inch lengths)

▲ Brown bacon in Dutch oven, remove bacon and set aside. Brown beef in bacon drippings, stirring often. Don't overcrowd. Warm brandy, ignite and pour over beef and stir. When flames die, remove beef and set aside with bacon. Sauté garlic in one tablespoon of butter. Add flour and stir until light brown, making a roux. Add the consommé and wine gradually, stir until smooth. Stir in herbs and seasonings, bacon, beef and garlic. Cover, simmer or bake at 325° for 1½ - 2 hours. Sauté onions and mushrooms in 2 tablespoons butter and add with carrots in the last 45 minutes of cooking (if added too soon, the onions and mushrooms will disintegrate).

Pass It On...Make up to 3-4 days ahead and reheat for 1 hour before serving. Serve with simple green salad with vinaigrette dressing and a warm crusty French bread.

MAE'S QUICK FIX BRISKET

Servings vary

Requires marinating overnight.

One brisket, any size
black pepper

garlic salt

▲ Trim brisket of excess fat, but leave some fat for self-basting during cooking. Rub brisket with plenty of black pepper and garlic salt. Cover with foil and marinate overnight in the refrigerator. Cook at 300° for 4 hours (no matter what size of brisket).

Pass It On...The best thing to do behind a person's back is to pat it.

BEEF BRISKET IN ONE HOUR

Servings vary

Note: Overnight recipe.

*1 beef brisket (size according to
    your need)*
favorite seasoning (no salt)

marinade of your choice
8-10 pounds rock salt
1 cup warm water

▲ Marinate overnight in teriyaki, soy sauce or your favorite marinade. Pre-heat oven to 500°. Cover bottom of a large baking pan (14x10-inch or larger) or throw-away aluminum baking pan with rock salt at least ¼-inch deep. Dampen with ¼ cup warm water. Place brisket on salt and cover with additional salt. Dampen with another ½ cup water. Cook at 500° for 1 hour. Break salt away in chunks and scrape excess from meat. Grill on charcoal or gas grill for 10 minutes and serve with your favorite barbecue sauce.

CORNED BEEF PIE

8-10 servings

*pie crust for a 7-inch or 8-inch
    double crust pie, unbaked*

Filling:
1 can corned beef
1 (10-ounce) can stewed tomatoes
1-2 tablespoons onion, chopped
oil

*1 tablespoon Cheddar cheese,
    grated*

▲ Break up the corned beef and add the tomatoes in a saucepan. Cook slowly over medium heat. Add 1 or 2 tablespoons of chopped onion cooked in a small amount of oil. Add 1 tablespoon grated Cheddar cheese. Cook all stirring often until it resembles sloppy joe mixture. Pour into crust and bake about 30 minutes at 350°.

Pass It On... "Corned Beef Pie was a favorite of our family from the time I was a little girl. Mother loved Bing Crosby, and she read in a magazine that this dish was made by his mother and enjoyed by her sons, Bing and Bob." - Jeanne Johnston Grimes Phillips, Delta Delta Delta National President 1976-80. Recipe also contributed by Ms. Phillips.

GRILLADES

An authentic taste treat from New Orleans

8 servings

4 pounds ½-inch thick veal or beef rounds
4 tablespoons bacon drippings or vegetable oil
½ cup flour
1 cup chopped onions
2 cups chopped green onions
1 cup chopped green peppers
¾ cup chopped celery
2 cloves garlic, minced
2 cups chopped tomatoes (fresh or canned)
⅔ teaspoon thyme
1 cup water
1 cup red wine
3 teaspoons salt
½ teaspoon black pepper
2 bay leaves
½ teaspoon hot pepper sauce
2 tablespoons Worcestershire sauce
3 tablespoons parsley, chopped
grits, cooked according to package directions

▲ Remove fat from meat and cut into serving-sized pieces, pound to ¼-inch thickness. Brown meat well in the drippings or vegetable oil in Dutch oven. Remove meat and add flour to make dark brown roux. Be sure to stir constantly. Add onions, celery, peppers and garlic; stir until vegetables are limp. Then add tomatoes and thyme. Cook 3 minutes. Add water and wine; stir well. Return meat to pot. Add spices and seasonings, except parsley. Lower heat and continue to stir and cook. Simmer covered for 1 hour if using veal. If using beef, cook 2 hours. Remove bay leaves and add parsley. Let grillades set several hours, or refrigerate overnight. Reheat and serve over grits for brunch, lunch or dinner.

Pass It On*...Serve with Peaches By Jiminey for dessert.*

NATCHITOCHES MEAT PIES

36 (4-inch) pies, or 48 (3-inch) cocktail

1 pound ground beef
1 pound ground pork
1 bunch green onions, chopped
1 small green pepper, chopped
1 garlic clove, minced

1 teaspoon salt
1 teaspoon pepper
½ teaspoon red pepper
2 tablespoons flour

Crust:
4 cups self-rising flour
½ cup shortening

1 egg, beaten
1 cup milk

▲ Cook beef and pork in large pan with onions, green pepper, garlic, salt and peppers until meat is browned. Sprinkle 2 tablespoons flour over meat and vegetables and stir. Cool to room temperature; drain excess juice and grease. Adjust seasonings for a spicier flavor. For crust: Sift flour, cut in shortening and stir in beaten egg mixed with milk. Form dough into balls and chill. Roll out dough on floured work surface; shape into thin circles. Fill each circle with 1 tablespoon meat mixture. Dampen edge of pastry circle and fold over to make semicircle pie. Prick each pie on top with fork twice after sealing and crimp edges with fork. Place on wax paper-lined cookie sheet and chill before cooking. Pies may be frozen at this point in a plastic storage bag. When ready to cook, fry in oil at 350° until each side is golden brown (about 5 minutes) or bake for 10-15 minutes at 350° after brushing with melted butter or beaten egg whites mixed with 1 tablespoon of water. Do not thaw before cooking.

Pass It On*...Brown ground meat with onions and green peppers. Freeze for busy days.*

"NEVER FAIL" ROAST BEEF

Perfect, regardless of when guests arrive

4-pound rib roast serves approximately 8-10

1 aged , well-marbled prime rib
  roast

salt and pepper to taste
parsley

▲ Let roast stand at room temperature for 1 hour. Preheat oven to 375°. Season roast and place in a shallow roasting pan. Do not cover or add water. Put roast in oven and cook for just 1 hour. Turn off heat but do not open oven door at any time until ready to serve. Regardless of time roast has been in oven (at least 2 hours), turn on oven to 375° 40 minutes before serving. Cook for 30 or 40 minutes. Open door and remove roast to serving platter. Garnish with parsley. The meat will be very brown and crisp on the outside, beautifully pink all the way through, medium rare and very juicy. Use same procedure for any size roast that has not been frozen.

EYE-OF-ROUND ROAST WITH ROSEMARY

5-pound roast serves 8 for dinner, 20 for cocktails

Note: Requires at least 4 hours refrigeration.

1 eye of round
seasoned salt
garlic salt

black pepper
1 teaspoon rosemary, crushed
1 teaspoon oil

▲ Rub entire surface of meat liberally with mixture of seasonings. Wrap in aluminum foil and refrigerate overnight, or at least 4 hours. Remove from refrigerator to reach room temperature. Brown in oil on all sides in skillet. Bake at 300° until desired doneness: rare—15 minutes per pound, medium—20 minutes per pound, well done—22 minutes per pound. Serve at room temperature.

BARBECUED EYE ROAST

A delicious, low fat way to enjoy beef

8 servings

6 pounds beef eye roast
1-2 large cloves garlic
1½ teaspoons Dijon mustard
1 teaspoon chili sauce

1 tablespoon freshly ground black
   pepper
1 teaspoon ground cloves
1 teaspoon fresh ginger, minced
¼ cup Kosher salt

▲ Trim all excess fat from eye roast. Cut garlic into quarters and insert into meat. Combine next 5 ingredients and spread over all meat surfaces. Let stand for 30 minutes. Rub ¼ cup salt into meat until surface is well-coated; let stand for 1 hour. Charcoal for 1 hour for medium rare, turning 3 times (about 20 minutes per side).

Pass It On...*Serve with Savory Mashed Potato Casserole and Rhubarb Pie.*

CABBAGE ROLLS

A famous Tulsa, Oklahoma restaurant favorite

4-5 servings

1 head cabbage (remove big leaves
   being careful not to tear them)
1 pound lean ground beef or
   ground turkey
1 cup instant rice, uncooked
2 cloves garlic, minced

1½ teaspoons salt
½ teaspoon allspice
¼ teaspoon pepper
½ teaspoon cinnamon
1 (6-ounce) can tomato paste
1 lemon

▲ Blanch cabbage leaves for 2 minutes in boiling water, drain and plunge into cold water. Combine ground beef, rice, tomato paste and all the spices in a bowl; knead to mix. Take each cabbage leaf and place about 3 tablespoons of the meat mixture on the edge of the leaf and roll once, then tuck outside edges of the leaf and keep rolling. They will look like little "packages." Spear each one with toothpick to secure. Place in electric skillet with 2 cups water and simmer. Simmer for 1 hour, adding 1 cup water every 15 minutes and turning the rolls after 30 minutes. Squeeze the juice of 1 lemon over the rolls the last 15 minutes.

MICROWAVE SIRLOIN TERIYAKI

Simple to make and excellent over rice

8 servings

½ cup soy sauce
¼ cup cider or apple juice
3 tablespoons honey
¼ teaspoon ginger root, minced
1-2 cloves fresh garlic, mashed

2 pounds boneless beef sirloin
  steak
1 tablespoon cornstarch
green onions
cooked rice

▲ Cut sirloin into thin strips (or use pre-cut fajita strips). Combine soy sauce, cider, honey, ginger root and garlic in bowl. Microwave on high for 1 minute, stir and add steak strips. Cover and refrigerate 8 hours or overnight. Make sure all meat is covered with juice. Drain marinade into cake pan, blend in cornstarch, add strips. Microwave on high for 8½ - 11 minutes until meat is desired doneness. Garnish with chopped green onions and serve over rice.

MAVERICK MARINATED FLANK STEAK

Super, simple and delicious

3-4 servings

1 large flank steak
¾ cup vegetable oil
½ cup teriyaki sauce
½ cup honey
2 tablespoons wine vinegar

2 tablespoons green onions,
  chopped
1 large clove garlic, mashed or
  minced
1½ teaspoons ground ginger (or
  fresh ginger root)

▲ Mix marinade ingredients together and marinate meat in refrigerator at least 24 hours in freezer storage bag. Flip several times so meat is well seasoned on all sides. Grill over hot coals 3-4 minutes on each side for medium rare. Always slice flank steak on the diagonal across the grain.

Pass It On*...Our family always has autumn picnics to mark the last cookout of the year. It's amazing how fast we can get the leaves raked with the smell of a hot fire burning in the grill and the promise of a juicy steak in the offing.*

BEEF TENDERLOIN BORDELAISE

For a truly special occasion

8-10 servings

4 pounds beef tenderloin

Sauce Bordelaise:

2 tablespoons butter	*6 ounces beef bouillon, undiluted*
1 medium onion, minced	*¼ teaspoon salt*
1 carrot, sliced	*⅛ teaspoon pepper*
sprig of parsley	*½ cup dry red wine*
6 or more whole peppercorns	*1 tablespoon parsley, snipped*
a few cloves	*½ pound mushrooms, sliced*
1 bay leaf	*2-3 tablespoons butter*
2 tablespoons flour	

▲ Buy well-trimmed tenderloin. On day of serving, brush with melted butter and season lightly with garlic salt, wrap in foil and refrigerate until an hour before baking. Remove from refrigerator and place unwrapped tenderloin on broiler pan in middle of oven at 425°. Bake for 30 minutes for medium rare (meat may look rare, but it continues to cook after it is removed from the oven). Slice and spoon some of sauce over top. Serve remaining sauce on the side. For Bordelaise sauce (make a day ahead): Sauté onion, carrot, parsley, peppercorns, cloves and bay leaf in butter until golden and tender. Add flour and cook over low heat until flour is lightly browned. Stir in bouillon, simmer until thick and smooth, about 10 minutes. Puree in food processor or strain. Add salt, pepper, red wine and snipped parsley. Refrigerate. Reheat to serve. If too thick, add more wine. If too thin, add flour. Add mushrooms that have been sautéed in butter.

VEAL CORDON BLEU

Easy to make and impresses guests

1 serving

2 veal cutlets
2 thin slices baked ham
2 thin slices Swiss cheese
1 egg
seasoned flour

Italian seasoned bread crumbs
1 tablespoon butter
2 tablespoons olive oil
1 cup undiluted canned beef
  bouillon

▲ Layer ingredients as follows: veal cutlet, ham, cheese, ham and other veal cutlet. Pinch edges to seal cutlets together enclosing ham and cheese. Dredge with seasoned flour, dip into beaten egg, coat with Italian seasoned bread crumbs. Sauté in 1 tablespoon butter and 2 tablespoons olive oil until browned. Pour 1 cup beef bouillon over and bake in 350° oven about 30 minutes.

Pass It On...Sometimes when I've had a tough day, the last thing I want to do is cook or drag myself up and out to a restaurant. For such occasions, I've invented "Cheater's Chicken" so I can literally cook dinner while watching TV or sipping a glass of wine. All I need is some chicken breasts, a package of rice and a glass baking dish. First, I look at the instructions on the rice package. If they call for a lot of liquid, I just mix it all at once in the dish. If the mixture isn't really soupy, I add water or milk or even a can of tomatoes, whatever sounds good at the time. Then I season the chicken breasts and lay them right on top of the rice mixture. I cover the whole thing with aluminum foil and slide it into the oven to bake at 350° for about an hour. Believe it or not, the chicken and rice will almost always be done at the same time. If the rice isn't done, take the chicken off and pop the rice back into the oven. If the rice gets done first, add more liquid while the chicken finishes cooking. The first time I did it, I had a fallback plan to order pizza. But it's almost foolproof, and by the time it's done, I've usually regained enough strength to toss a salad and sit down to eat.

VEAL EPICUREAN

4-6 servings

1 tablespoon cooking oil
1 tablespoon butter
2 pounds veal steaks
3 teaspoons flour
¾ teaspoon salt
⅛ teaspoon pepper
¼ cup chicken broth

½ onion, coarsely chopped
½ cup dry Vermouth wine or other
   dry white wine
2 tablespoons chopped parsley
1 bay leaf
hot cooked rice

▲ Heat oil and butter in skillet, add meat and brown. Remove meat and blend in flour, salt and pepper. Add chicken broth. Cook and stir until mixture boils. Reduce heat, add onions, wine, parsley and bay leaf. Add meat, cover and simmer for 25 minutes, stirring occasionally. Remove bay leaf and serve over hot rice.

BUTTERFLIED BARBECUED LEG OF LAMB

6 servings

3½-4 pounds boneless leg of lamb
½ teaspoon garlic powder
1 teaspoon bouquet garni

2 teaspoons Mei Yen seasoning
⅓ cup olive oil
3 tablespoons red wine vinegar

▲ Spread meat out flat and cut off excess fat and gristly pieces. Combine garlic powder, bouquet garni and Mei Yen seasoning. Rub well into meat. Place in glass baking pan or large bowl. Combine olive oil and vinegar; pour over lamb and turn until thoroughly coated. Marinate several hours at room temperature or overnight in the refrigerator. Barbecue over glowing coals for 45 to 50 minutes, turning every 10 to 15 minutes and brushing with marinade. Place meat on platter or cutting board and cut into ¼-inch slices. Spoon any remaining marinade and meat juices over slices of lamb and serve at once.

Pass It On*...This is wonderful served with Armenian Rice or Barley Mushroom Casserole.*

ITALIAN MEATBALLS

6-8 servings

1½ pounds ground beef
2 tablespoons onion, chopped
2 tablespoons celery leaves,
   chopped
½ cup Italian bread crumbs
¼ cup milk

1 egg, slightly beaten
½ teaspoon salt and pepper
1 clove garlic, minced
½ cup Parmesan cheese, freshly
   grated

▲ Combine all ingredients, shape in balls and brown in hot skillet. Drain off fat. Add meat balls to your favorite spaghetti sauce and simmer 30 minutes longer.

Pass It On...I keep Madeira wine in my kitchen to deglaze pans which have sautéed chicken or beef.

SOUR CREAM AND HORSERADISH SAUCE

Wonderful for a beef dish

1-1½ cups

4 tablespoons horseradish sauce
¾ cup sour cream

1 teaspoon prepared Dijon
   mustard

▲ Mix all ingredients together and chill.

Pass It On...Nice to complement a beef dish. Add 1 teaspoon unflavored gelatin, softened, for a mousse to serve with cold roast beef or ham. Or thin with milk and heat over low heat. Pour over steamed vegetables such as a mixture of broccoli, carrots and cauliflower.

MJ'S TERIYAKI MARINADE

1½-2 cups

Note: Make 1-6 days in advance.

⅓-¼ cup soy sauce
⅔-¾ cup water
1 clove garlic
1 tablespoon sugar

2 teaspoons seasoned salt
1 tablespoon shaved ginger root
beef, cut in 2-inch chunks

▲ Blend first 6 ingredients well. Marinate meat 1-6 days before broiling, making enough basic recipe to cover meat totally. Use for fajita (skirt steak), flank steak, arm, round or chuck roast (cut roast in 2-inch square chunks).

Pass It On...Extra meat may be broiled, then frozen or may be frozen before cooking.

BAKED HAM WITH PINEAPPLE STUFFING

6 servings

½ cup margarine
1 cup sugar
4 eggs or 4 egg substitutes

1 can (1 pound, 4 ounces) crushed
*   pineapple, drained*
5 slices white bread, cubed

Ham:
1 ham, fully cooked (or canned
*   ham)*

brown sugar
1 can beer

▲ Heat oven to 300°. Place ham in broiler pan and sprinkle with brown sugar and baste with can of beer. Repeat basting every 20 minutes for 2 hours of cooking. For pineapple: Cream margarine and sugar. Add 1 egg at a time; beat after each egg. Stir in pineapple. Fold in bread cubes. Bake in greased 1½-quart casserole at 350° for 1 hour.

Pass It On...*Originality is simply a fresh pair of eyes.*

POLISH SAUSAGE

Delicious with potato pancakes, fresh applesauce and a light dessert

10 servings

2 tablespoons bacon fat
3 large onions, chopped
2 cups carrots, diced
1 large apple with skin, diced
½ cup parsley, chopped
1 bay leaf
½ teaspoon garlic salt

1 cup chicken broth
8 cups sauerkraut, rinsed and
*   drained*
½ cup white wine
2 tablespoons brown sugar
1 ring smoked Polish sausage

▲ Place bacon fat in a large skillet and add the next 7 ingredients. Simmer covered for 20 minutes. Add sauerkraut, white wine, and brown sugar. Stir in 1 ring of smoked Polish sausage, cut on the diagonal into 1½-inch pieces. Smoked beef sausage also may be used. Bake in a covered casserole for 1 hour at 400°.

ALSATIAN PORK CASSEROLE

Great on a cold night in front of the fire

4 servings

4 thick pork chops or country
spare ribs
1 tablespoon oil
1 pound bagged sauerkraut,
reserve juice
1 Granny Smith apple, peeled and
sliced

1 onion, peeled and sliced
1 teaspoon caraway seeds
¼ cup white wine (Vermouth is
good)
oil

▲ Brown meat in a bit of oil. Spread sauerkraut in bottom of ovenproof dish. Arrange apple and onion over kraut and sprinkle with caraway seed. Place meat on top. Baste with sauerkraut juice and wine. Bake at 350° for 1-1½ hours until nicely browned.

***Pass It On**...Sauerkraut brings back memories of Thanksgiving at my husband's Uncle Bill's house. We ate fresh homemade sauerkraut taken straight from the keg along with kneffles which were little German noodles dropped into beef broth and served with the sauerkraut which was usually cooked with fresh pork. I watched my mother-in-law cook the wonderfully tasty kneffles many times, but I never could copy her because she used half an egg shell to measure liquid.*

DELTA'S PARTY PORK

12-16 servings

1 tablespoon olive oil
1 tablespoon fresh rosemary (or 1
teaspoon dried), minced
1 tablespoon fresh thyme (or 1
teaspoon dried), minced
1 tablespoon fresh sage (or 1
teaspoon dried), minced

½ teaspoon salt
½ teaspoon freshly ground pepper
¼ teaspoon allspice
4 pounds boneless pork loin roast,
trimmed
1 tablespoon olive oil

▲ Combine all seasonings in small bowl. Rub on outside of pork. Brown pork in 1 tablespoon olive oil in hot skillet. Remove from skillet and place in oven-proof dish. Bake at 375° until internal temperature is 160°. Let stand 10 minutes before slicing.

PINEAPPLE PORK SWEET AND SOUR

A San Francisco treat

6 servings

Pork:

*2 pounds pork tenderloin, cut into
one-inch pieces*

2 eggs, beaten
seasoned flour

Sauce:

2 teaspoons soy sauce
1 cup sugar
⅔ cup pineapple juice
½ cup ketchup
1 cup white vinegar

*1 cup canned pineapple chunks,
drained*
*1 medium green pepper, cut into
one-inch squares*

▲ Dip pork pieces in egg, then in flour and fry in deep fat until brown. Drain and keep warm. Blend soy sauce, sugar, juice, ketchup and vinegar until sugar is dissolved. Place in wok or skillet and bring to a boil. Make paste of cornstarch and water and add to mixture, stirring constantly. When mixture thickens, add pork, pineapple and green peppers; cook about 5 minutes.

Pass It On...Serve with hot steamed rice and sautéed fresh snow peas. When preparing fried or other meats with coating, refrigerate for one hour between flouring and coating. The coating will adhere better.

CANTONESE PORK TENDERLOINS

4-6 servings

2-4 pork tenderloins
½ cup peanut oil
¼ cup hoisin sauce
¼ cup soy sauce
½ cup rice vinegar

1 tablespoon sesame oil
4 whole green onions, chopped
4 cloves garlic, minced
*2 tablespoons fresh ginger root,
minced*

▲ Combine all marinade ingredients and mix well. Pour over pork and marinate for 1-2 days in refrigerator. Grill over hot coals 9-11 minutes on each side, basting frequently with marinade.

Pass It On...May be prepared in broiler.

GOOD 'N EASY BARBECUE RIBS

4-5 servings

1 tablespoon celery salt
1 tablespoon chili powder
1 tablespoon salt
¼ cup dark brown sugar
1 teaspoon paprika

2-3 pounds country style or baby
*   back pork ribs or beef ribs*
1 (10½-ounce) can tomato soup
¼ cup vinegar (red wine or cider)

▲ Mix first 5 ingredients. Rub over meat. Heat together tomato soup and vinegar in saucepan and add any leftover dry ingredients. Ribs can be grilled outside using the sauce to baste or cooked with sauce in an oven baking bag for 1 hour at 350°.

Pass It On...Words of wisdom from my mother, "If you're dressed ready to go out and find a spot on your garment with no time to change, put a decorative pin over it."

BLACK RUSSIAN BARBECUE SAUCE

Great with any meat

3 cups

4 tablespoons butter
1 medium onion, chopped
2 cloves garlic, minced
2 tablespoons white vinegar
1 cup strong black coffee into
*   which 2 teaspoons cocoa has*
*   been dissolved*
½ cup beer
1 cup chili sauce
¼ cup soy sauce
freshly squeezed juice of ½ lemon
grated peel of ½ lemon

2 tablespoons Worcestershire
*   sauce*
2 tablespoons steak sauce
several dashes of hot pepper sauce
1 tablespoon dry mustard
½ teaspoon each of celery seed,
*   thyme, turmeric, marjoram,*
*   paprika, red pepper and ginger*
2 tablespoons horseradish
2 bay leaves
2 teaspoons cornstarch

▲ Melt butter. Add onion and sauté until tender; add garlic and sauté for 2 minutes more. Add vinegar. Reduce heat and combine the remaining ingredients. Simmer for at least 1 hour, stirring occasionally. Remove bay leaf and serve or store in refrigerator.

HICKORY COOKED BARBECUE BACK RIBS

½ pound ribs per person for moderate appetites

Note: Requires hickory chips to be soaked overnight.

**6-15 pounds pork back ribs, in
    slabs**

Sauce:

1 (14-ounce) bottle ketchup
½ ketchup bottle of water
**½ (5-ounce) bottle Worcestershire
    sauce**
2 tablespoons cider vinegar
1 tablespoon chili powder

½ cup dark brown sugar
½ cup white sugar
2 small onions, grated
1 teaspoon salt
¼ teaspoon pepper

▲ For sauce: Mix all ingredients and bring sauce to a slow boil. Cook slowly until slightly thickened. This may be made ahead of time and stored in the refrigerator. For ribs: Fill a one pound coffee can ¾ full with hickory chips. Fill with water and soak overnight. Spread chips over hot charcoal fire. Brown slabs of ribs on both sides over charcoal fire. Season with salt and pepper to taste. Cut slabs into individual servings (2 or 3 ribs) and layer in roaster pan with barbecue sauce on each serving. Cover and bake at 300° for about 15 minutes per pound. For boneless barbecue spare ribs: Simmer until bones pull out easily and then proceed as above. Meat can be cut into bite-size pieces for serving at cocktail parties.

BARBECUE SAUCE FOR RIBS OR CHICKEN

A wonderful "sweet and sour" barbecue sauce

6-8 servings

1 cup mustard
½ cup molasses
½ cup Worcestershire sauce

½ cup apple cider vinegar
hot pepper sauce

▲ Mix mustard and molasses in saucepan on low heat. Add Worcestershire and molasses to mix. Add hot pepper sauce to taste.

BRANDIED CHICKEN

4-6 servings

5 tablespoons butter or margarine,
    softened
3 medium red tart apples,
    unpeeled, cored, and sliced (3
    cups)
2 large white onions, thinly sliced
3 boneless chicken breasts, halved
1 teaspoon salt

¼ teaspoon pepper
1 cup Swiss cheese, shredded
½ cup Parmesan cheese, grated
¼ cup unseasoned bread crumbs
½ leaf thyme, crumbled
2 tablespoons brandy, apple jack,
    or apple cider (or to taste)

▲ Coat a 6-cup baking dish with 1 tablespoon butter. Sauté apples and onions in remaining butter until tender (do not brown). Spoon evenly into prepared baking dish. Rub chicken breasts with salt and pepper. Arrange down center of apple mixture. Combine cheeses, bread crumbs and thyme. Sprinkle over chicken and apple mixture. Drizzle brandy over all. Bake in 350° oven uncovered for 35 minutes or until cheese is golden brown and chicken is tender.

Pass It On...*Try with boneless pork chops for a different flavor or use Winesap or Granny Smith apples.*

CHICKEN BUNDLES

4 servings

1 (17¼-ounce) package frozen puff
    pastry sheets
2 cooked chicken breasts, skinned
    and boned
2 tablespoons peanut oil
¼ cup onion, chopped
¼ cup mushrooms, chopped

½ cup sour cream
1½ teaspoons prepared mustard
½ teaspoon garlic salt
¾ teaspoon salt
¼ teaspoon pepper
¼ pound Monterey Jack cheese,
    sliced

▲ Thaw pastry sheets until flexible. Chop chicken into small bite-size pieces. Heat oil in skillet; add onions and mushrooms. Sauté 3-4 minutes. Mix sour cream, mustard and seasonings; add to onion and mushroom mixture. Cut pastry sheet in half. Place mound of ¼ chicken in center, spoon skillet mixture over chicken, top with slice of cheese and cover with ends of pastry. Crimp sides of pastry to seal chicken inside. Place on lightly greased cookie sheet and bake at 350° for 20-25 minutes.

ELEGANT CHICKEN AND ARTICHOKE BAKE

6 servings

*1 (10-ounce) package frozen
  chopped spinach, cooked and
  drained*
*2 cups cooked long grain white
  rice (not minute)*
1 egg, slightly beaten
4 tablespoons butter, softened
*1 (14½-ounce) can artichoke
  hearts*
*1½ cups chicken, cooked and
  shredded* cut in pieces

1½ cups ~~Monterey Jack~~ Mozavella *cheese,
  grated*
~~½ pound fresh mushrooms, sliced~~
½ medium onion, chopped
2 tablespoons flour
1 clove garlic, crushed
1 teaspoon prepared mustard
salt and pepper
1 cup milk

▲ Grease a 9-inch pie plate. Squeeze spinach to remove all excess moisture.
Combine spinach, rice and egg in medium bowl. Add 2 tablespoons butter
and mix well. Press into prepared pie plate, covering bottom and sides.
Cover and chill for 30-60 minutes. Drain artichokes and blot dry. Cut each
into 2 or 3 pieces. Arrange over rice and spinach crust. Place chicken and
cheese over artichokes. Melt remaining 2 tablespoons butter in skillet over
low heat, then sauté mushrooms and onions over medium heat until tender.
Stir in flour, garlic, mustard and salt and pepper to taste. Add milk gradually. Cook until mixture thickens. Pour over pie. (At this point, dish may be
refrigerated.) Bake uncovered at 350° for 45 minutes.

*Pass It On...Recipe may be doubled and placed in 9x13-inch casserole.
My grandmother always told me casseroles can be made ahead and
refrigerated. I just have to remember to take them out of the refrigerator
30 minutes before baking or to place the dish in an oven that hasn't been
preheated.*

CHICKEN AND ASPARAGUS ENCHILADAS

A delicious and different dish

6 servings

12 (8-inch) flour tortillas
½ cup onion, chopped
½ cup flour
2 (14½-ounce) cans chicken broth
½ cup green taco sauce
3 cups chicken, cooked and chunked
2 pounds fresh asparagus (if asparagus is thick, steam briefly before rolling into tortillas)

½ cup margarine
1 cup sour cream
⅓ cup Parmesan cheese, grated
2½ cups Monterey Jack cheese, shredded
green onions, chopped
black olives, sliced
tomatoes, chopped

▲ In saucepan, melt margarine and whisk in flour. Add chicken broth and cook until thickened. Remove from heat and stir in sour cream and green taco sauce. Set aside. Divide the chicken, Monterey Jack cheese, onion and asparagus among the 12 tortillas. Top each with 2 tablespoons sauce; roll up and place seam side down in a 9x13-inch greased pan. Top with remaining sauce and Parmesan cheese. Bake in a 400° oven 25 minutes or until hot and bubbly. Garnish with chopped green onion, sliced black olives, and chopped tomatoes.

Pass It On...For centerpieces when serving Tex-Mex, I put flowers in long vases stuck in cowboy boots (clean, of course) and use bandannas as napkins. I've also stuck bandannas in the pockets of men's jeans made into placemats. I use pinking shears to cut the front or back top panel into the size I want.

BROILED CORIANDER HONEY CHICKEN

Wonderful with cauliflower or zucchini

6 servings

4 pounds chicken parts (breasts halved, legs and thighs separated)
6 tablespoons soy sauce
1 tablespoon honey
1 tablespoon ground coriander seed

1-2 garlic cloves, minced
2 teaspoons fresh ginger root, finely grated
¼ teaspoon turmeric
¼ teaspoon cayenne pepper

Hot Sweet and Sour Peanut Sauce:
4 tablespoons natural peanut butter, chunky or smooth
4 tablespoons soy sauce
2 tablespoons fresh lemon juice
1 tablespoon dark brown sugar, firmly packed

½-1½ teaspoons cayenne pepper to taste
fresh coriander sprig for garnish, if desired

▲ Make 2 slits in each chicken piece, cutting to bone, but not through an edge. In separate bowl, whisk together next 7 ingredients; add chicken and coat well. Marinate at least 1 hour, turning occasionally. Broil chicken, skin side down on oiled rack about 6 inches from heat, turning and basting for 15 minutes or until golden brown. Breast pieces will be done first. Transfer to platter and serve with dipping sauce. For Hot Sweet and Sour Peanut Sauce: In a small bowl whisk peanut butter, soy sauce, lemon juice, brown sugar and cayenne pepper. Transfer to a small serving bowl. Garnish with coriander sprig. Makes ⅔ cup.

CRANBERRY CHICKEN BAKE

4-6 servings

**flour seasoned with salt and
    pepper**
**1 frying chicken, cut up - or one
    chicken breast per person**
1 cup sugar

2 tablespoons canola oil
2 cups canned pineapple juice
2 tablespoons lemon juice
2 cups fresh cranberries

▲ Roll chicken in seasoned flour and brown in hot oil. Arrange chicken pieces in single layer in shallow baking dish. Combine sugar and juices; boil 5 minutes. Add cranberries and boil another 5 minutes or until skins pop. Pour sauce over chicken and bake at 350° about 45 minutes, basting several times.

CHICKEN BREASTS DIJON

A great low calorie, low fat dish

2-4 servings

**2 whole medium chicken breasts,
    boned, skinned, and split**
non-stick cooking spray
⅔ cup hot water
**1 teaspoon chicken bouillon
    granules**

4 tablespoons white wine
3 teaspoons Dijon mustard
½ teaspoon dried basil, crushed
**½ teaspoon dried tarragon,
    crushed**
dash of pepper

▲ Rinse chicken and pat dry. Halve each chicken breast. Spray a cold, large skillet with non-stick cooking spray and heat skillet over medium-high heat. Add chicken pieces and cook, turning once until golden brown, about 4 minutes. While chicken cooks, combine hot water with remaining ingredients and stir to mix. Remove skillet from heat and add bouillon mixture to the chicken. Heat to a boil, reduce heat, cover and simmer for 5 to 6 minutes. If you desire sauce thickened, remove chicken to serving dish and mix 1 tablespoon cold water and 1 teaspoon of cornstarch. Then add to sauce in pan and stir until it boils and thickens. Pour over chicken.

Pass It On...*Serve with tiny red-skinned new potatoes and pea pods for a deliciously healthy meal. Also great served with pasta to spoon the sauce over.*

ITALIAN CHICKEN FOR TWO

A green salad and crusty French bread complete this quick, easy meal

2 servings

2 skinless, boneless chicken breast halves
flour seasoned with salt, pepper, paprika
1 clove garlic, minced

2 tablespoons olive oil
1 cup white wine
Italian seasoning mix
⅓ cup Parmesan cheese, grated

▲ Roll chicken breasts in seasoned flour and brown with garlic in olive oil. Add wine and sprinkle with Italian seasoning. Cover and place in 350° oven for 30 minutes. Remove chicken breasts and reduce cooking liquid until syrupy. Serve over cooked spaghetti or linguine topped with reduced liquid and grated Parmesan cheese.

Pass It On...*Things to always have on hand in case of unexpected company or just a long day at work: eggs, onions, dried parsley flakes and other herbs; pecans, almonds or walnuts; canned or fresh mushrooms; canned or fresh tomatoes; black olives; pasta and canned pasta sauce; cheeses; cream cheese and cheese spreads; flavored crackers; microwave popcorn; frozen chicken breasts; casseroles; bread or yeast rolls; ground meat, bacon or sausage; and cans of tuna fish.*

ORIENTAL CHICKEN STIR-FRY

4-6 servings

3 tablespoons oil
3 whole broiler-fryer chicken breasts, boned and cut into 1-inch chunks
3 cups broccoli florets
1 medium sweet red pepper, cut into 1-inch squares
½ pound mushrooms, sliced

3 tablespoons thinly sliced scallions
1 cup chicken broth
3 tablespoons dry sherry
1 tablespoon cornstarch
1 tablespoon soy sauce
½ teaspoon hot pepper sauce
½ cup cashew nuts
hot cooked rice

▲ In a wok or large skillet heat oil. Add chicken and cook over moderate heat, stirring frequently for 5 minutes until chicken is white. Remove from wok. Place broccoli, red pepper, mushrooms and scallions in wok. Cook 3 minutes, stirring constantly. In small bowl mix chicken broth, sherry, cornstarch, soy sauce and hot pepper sauce. Return chicken to wok along with chicken broth mixture. Cook stirring constantly 5 minutes until sauces thickened slightly. Sprinkle with cashew nuts and serve over hot rice.

IMPERIAL CHICKEN PARMESAN

An easy and elegant way to bake chicken

6 servings

1½ cups plain bread crumbs
½ cup Parmesan cheese, freshly
grated
1 tablespoon salt

1 teaspoon pepper
6 chicken breast halves, skinned
and boned
1 cup butter or margarine, melted

▲ Combine bread crumbs, cheese, salt and pepper. Dip chicken in melted butter and then in crumbs, coat heavily. Place breast, meat side up in a baking dish and bake in 350° oven for 30-35 minutes uncovered. Do not turn chicken.

Pass It On*...May be prepared ahead and refrigerated or frozen, then baked. To reheat after thawing, bake in 325° oven until hot.*

PERFECT ROAST CHICKEN

Great for picnics

4 servings

1 (4-pound) whole chicken
juice from ½ lemon
¼ cup butter

2½ teaspoons salt
1½ teaspoons freshly ground black
pepper

▲ Wash chicken. Rub lemon juice inside chicken onto bone structure. Cream butter, salt and pepper together and place in cavity. Truss the bird and rub one side with butter. Roast, buttered side up on rack in shallow pan at 400° for 30 minutes. Brush other side with butter and roast this side up for 30 minutes. Turn chicken, baste well with juices and sprinkle with additional salt and pepper if desired. Roast 15 minutes more and baste several times. Test for doneness: if thigh juices run clear, it is done (165° on meat thermometer). Carve into quarters.

Pass It On*...Serve with Oven-Roasted Garlic Rosemary Potatoes and salad.*

CHICKEN SATAY

3-4 dinner, 6-8 for cocktails

Note: Requires 6 hours to marinate.

¼ cup smooth peanut butter
2 tablespoons onion, minced
2 tablespoons lemon juice
1½ teaspoons soy sauce
½ teaspoon coriander
1 clove garlic, minced

⅛ teaspoon cayenne pepper
2 tablespoons fresh parsley,
* minced*
1 pound boneless skinless chicken
* breasts, cut into 1-inch pieces*
* or strips*

▲ Combine first 8 ingredients and pour over chicken, mixing well. Marinate 4-6 hours. Thread on skewers and grill or broil for 10-15 minutes, until just cooked.

Pass It On...As newlyweds, my best friend and I thought it was hard to cook for our husbands when most recipes served eight. We decided to each invite one other couple to join us in a Supper Club. We agreed to cook only new recipes and to be fearless. We shared many memorable meals from just plain bad to really superb as our skills grew. All eight of us eventually became accomplished cooks and more. One ultimately opened his own restaurant and became a nationally recognized wine expert, lecturer and writer. Another began a catering business and gourmet food shop. Though we have scattered to different cities, we get together for Supper Club now and then - and it's still the best.

Pass It On...For unexpected entertaining, I keep special canned goods like white meat chicken, shrimp, smoked oysters, caviar, pate, white meat tuna, salmon, olives, cornichons and sweet pickles handy. It's easy to open the cans and turn them out on pretty trays covered with curly lettuce leaves or parsley. Serve with crisp crackers, melba rounds, rounds of thinly sliced and oven dried French bread or baked tortilla or pita triangles and let your guests blissfully graze!

CHICKEN SALTIMBOCCA

An Italian specialty

6 servings

*3 large chicken breasts, skinned,
    boned, and halved lengthwise*
*6 thin slices cooked ham (may use
    sandwich slices or prosciutto
    ham)* substi.velveeta
3 slices mozzarella cheese, halved
*1 medium tomato, seeded and
    chopped*

½ teaspoon dried sage, crushed
1 cup fine dry bread crumbs
*2 tablespoons Parmesan cheese,
    grated*
2 tablespoons snipped parsley
½ cup butter or margarine, melted

▲ Place chicken breasts, one at a time, in a large plastic bag or plastic wrap. Place on cutting board. Working from the center out, pound lightly with meat mallet to 5x5-inches. Remove from plastic bag. Place a ham slice and half a slice of cheese on each cutlet, trimming to fit. Top each with the chopped tomato and a dash of sage. Tuck in sides, roll up jelly-roll style, pressing to seal well. Combine bread crumbs, Parmesan cheese and parsley. Dip chicken in butter, then roll in crumbs. Place in a shallow 8x11-inch pan. Bake uncovered at 350° for 40 to 45 minutes.

Pass It On*...Serve with pasta, green beans, salad and Tiramisu for dessert.*

CHICKEN YUCATAN

2 servings

2 ribs celery
1 small-medium onion
1 clove garlic
½-1 jalapeño, seeded
2 tablespoons oil

seasoned flour
4 tablespoons olive oil
2 chicken breast halves
1 cup orange juice

▲ Chop all vegetables (or put them all in food processor) into ¼-inch pieces. Sauté vegetables in 2 tablespoons oil until soft, then remove from pan and set aside. Dredge chicken breasts in seasoned flour. Add 2 tablespoons olive oil to same skillet and sauté chicken breasts until lightly browned. Place sautéed vegetables on top of chicken breasts and pour orange juice over all. Bake at 350° for about 45 minutes.

Pass It On*...Instead of making seasoned flour each time a recipe calls for it, I keep a ready-to-use mixture in a container in the refrigerator. I pour some out on a sheet of waxed paper, use what I need, and pour the rest back into the container for later use as necessary.*

CHICKEN AND WILD RICE CASSEROLE

Perfect for company

10-12 servings

2 large broiler chickens
1 cup water
1 cup dry sherry
1½ teaspoons salt
½ teaspoon curry powder
1 medium onion, diced
½ cup diced celery

1 pound fresh mushrooms or 2
small cans of mushrooms
¼ cup margarine
2 packages long grain wild rice
1 cup dairy sour cream
1 can (10½-ounces) cream of
mushroom soup

▲ In a deep kettle add chicken, water, sherry, salt, curry powder, onion and celery. Bring to a boil; cover, reduce heat, simmer 1 hour. Remove chicken and strain broth. Refrigerate chicken and broth. When cool, cut up chicken into bite-size pieces. Sauté mushrooms in margarine until brown. Use chicken broth to cook rice (use package directions for firm rice). Combine chicken, rice and mushrooms, saving some mushroom caps to decorate top of casserole. Blend sour cream and mushroom soup and toss with chicken mixture. Put mixture into casserole dish (use 2 rectangular glass baking dishes) and place mushroom caps on top of mixture in a circle to decorate. Cover and refrigerate for several hours or overnight. Bake at 350° for 1 hour.

Pass It On...When I make a casserole, I double the recipe and make one for the freezer or a friend.

CORNISH HENS À L'ORANGE

4 servings

4 Cornish hens
2 cans pineapple chunks
salt
pepper

cinnamon
Grand Marnier
orange zest to garnish

▲ Thaw hens, rinse and pat dry. Salt and pepper the cavities, and sprinkle with cinnamon. Fill each cavity with well-drained pineapple chunks and close with skewers. Place hens on rack in a 9x13-inch pan. Baste with Grand Marnier and bake in preheated 325° oven. Rebaste every 15 minutes for approximately 1 hour and 15 minutes of cooking time. In the final 15 minutes, arrange orange zest over tops of hens and baste once more.

WHITE CHILI

6 servings

Note: Requires 4 hours to soak.

1 pound dried, white beans
2 tablespoons olive oil, divided
1 pound ground chicken or turkey
1 teaspoon ground cumin
1 medium onion, peeled and
*   minced*
1 medium bell pepper, finely
*   chopped*
2 cloves garlic, minced
1 (4-ounce) can chopped green
*   chilies*

6 cups chicken broth
salt
white pepper
¹/₄-¹/₂ teaspoon hot pepper sauce
¹/₄ teaspoon cayenne pepper
¹/₂ teaspoon water
¹/₂ cup plain low-fat yogurt
cilantro or parsley
salsa

▲ Cover beans with water in large saucepan. Bring to boil, reduce heat and simmer 15 minutes. Set aside to soak for 4 hours or overnight. Drain. Brown chicken in 6-quart Dutch oven in 1 tablespoon olive oil, add ½ teaspoon cumin, break up chicken into bite-size pieces as it cooks. Remove chicken from pan. Add remaining oil, onion, bell pepper and garlic and sauté 5 minutes. Add beans, chicken, ½ teaspoon cumin, chilies and chicken broth. Bring to a boil, reduce heat, cover and simmer 1 to 1½ hours, stirring occasionally. Add a little water if chili becomes too thick. Season with salt, pepper and hot pepper sauce 30 minutes before end of cooking time. Stir cayenne pepper in ½ teaspoon water and into yogurt. Ladle chili into bowls, garnish with cayenne/yogurt mixture, parsley and salsa.

Pass It On...*Microwave ground beef or turkey in a plastic colander with a plate underneath to catch the fat.*

BRANDIED CRANBERRY SAUCE

Perfect for the holidays

12 servings

1 (16-ounce) package fresh
*   cranberries (4 cups)*

2 cups sugar
¹/₃ cup brandy

▲ Sort, wash and drain cranberries. Spread in 13x9x2-inch baking pan. Sprinkle sugar evenly over the cranberries. Cover and bake at 300° for 1 hour. Stir occasionally during the baking time. Remove from oven, stir in the brandy. Cool and store in covered container in the refrigerator.

CHICKEN DIJON

4 servings

4 skinless, boneless chicken breast
halves
2 tablespoons Dijon mustard
½ cup nonfat evaporated milk
2 egg yolks

1 teaspoon balsamic vinegar
1 clove garlic, crushed
½ teaspoon tarragon
freshly ground pepper

▲ Arrange chicken breasts slightly apart in a greased or sprayed baking dish. Spread ½ teaspoon mustard on each piece. Cover loosely with foil and bake 20 minutes in 400° oven. Combine remaining ingredients, including remaining mustard, in top of a double broiler over 2 inches of simmering water. Cook sauce several minutes, stirring constantly. Remove from heat when sauce begins to thicken. Place chicken breasts on serving plate and pour sauce over.

CHICKEN VERONIQUE

The grapes make this different

6 servings

¾ cup cracker or bread crumbs
½ teaspoon salt
¼ teaspoon pepper
¼ teaspoon crushed tarragon
2 chicken breasts, skinned, boned
and split

½ cup melted butter
¼ cup minced onion
½ cup chicken broth
½ cup dry white wine
½ pound sliced mushrooms
2 cups red seedless grapes

▲ Combine crumbs, salt, pepper and tarragon. Dampen chicken and coat with crumb mixture. Let set for 15 minutes. Brown chicken in ¼ cup melted butter in skillet. Transfer chicken to shallow baking dish. Add onions to drippings and sauté. Add chicken broth and wine to onion mixture, bring to a boil. Add sauce to chicken and bake at 375° for 35 minutes. Sauté mushrooms and grapes in remaining ¼ cup butter. Spoon over baked chicken and bake an additional 10 minutes.

CHRISTMAS SCALLOPED OYSTERS

8-10 as main course, 14-16 as appetizer

2 quarts oysters, freshly shucked
½ cup unsalted butter
1 package saltine crackers
2 cups Parmesan cheese, freshly
*   grated*
Worcestershire sauce

dry sherry
white pepper
Tabasco sauce
1 pint half-and-half
liquor from oysters

▲ Drain oysters over sieve, reserving liquor. In a mixing bowl, combine the half-and-half and enough oyster liquor to make 2 cups liquid. Add a dash of Worcestershire sauce, a generous slosh of sherry (about ¼ cup), and a small dash of Tabasco. Mix well. In a large casserole, make a layer of oysters to cover bottom. Crumble saltines over it to make a fairly thick layer of cracker pieces. Scatter grated Parmesan cheese over the crackers. Dust with pepper. Repeat twice more, finishing with cracker and cheese layer. With a long teaspoon or skewer, make several holes in the casserole deep enough so that the utensil touches the bottom of the dish. Pour liquid mixture over casserole until it appears around the edges of the oyster-cracker mixture. Bake uncovered at 325° until entire casserole bubbles. This could take from 30 minutes to an hour depending on the depth of the dish. Give it enough time.

Pass It On*... "If using as an appetizer, pack in individual ramekins or on large scallop shells. Reduce baking time. Three generations of my family have served these oysters on Christmas Eve as an entree, usually with a green salad dressed with oil and lemon juice and served with a crusty French bread. Citrus ambrosia makes a good dessert, and a dry white wine is a nice accompaniment." - Anne Rivers Siddons, author of* Outer Banks, Heartbreak Hotel and Colony.

CHEESY CATFISH

A healthy choice

6 servings

1 cup cheese crackers, finely crushed	1 teaspoon pepper
	1 teaspoon salt
1 cup Parmesan cheese	6 catfish fillets
2 tablespoons parsley, chopped	½ cup margarine, melted

▲ Combine cracker crumbs, Parmesan cheese, parsley, pepper and salt. Dip fish fillets in melted margarine and roll in cracker mixture. Place fillets on baking sheet that has been lined with aluminum foil. Bake in 400° oven for 20 minutes or until fish are golden brown. Top with parsley and/or more cheese.

Pass It On...Mom, when trying to encourage her children to overcome shyness, would ask, "What's the worst that could happen?" Somehow it was always less traumatic than what we had imagined it to be.

MISSISSIPPI DELTA CATFISH

4 servings

4 catfish fillets	2 tablespoons wine vinegar
3 tablespoons soy sauce	Cajun seasoning
3 tablespoons Worcestershire sauce	lemon pepper seasoning
	¼ cup oil
2 tablespoons lemon juice	¼ cup butter

▲ Mix soy sauce, Worcestershire sauce, lemon juice and wine vinegar. Pour over catfish fillets. Marinate several hours. Coat fillets heavily with Cajun seasoning on 1 side and lemon pepper seasoning on the other side. Using a 12-inch non-stick skillet, pan fry slowly in oil and butter until brown (about 5-10 minutes each side).

Pass It On... "The history of any people can be studied through its building. How much we learn about builders when we examine why they build, how they build, and what they build." - Jean Hunt Gaines, Delta Delta Delta National President 1984-88.

IMPERIAL CRAB

5 servings

1 pound crab meat
1 cup mayonnaise
2 teaspoons Worcestershire sauce

½ green pepper, chopped
5 individual baking shells
5 tablespoons bread crumbs

▲ Sauté green pepper in skillet, then mix with crab, mayonnaise, pepper and Worcestershire sauce. Place in 5 individual baking shells, and sprinkle buttered crumbs on top. Bake 15 minutes in a moderate oven.

Pass It On...It's good to have money and the things that money can buy, but it's good to check once in a while to make sure you haven't lost the things that money can't buy.

THE BEST MARYLAND CRABCAKES

4 servings

1 pound cooked lump crab meat
½ cup soft bread crumbs
½ cup mayonnaise
cayenne pepper to taste
1 teaspoon Worcestershire sauce
1 egg, lightly beaten

1 tablespoon fresh flat leaf parsley,
    chopped
1 teaspoon lemon rind, grated
salt to taste
1 tablespoon canola oil
1 tablespoon butter

▲ Pick crab meat over carefully to remove any bits of shell, being careful not to break up large chunks. Thoroughly blend bread crumbs, mayonnaise, cayenne, Worcestershire, egg, parsley and lemon rind. Gently fold in lumps of crab. Season with salt. Shape lightly into 8 crab cakes. Chill before frying. Heat oil in heavy skillet. Add butter. Fry crab cakes until lightly browned on both sides.

Pass It On...To make bread crumbs, chop stale bread or crusts in food processor, blender or with a knife.

MOLDED CRAB LOUIS

A spectacular dish for a summer ladies' luncheon

6-8 servings

1 (12-ounce) can mixed vegetable juices or well-seasoned tomato juice
1 (3-ounce) package lemon flavored gelatin
¼ cup water
2 tablespoons sherry
3 tablespoons lemon juice
1 teaspoon onion, grated

½ cup celery, thinly sliced
2 hard-cooked eggs, chopped
2 cups fresh, frozen, canned, or imitation crab meat
salt and pepper to taste
½ cup mayonnaise
2 tablespoons chili sauce
shredded lettuce

▲ Heat vegetable juices and pour over lemon-flavored gelatin, stirring until gelatin is dissolved. Mix in water, sherry, lemon juice and onion. Chill until syrupy, then fold in celery, hard cooked eggs, crab, salt and pepper, and mayonnaise mixed with the chili sauce. Spoon into a medium-sized ring mold or 8 individual molds. Chill until firm (at least 12 hours). Turn out and serve on a bed of shredded lettuce. Make at least 12 hours ahead to ensure a good jell. Garnish with spiced beets, deviled egg halves, asparagus spears, olives, green or red pepper slices.

Pass It On*...When called for in cooking, I always use a wine I'd be willing to drink, not "cooking sherry."*

HALIBUT WITH PESTO

Servings vary

halibut steaks
olive oil
salt

freshly ground pepper
pesto
tomatoes

▲ Brush one-inch thick halibut steaks with olive oil and season with salt and freshly ground pepper. Grill 5 minutes on each side. Top with pesto and freshly diced tomatoes.

Pass It On*...When love and skill work together, expect a masterpiece.*

125

POACHED HALIBUT WITH LEMON BUTTER

4 servings

Court Bouillon:

¼ cup carrot, chopped
¼ cup celery, chopped
¼ cup onion, chopped
1 fresh lemon grass stalk
1 cup white Riesling wine
1 garlic clove

pinch of thyme
1 bay leaf
juice of half a lemon
2 peppercorns
4 cups water

Sauce: (may be made ahead)

1 teaspoon shallots, chopped
2 cloves garlic, chopped
¼ cup Court Bouillon
¼ cup white Riesling wine
pinch of thyme
1 bay leaf
1 peppercorn
juice of half a lemon

½ cup heavy cream
6 tablespoons unsalted butter,
*   softened*
zest of half a lemon
approximately 1 teaspoon fresh
*   parsley, chopped*
salt to taste
pepper to taste

Halibut:

4 (6-ounce) halibut fillet pieces,
*   boned and skinned*

approximately 1½ cups Court
*   Bouillon*
fresh chives

▲ For Court Bouillon: Combine carrot, celery, onion, lemon grass, wine, garlic, thyme, bay leaf, lemon juice, peppercorn and water in a saucepan. Bring mixture to a boil. Reduce heat and simmer for 10 minutes. Strain. To prepare the sauce: Combine shallots, garlic, ¼ cup Court Bouillon, wine, thyme, bay leaf, peppercorn and lemon juice in a small saucepan. Reduce to about half. Strain. Stir in heavy cream and reduce again until sauce coats the back of a spoon. Remove from heat and fold in butter, 1 tablespoon at a time. Stir in zest and parsley. Add salt and pepper to taste. Place halibut fillets in a shallow baking dish. Cover with approximately 1 cup Court Bouillon. Cover. Bake in a 350 ° oven for approximately 10 minutes or until fish flakes easily with a fork. Fish can also be poached in a large skillet if preferred. To assemble: Place one-fourth of the sauce on an individual dinner plate. Place fish on top of sauce and garnish with fresh chives.

Pass It On...My mother once steamed a fish in the dishwasher. Delicious!

POACHED SALMON WITH CUCUMBER SAUCE

6 servings

Note: Requires 2 hours chilling.

6 fresh salmon steaks
1 quart water

1½ tablespoons salt
2 tablespoons lemon juice

Sauce:

1 cup cucumber, grated (peeled
* and seeded)*
½ cup sour cream
¼ cup mayonnaise
1 tablespoon parsley, minced
2 teaspoons onion, grated

2 teaspoons cider vinegar
¼ teaspoon salt
pinch of pepper
lemons
fresh dill

▲ To poach salmon: In a large skillet, heat water, salt and lemon juice to boiling. Reduce heat and simmer salmon steaks 3 at a time for 10 minutes, or until steaks turn light pink in color. Remove steaks with slotted spatula and chill for at least 1 hour. To make sauce: Grate enough cucumber to make 1 cup and drain well. Add the remaining ingredients and stir well. Chill for at least 1 hour. Serve salmon with sauce and garnish with lemon quarters and dill.

Pass It On...We celebrate Christmas Eve at my parents' or godparents' home, switching every year, with a huge buffet highlighted by beefsteak tartar and cold salmon and shrimp served festively at a beautifully set table. While stuffing ourselves Christmas Eve, we enjoy knowing Christmas dinner will be a delicious sit down formal affair with the best china and crystal and special European dishes. (Both my parents and godparents are from Europe). I always anticipate holidays full of warm, fuzzy memories and thoughts of happy futures.

SALMON STEAKS WITH CAPER SAUCE

A super summer dinner

2 servings

2 tablespoons plain low-fat yogurt
2 tablespoons mayonnaise
1 teaspoon capers, drained
½ teaspoon white wine vinegar
¼ teaspoon lemon pepper
seasoning
2 (4-ounce) salmon steaks
vegetable cooking spray

1 small onion, thinly sliced
2 tablespoons dry white wine
1 tablespoon fresh dill, chopped or
1 teaspoon dried whole
dillweed
lemon slices (optional)
fresh dill sprigs (optional)

▲ Combine first 5 ingredients. Mix well. Cover and chill. Rinse salmon and pat dry. Place in a 1-quart baking dish coated with cooking spray. Arrange onion slices over salmon. Pour wine over salmon and sprinkle with dill. Cover and bake at 350° for 15-20 minutes or until salmon flakes easily. Remove onion and dill and transfer salmon to serving plates. Spoon 2 tablespoons chilled caper mixture over each salmon steak. Garnish with lemon slices and fresh dill if desired.

***Pass It On**...I use white vermouth to add a lovely flavor when dry white wine is called for.*

COQUILLE ST. JACQUES

A scrumptious dish

8 servings

2½ pounds scallops
½ pound mushrooms, sliced
juice of 2 lemons
2 tablespoons shallot, minced
½ cup fresh chives, chopped
¼ cup white wine

2 cups fish or chicken stock
3 tablespoons flour
4 egg yolks
3-4 drops hot pepper sauce
½ cup heavy cream
paprika

▲ Put first 6 ingredients in saucepan and cook over medium heat until scallops are poached (about 5 minutes). Mix flour and fish stock and add to scallop mixture. Cook and stir until sauce is smooth. Add egg yolks, hot pepper sauce and heavy cream; blend well. Put into scallop shells or casserole and top with paprika. Place under broiler for a few minutes until glazed.

***Pass It On**...Thaw fish in milk for added flavor.*

SHRIMP CREOLE

4 servings

3 tablespoons oil
⅔ cup onion, chopped
¾ cup celery, chopped
1 cup green pepper, chopped
1 tablespoon flour
16 ounces canned tomatoes
1½ teaspoons salt

red pepper
black pepper
1 pound medium shrimp, peeled
   and boiled
1 (3-ounce) can mushrooms
juice of ½ lemon
hot rice

▲ Heat oil. Sauté onion, celery and green pepper. Add flour and cook a little. Add tomatoes, salt, red and black pepper to taste. Cook over medium heat about 10 minutes. Just before serving add shrimp, mushrooms and lemon juice. Heat through and serve over hot rice.

GRILLED YELLOW FIN TUNA STEAKS

Excellent flavor and low in calories

4 servings

4 tuna steaks
¼ cup light soy sauce
¼ cup orange juice
1 tablespoon lemon juice
2 tablespoons ketchup

½ teaspoon garlic powder
½ teaspoon leaf oregano
dash pepper
2 tablespoons parsley
2 tablespoons vegetable oil

▲ Preheat grill (or broiler). Mix all ingredients and pour over rinsed tuna steaks. Marinate at least 30 minutes. Cook fish over moderately hot coals for 5 to 6 minutes. Baste with marinade. Turn with pancake turner. Cook 4 or 5 minutes longer. If broiling, broil 4 inches from heat, 4 minutes on each side. For easier turning, use a hinged wire grill.

SEAFOOD BOMBAY

A unique, tropical dinner

4 servings

2 medium-sized fresh pineapples
2 pounds assorted seafood such as
    shrimp, scallops and lobster
2 sticks butter
1 tart green apple, cored and
    chopped
1 medium onion, chopped
2 ribs celery, chopped
4 tablespoons chutney

2 teaspoons curry powder
2 teaspoons flour
1½ cups chicken broth, heated
¼ cup sherry
½ cup cream
garnish of banana chips, toasted
    almonds, shredded coconut
coconut rice

▲ Slice pineapples (including tops) in half lengthwise and remove pulp. Place shells on baking sheet. Combine apple, onion and celery and fry in half the butter until cooked. Add chutney, curry powder and flour. Cook 3-4 minutes on low heat, stirring constantly. Continue stirring as hot chicken broth is added until mixture is thick and creamy. In another pan melt the remaining butter. Add seafood and stir-fry about 4 minutes, then add sherry. Combine with creamy sauce mixture. Remove from heat and add cream. Preheat pineapple shells in 300° oven for 5-6 minutes. Place ½ cup coconut rice in each shell, then fill with seafood mixture. Return to oven until heated through (about 10 minutes). Sprinkle top with banana chips, toasted almonds and shredded coconut. Serve with additional coconut rice and spinach salad with pineapple, almonds and mushrooms. For coconut rice: cook rice, following package instructions substituting coconut milk for water.

Pass It On…You may also substitute chicken for the seafood.

TOMATO BASIL CHEESE SAUCE FOR PAST

8-10 servings

3 cups ripe tomatoes, chopped
¾ cup fresh basil, chopped
3 tablespoons onion, minced
1 garlic clove, minced
1 cup ricotta cheese

¼ cup olive oil
salt and pepper to taste
1 pound pasta, cooked according
  to package instructions

▲ Combine the first 4 ingredients, then stir in ricotta, oil and seasonings. Pour sauce over hot pasta, mix well and serve at once.

SPICY MARINARA

2½ cups or enough for 1 pound pasta

⅓ cup Italian extra virgin olive oil
4 garlic cloves, chopped fine
½ cup dry white or red wine
½ teaspoon crushed red pepper
20 ounces ripe tomatoes, peeled
  seeded and chopped or 28-
  ounce can of imported Italian
  tomatoes

1 pinch seasoned salt
1 pinch sugar
2 tablespoons chopped fresh basil

▲ In a heavy saucepan, heat the olive oil over medium heat. Sauté garlic until it begins to color slightly. Pour in wine and cook until a good bit of the liquid evaporates. Add the crushed red pepper, tomatoes, salt and sugar and cook over low heat for 20 minutes, until sauce thickens slightly. Add basil and cook 5 minutes more.

Pass It On...Omit the red pepper for a milder marinara.

PASTA

Plain and easy with fantastic flavor

2 servings

6 ounces dried spaghetti
2 tablespoons olive oil
4-5 teaspoons garlic, minced
3 tablespoons spaghetti water

salt and pepper to taste
1 tablespoon fresh parsley, minced
Parmesan cheese, grated

▲ Cook spaghetti according to package directions. Heat oil and sauté garlic, add water. Drain spaghetti and toss with sauté of garlic garnishing with parsley and cheese.

Pass It On...*To prevent water from boiling over, add 1 tablespoon of cooking oil when preparing spaghetti, noodles, rice or other pasta.*

HINTERBERGER'S PASTA WITH CLAMS

4-6 servings

½ cup plus 1 tablespoon olive oil
¼-½ teaspoon dried red pepper flakes
1 large onion, chopped
4 cloves garlic, minced
⅓ pound fresh mushrooms, sliced and sautéed in 1 tablespoon olive oil and 1 tablespoon butter
½ cup fresh basil, chopped or 1 tablespoon dried basil

1 tablespoon oregano
salt and freshly ground pepper to taste
2 (4½-ounce) cans chopped clams, reserve liquid
½ cup white wine
½ cup black olives, sliced
1 pound dried spaghetti
1 cup parsley, chopped
Romano and/or Parmesan cheese, freshly grated

▲ Pour the olive oil into a large skillet and heat slowly over low heat. Add pepper flakes, onion and garlic. Cook slowly about 20 minutes or until the onions are soft. Add basil, oregano, salt and pepper, liquid from the clams and wine. Continue to simmer until some of the liquid is reduced. Add mushrooms and keep warm. Bring a large kettle of water to boil, adding 1 tablespoon salt and 1 tablespoon oil. Cook spaghetti until just al dente, about 5 minutes then drain well. As pasta is cooking, add the clams, parsley, olives and 3 tablespoons of cheese to sauce. Simmer about 5 minutes. Drain and stir pasta into the sauce and toss until well mixed. Sprinkle generously with grated cheese and serve directly from the skillet.

SPICY PEANUT NOODLES

A terrific, spicy dish

8 servings

1 teaspoon dry red pepper, crushed
¼ cup corn oil
3 tablespoons sesame oil
3 tablespoons honey
2 tablespoons soy sauce
8 ounces dry spaghetti

2 tablespoons cilantro, chopped
¼ cup roasted peanuts, chopped
¼ cup green onions, minced
1 tablespoon sesame seeds, roasted
sesame seeds for garnish

▲ In a saucepan, stir red pepper and oils over medium heat for 2 minutes. Add honey and soy sauce. Stir to combine and set aside. Cook spaghetti in boiling salted water until tender, about 9 minutes. Drain well and combine with soy sauce mixture. Cover and refrigerate for at least 4 hours or overnight. When ready to serve, add chopped cilantro, peanuts and onions to noodles. Toss together. Sprinkle with sesame seeds and garnish with whole cilantro leaves.

Pass It On...*Can also be served as an appetizer.*

AEGEAN PASTA

Equally delicious served hot or at room temperature

12 servings

2 pounds shrimp, cleaned and
butterflied
½ pound butter
1 tablespoon oil
6-8 scallions (or green onions),
chopped

1 pound (or two 9-ounce packages)
spinach linguine
freshly ground black pepper to
taste
chopped fresh basil to taste
8-16 ounces Feta cheese
cherry tomatoes for garnish

▲ Sauté shrimp in butter and olive oil. Add scallions and sauté. Cook linguine and drain. While linguine is hot, toss with shrimp mixture, black pepper, basil and crumbled Feta cheese until cheese melts and mixture is creamy. Garnish with cherry tomatoes.

PIZZA ON THE GRILL

4 servings

1 package dry yeast
¾ cup lukewarm water
2 cups flour (a combination of
 white and wheat, if possible)
1 teaspoon salt
1 teaspoon sugar
4 medium tomatoes, quartered
2 cloves garlic, sliced

1 tablespoon olive oil
2 tablespoons fresh basil
2 cups fresh mushrooms, sliced
1 medium onion, sliced
1 cup mozzarella cheese, shredded
¼ cup Romano cheese, freshly
 grated

▲ Soak yeast in water for 5 minutes. Add flour, salt and sugar. Mix to blend. Knead for 2 or 3 minutes until flour is well blended. Preheat charcoal grill to very hot (550°), adjust grill grid to 8 inches above heat. Roll to fit 12-inch pizza pan (to save time, use frozen pizza or pre-made pizza crust). Place tomatoes, garlic, olive oil and basil in blender and blend until smooth. Spread on dough, then top with mushrooms, onions and cheeses. Cover and bake for 5 minutes. With a large spatula, slide pizza directly onto grill grid and cook an additional 10 minutes or until the bottom side of crust is nicely browned. Serve immediately or hold in warm oven until time to be served.

Pass It On...When my family wants to entertain but doesn't have the time or energy to do all the cooking, we "Entertain by Committee" and invite friends for a salad luncheon, potato bake, pizza party, omelet or crepe soiree or taco fiesta. Each guest simply selects one or two items and brings them. Choices for a salad luncheon include already chopped, sliced, grated or torn ingredients such as greens, cheese, cooked meat, tomatoes, mushrooms, olives, radishes, cucumbers, onions, carrots, peppers, raisins, nuts, seeds, bacon bits, croutons or salad dressing. I keep a list of what's coming, so we know what to add. We also provide the basics when doing potatoes, pizzas, omelets, crepes or tacos along with drinks and dessert. It's always fun to see all the ingredients spread out on the table and the different combinations chosen by each "guest."

PASTA À LA HOT SPRINGS

4 servings

1 cup frozen peas
1 pound Italian imported pasta,
  preferably bow ties or penne
  rigate
5 cloves garlic
½ cup extra virgin olive oil and
  sunflower oil and canola oil,
  mixed in equal parts

1 cup fresh mint or basil
½-1 teaspoon cayenne pepper,
  blended in olive oil
½ cup butter (or half margarine
  and half butter)
salt to taste
½ cup Parmesan cheese, freshly
  grated or processed

▲ Cook peas and pasta according to package directions. Three minutes before end of cooking time, pour oils in small pan at medium heat; add garlic, sliced in large segments, and sauté the garlic until translucent. Lower heat, add cayenne oil, then add butter. Drain pasta, saving 1 cup of hot water. In cooking pot, blend all the ingredients, and add the fresh mint (chopped fine), and if it is not moist enough, add the hot water. Serve in large dish, sprinkle with generous amounts of Parmesan cheese, and garnish with twigs of additional mint.

Pass It On...The origins of this recipe lie deep in my early memories. When I was a child in the 1940's, my parents would take us to vacation in a small village high in the Apennines, the mountain range that is the backbone of Italy and separates the region of Tuscany from the region where I was born, Romagna. Those hills, so similar in nature to the ones that surround Hot Springs, Arkansas, would produce sweet basil in abundance each summer, so basil became the predominant herb of choice of that region. Having difficulty in finding a steady supply of basil in Hot Springs, I tried substituting wild mint that grows like a weed there, and by this change, created this thrilling pasta recipe.

MEDITERRANEAN PASTA

4 servings

1 pint large red cherry tomatoes,
plus herbs for seasoning,
ovendried

1 pound pasta - fettucini or
linguine
¾ cup Kalamata olives, sliced
1 cup Feta cheese, crumbled

Pesto:
2 cups fresh basil, washed, dried,
and stems removed
½ cup Parmesan or Romano
cheese, grated

¼ cup walnuts, chopped
4 cloves garlic, minced
¾ cup virgin olive oil

▲ For ovendried tomatoes: Heat oven to 425°. Slice 1 pint of large cherry tomatoes in half and place cut side up on lightly greased cookie sheet. Sprinkle with your favorite fresh herbs, if desired. Place in oven and immediately reduce temperature to 250°. Keep in oven for 2-2½ hours. Remove and cool. Use like sundried tomatoes. For pesto: In blender place 2 cups fresh basil leaves, washed and dried and stems removed. Add ½ cup grated Parmesan or Romano cheese, walnuts and garlic clove. Blend until smooth, adding ¾ cup olive oil in steady stream. For pasta: Cook pasta in large pot of boiling water until al dente. Drain and toss with pesto, tomatoes and olives. Top with 1 cup crumbled Feta cheese.

Pass It On...I have a favorite quick dinner that gets a lot of use at my house. I always keep a selection of dried pasta on hand. Also, I keep canned chicken, mushrooms, olives, pesto mix, jars of marinara sauce, fresh garlic, sun-dried tomatoes, capers, pine nuts, dried red pepper flakes and Italian herb seasoning on my "10 minute shelf". I select the pasta of the evening and while it is cooking, I choose the rest of the ingredients from the shelf. When pasta is cooked, I drain it and mix in the seasonings along with 1 cup half-and-half, ½ pound crumbled goat cheese or Parmesan cheese, freshly ground black pepper and shredded fresh basil. I usually serve sliced tomatoes and buttered slices of French baguette sticks. I try to be creative — almost any combination on hand will work with pasta to make a quick and delicious meal.

DILLED SHRIMP PASTA

6 servings

2 cups heavy cream
4 tablespoons sweet butter
2 teaspoons salt
pinch of nutmeg

1 tablespoon Parmesan cheese
⅓ cup dill weed
1 pound cooked shrimp
1 package pasta

▲ Bring cream and ½ of the butter to simmer in an uncovered medium saucepan. Add 1 teaspoon of salt and nutmeg. Add Parmesan cheese and dill weed. Continue simmering until the mixture is reduced to one third. Stir and remove from heat. Add shrimp. Cook pasta according to package directions; drain and toss with remaining butter and salt. Serve with shrimp mixture over pasta.

PENNE AND PESTO

4 servings

1 cup fresh basil leaves
2 teaspoons garlic, minced
¼ cup pine nuts (pignolia nuts)
½ cup Parmesan cheese, freshly
    grated

½ cup virgin olive oil
1 pound penne pasta
⅓ cup butter
pepper to taste

▲ Chop basil leaves, garlic, pine nuts and Parmesan cheese in food processor. Add olive oil slowly until a thick consistency. Add pepper to taste. Cook pasta according to package directions and drain. Toss with butter and pesto mixture. Serve with extra Parmesan cheese and fresh basil leaf garnish.

Pass It On...Pine nuts (sometimes called pignolia nuts) can be found with regular packaged nuts at the grocery store but are normally quite expensive. Usually pine nuts can be purchased in bulk at "whole foods" markets. They freeze well. Sunflower seeds make a suitable substitution.

GRAN'S BEST CHICKEN SPAGHETTI

12-15 servings

4-5 pounds chicken pieces
8-10 cups water, lightly salted
bouquet garni of celery leaves and
stems, green onions and tops,
whole peppercorns
1 (24-ounce) package spaghetti
1 stick butter
1 (8-ounce) can sliced mushrooms

1 large onion, chopped
1 green pepper, chopped
¾ cup flour
4 cups milk
¼ pound American cheese
½ pound Old English cheese
salt and pepper to taste

▲ In a large pot bring water to boil. Tie celery, onion and peppercorns in several layers of cooking cheesecloth or nylon net. Add chicken and bouquet garni to boiling water. Reduce heat and simmer about 45 minutes. Let chicken cool in broth. When cool enough to handle, remove chicken from broth and separate skin and bones from meat. Shred meat and set aside. Remove bouquet garni and strain broth. Chill until fat rises to the top and can be removed. Return broth to the large pot and bring to a boil. Add spaghetti and cook until most of the liquid has been absorbed.

Melt butter in a large saucepan. Add vegetables and sauté until tender. Add flour and cook 1 minute. Slowly add milk stirring constantly until mixture thickens. Add cheeses stirring until melted and thoroughly combined.

Combine spaghetti, cheese sauce and reserved chicken. Spoon into 2 greased or sprayed 2-quart casseroles. Casserole may be covered with foil and frozen at this point but should be thawed before baking. Bake uncovered at 350° about 30 minutes or until hot and bubbly. Serve with Parmesan cheese, a green salad and hot crusty garlic bread.

Pass It On...*My gran told me, "Always hold your head up because nobody will hold it up for you."*

Vegetables

U.S. POSTAGE 11c
VISIT THE U

Fire and Ice

RECIPE FOR Black Eye Peas

FROM THE KITCHEN OF

Recipe Saute 2 T. Olive Oil

1 Bunch green onions chop
with tops

one green bell pepper

(oranime) 3 (4" stems lemon grass)
recipe in

My Recipe by Evaleen

Macaroni And Cheese

Sauce:

3 tablespoons margarine
3 tablespoons of flower
1 1/4 cups milk
1 egg
1 teaspoon of dry mustard
1 teaspoon of salt
1 teaspoon of pepper
3 cups Ceddar cheese
8 ounces mackaroni

to Mar Mar

WORLD'S BEST CORNBREAD DRESSING

10-12 servings

2 cups chopped celery
3 cups chopped onion
1 cup butter or margarine
2 (9-inch) pans cornbread (use
your own favorite recipe)
6 slices white bread

2-3 cups canned chicken broth
6 eggs, beaten
salt
pepper
poultry seasoning

▲ Sauté onion and celery in butter until limp. Crumble cornbread into mixture. Tear white bread into small pieces and add to the mixture. Add 1½-2 cups of chicken broth and mix together. Add 6 beaten eggs. Season to taste with salt, pepper and poultry seasoning. Grease a three-quart casserole or 2 (9x13-inch) pans with cooking spray. Pour dressing into pans and cover with tin foil. Bake for 45-50 minutes at 350°. You may need to add broth during cooking, if too dry.

Pass It On... "Always position yourself for good things to happen." - Donna Axum Whitworth, Miss America 1964. Ms. Whitworth also contributed the above recipe.

STUFFED ACORN SQUASH

6 servings

3 medium acorn squash
1 egg, beaten
1 chicken bouillon cube
⅓ cup boiling water
¼ cup onion, chopped

2 tablespoons butter or margarine
½ cup herb seasoned stuffing mix,
crushed
½ teaspoon salt
dash of pepper

▲ Cut squash lengthwise, remove seeds. Bake, cut side down on baking sheet at 400° for 30 minutes or until tender. Cool and scoop squash from shells (reserve shells). Mash squash; add egg and bouillon dissolved in boiling water, stir, adding more water if necessary. Cook onion in butter until tender, but not brown. Add to squash mixture. Stir in stuffing mixture, (reserve ¼ cup); add seasonings and mix well. Fill shells with squash mixture, it will be thin, top with reserved stuffing. Bake at 400° for 25 minutes, or until lightly browned.

Pass It On...We have a "Thank You Box". Throughout the year, family members write on slips of paper things they are thankful for. The items can be simple, like the cookies didn't burn, or major, such as successful surgery. On Thanksgiving Day, we open the box, read the slips and relive the memories.

BOSTON BAKED BEANS

A good meal in itself

12-15 servings

*1 pound dried beans (navy, pea or
  marrow)*
fresh water
*¼ pound meaty salt pork or
  boneless pork chop (optional)*
⅓ cup dark brown sugar

⅓ cup molasses
⅓ cup chili sauce
1 teaspoon salt
1 teaspoon dry mustard
1 teaspoon cider vinegar
2 whole small onions, peeled

▲ Pick over beans and place in large saucepan. Soak beans in water; cover overnight (or follow quick method on package). Pour off water and cover with fresh water. Simmer until skins crack when blown upon - about one hour. Drain, reserving bean liquid. Place ½ of beans in three quart bean pot. Score and wash the salt pork (strip of fat/strip of lean) and press down into bean pot. Press the two small whole onions into bean pot. Add the remaining beans. Mix the dark brown sugar, molasses, chili sauce, salt, dry mustard and cider vinegar with the reserved bean liquid; pour into pot to just cover the beans, adding the rest or boiling water as necessary to keep moist. Cover and bake in a 250° to 300° oven for 6 to 8 hours (uncover the last ½ hour so the pork browns nicely).

Pass It On... "*We Tri Deltas owe a great debt to fraternity leaders who would not accept a philanthropy unrelated to our purpose and aim but who convincingly saved the choice of philanthropy until need was demonstrated for the most fitting logical service a college fraternity can render society." - Zoe Gore Perrin, National President of Delta Delta Delta 1942-46. The above recipe was contributed by friends of the late Ms. Perrin.*

SOUTHERN-STYLE CUBAN BLACK BEANS

8-10 servings

1 white onion, finely chopped
2 cloves garlic, minced
1 green pepper, seeded and finely
chopped
¼ cup virgin olive oil
1 pound dried black beans, soaked
for at least 4 hours and
drained
6 cups water
1½ cups chicken stock

¼ cup red wine
1 tablespoon salt
1 tablespoon freshly ground
pepper
1 ham hock
1 teaspoon white vinegar
bouquet garni (2 green onions, 2
sprigs fresh coriander, 2 sprigs
fresh parsley, 1 bay leaf in
cheese cloth or tied together)

▲ In a heavy Dutch oven, sauté the onion, garlic and green pepper in the olive oil until they become limp. Add the beans, stir well; then add water, chicken stock, wine, salt, pepper, ham hock and bouquet garni. Bring mixture to a boil over moderate heat. Lower heat, add vinegar and simmer the beans, covered, for 2 hours. Uncover the beans and cook until sauce thickens. Remove 1 cup of the beans and mash them until soupy. Return the mashed beans to the pot and cook another 10 minutes.Remove bouquet garni and adjust seasoning. Serve with white rice.

FIRE AND ICE BLACKEYED PEAS

A spicy taste with cool yogurt

6-8 servings

3 tablespoons olive oil
1 bunch green onions with tops,
chopped
1 green bell pepper, chopped
3 4-inch stems fresh lemon grass
1 tablespoon garlic, minced
salt and pepper to taste

2 (15½-ounce) cans blackeyed
peas with juice
¼ cup picante sauce
handful of fresh cilantro leaves,
chopped
plain yogurt

▲ Cut lemon grass into very small pieces. Lemon grass may be found in most Oriental food supply stores. Combine first six ingredients and lightly sauté. Add blackeyed peas and simmer 10 minutes. Add cilantro and picante sauce. Serve topped with a swirl of 1-2 tablespoons of yogurt.

Pass It On*...To bring luck to each new year, my great-grandmother boiled a silver dollar and placed it in the bottom of the blackeyed peas. On the first serving, she allowed everyone only one dip and no seconds until all firsts were eaten. The peas always disappeared quickly, at least until someone snagged the prize.*

HERBED GREEN BEANS

8 servings

1 pound green beans	**dried onion flakes (or minced**
olive oil	**fresh onion)**
dried basil flakes (or shredded	**garlic salt**
fresh basil leaves)	

▲ Cook green beans in boiling water until crisp and tender. Drain. Coat lightly with olive oil and mix with herbs and garlic salt to taste.

Pass It On...*Extra herbs enhance oil-reduced recipes.*

SWISS GREEN BEANS

Great with turkey and dressing for Thanksgiving or Christmas

8 servings

3 tablespoons butter	**1 pint sour cream**
2 tablespoons flour	**3 cans French style green beans**
¼ teaspoon pepper	**3 cups corn flakes, crushed**
1 teaspoon salt	**¼ pound Swiss cheese, grated**
⅓ cup onion, chopped	**¼ cup butter**

▲ Melt 3 tablespoons butter, stir in flour, salt, pepper and sour cream over low/medium heat. Stir until thick and smooth. Add onion and well-drained beans. Pour into greased casserole. Combine cheese, corn flakes and about ¼ cup melted butter. Cover the top of the casserole with mixture. Bake at 400° for 20-25 minutes.

Pass It On...*When our three children were 5, 8 and 10, we decided each family member should be responsible for one part of Thanksgiving Dinner. I claimed the turkey and dressing. My husband promised to bake cream pies. Marshall decided on salad and Michael on bread. That left 5-year-old Holly with the vegetable. Every person chose a specific recipe, made out a grocery list and prepared the food (with a little help). Years later, the tradition continues, and while I had envisioned swapping courses occasionally, the kids insist on the same job every Thanksgiving, even Holly's green beans.*

SWEET-SOUR GREEN BEANS

Good by itself or served cold as a salad

6-8 servings

1 pound green beans
4 slices bacon
1 medium onion, chopped
2 teaspoons flour

½ cup water
⅓ cup vinegar
2 teaspoons sugar

▲ Wash green beans and cut into two-inch pieces. Cook beans until crisp-tender. Drain. In large skillet, cook bacon until crisp. Drain on paper towels and crumble. Sauté onion in 2 tablespoons of pan drippings until tender. Stir in flour. Cook and stir until bubbly. Stir in water, vinegar and sugar. Heat to boiling and cook until slightly thickened. Add beans and heat through, tossing occasionally. Sprinkle with salt, pepper and bacon.

Pass It On...*To make a pretty plate, my Aunt Martha ties bundles of green beans with lemon rind, green onion or steamed red and green pepper.*

GERMAN BEETS

6-8 servings

4 cups beets, cooked and sliced
2 medium onions, sliced
¾ cup sugar
4 tablespoons margarine, melted
⅓ cup vinegar

2 teaspoons cornstarch
⅓ cup water
¼ teaspoon salt
pinch of pepper

▲ Sauté onions in margarine until tender, but not brown. Stir in sugar, cornstarch, salt and pepper; add water and vinegar. Simmer until thickened, stirring constantly. Add beets. Keep hot over hot water for about 30 minutes to blend the flavor of the sauce through the beets.

BROCCOLI EXTRAORDINAIRE

4 servings

1½ pounds broccoli
3 tablespoons olive oil

2 large cloves garlic, minced
4 sun-dried tomatoes

▲ Wash broccoli and peel stalks. Chop stalks into ½-inch slices; separate florets. Place in steamer, cover and steam 5 to 10 minutes or until al dente. Just before serving, heat oil in large skillet over medium-low heat. Add garlic, and cook 1 minute. Add broccoli and toss to coat. Cook, stirring frequently, about 4 minutes or until heated through. Toss with the sun-dried tomatoes and serve hot.

WINTER BROCCOLI CASSEROLE

8 servings

2 (10-ounce) packages frozen cut
    broccoli or broccoli spears
¼ cup butter or margarine
1 tablespoon garlic, minced
½ pound fresh mushrooms, sliced
1 (6-ounce) can tomato paste

1 (14½-ounce) can beef broth
¼ cup flour
½ cup Parmesan cheese, grated
salt
pepper

▲ Cook broccoli according to package directions, and arrange in a buttered two-quart casserole. In a saucepan, melt butter and sauté garlic and mushrooms. Pour mushrooms over broccoli. In another saucepan combine tomato paste and beef broth. Slowly whisk in flour, and season with salt and pepper. Add ¼ cup Parmesan cheese and simmer over low heat 15 minutes. Pour sauce over broccoli and mushrooms; sprinkle remaining Parmesan cheese over top of casserole. Bake uncovered at 350° for 30 minutes.

Pass It On...Sauté vegetables in white wine instead of oil for a healthier dish.

GREEN CHILE RICE

4-6 servings

Note: Microwavable.

2½ cups water
1 cup rice
salt to taste
2 cups sour cream

½ pound Monterey Jack cheese,
  grated
1 (7-ounce) can diced green chilies
3 tablespoons butter
¼ cup Parmesan cheese, grated

▲ Cook rice according to package directions. Let cool. Mix rice with sour cream and salt. Spread half of the rice in a one-quart casserole. Sprinkle with Monterey Jack cheese and chilies. Add the rest of the rice. Dot with butter, and sprinkle with Parmesan cheese. Bake in a 350° oven for 30 minutes or cook in microwave on high power for 10 minutes.

Pass It On...Success or failure is caused more by mental attitude than by mental capacity.

BRUSSELS SPROUTS IN CREAM

6-8 servings

1½ pounds Brussels sprouts
1 pint sour cream

½ cup onion, chopped
2 tablespoons margarine

▲ Cook Brussels sprouts until tender (about 15 minutes). Sauté onion in margarine until brown. Combine with sour cream. Add Brussels sprouts. Serve hot.

ZESTY CARROTS

4-6 servings

Note: Can be made ahead and baked just before serving.

1 pound carrots
1 cup mayonnaise
½ cup milk
1 tablespoon horseradish

1 teaspoon salt
½ teaspoon pepper
2 tablespoons lemon juice
¼ teaspoon nutmeg

▲ Cut carrots into thick slices on the diagonal and cook in boiling water until just tender, 10 to 15 minutes. Mix all other ingredients for sauce. Place carrots in one-quart casserole, cover with sauce. Bake 15 minutes at 350°.

CARROT TIMBALES

4 servings

4 ramekins or custard cups
1 pound carrots, peeled and cut
*   into medium slices*
1 tablespoon butter
3 eggs

½ cup milk
salt
pepper
sugar

▲ Generously butter four ramekins or custard cups. Place carrots in saucepan of boiling, salted water. Cover and cook until carrots are very tender. Drain well, then puree in food processor or blender until very smooth. Melt butter in same pan, add puree and cook over low heat, stirring often until excess moisture evaporates. Remove from heat. Whisk eggs and milk together, then gradually add to puree. Season to taste with salt, pepper and sugar. Divide mixture into baking cups. Tap each to pack down, smooth top. Set cups in roasting pan and add boiling water to pan to come halfway up sides of cups. Bake at 400° 35-40 minutes or until firm. Remove cups from hot water with tongs and allow to cool about 3-5 minutes. When cool enough to handle, run thin bladed knife around edge of molds. Invert on serving plate and tap to loosen. Gently lift mold.

Pass It On...Any vegetable can be substituted - spinach, beets, turnips, broccoli, etc. Serve as a vegetable or as an appetizer surrounded by a ribbon of your favorite sauce - tomato or mushroom sauce, for example.

RED CABBAGE

4-6 servings

1 medium head red cabbage
1 cup light sour cream
1 tablespoon lemon juice

1 tablespoon onion, grated
¼ teaspoon thyme
salt to taste

▲ Shred cabbage and cook in a small amount of water for about 10 minutes. Drain. Add sour cream, lemon juice, onion and thyme. Heat and mix together. Add salt to taste.

CRUNCHY CELERY CASSEROLE

8-10 servings

Note: Can be made ahead and refrigerated. Bake one hour before serving.

4 cups celery, diced

1 can sliced water chestnuts

¼ cup pimientos, diced (2 ounces)
or ¼ cup carrot, grated

1 can undiluted cream of chicken
soup

½ cup browned bread crumbs
tossed in 2 tablespoons butter

¼ cup toasted almonds, slivered or
sliced

▲ Cook diced celery about two minutes in butter, oil or water. Mix together cooked celery, sliced chestnuts, pimiento (or carrots) and soup. Put into 10x10x2-inch deep casserole. Top with bread crumbs browned in butter. Sprinkle almonds over top. Bake at 350° for 35 minutes uncovered.

***Pass It On**...Self confidence is the first requisite to great undertakings.*

CALICO CORN

4-6 servings

3 ears of fresh corn, kernels cut
from the cob

½-1 large onion, thinly sliced

½ red bell pepper, thinly sliced
lengthwise

½ yellow bell pepper, thinly sliced
lengthwise

½ (10-ounce) package fresh
spinach, washed and shredded

1 tablespoon olive oil

2 teaspoons dried dill weed

salt and pepper

▲ Prepare all vegetables - if peppers and onion strips seem too long, cut in half. Heat oil in skillet and sauté corn about 5 minutes. Add onions and peppers and sauté about 5 more minutes - these should be cooked through, but not limp. Season with dill, salt and pepper. Add spinach, toss well and cook just until it wilts.

***Pass It On**...To remove silk from corn on the cob, first rub with a dampened paper towel.*

FRESH CORN PUDDING

Best when made with fresh corn

6 servings

*2 cups corn, cut from cob (about 4
   medium ears)*
*1 tablespoon red bell pepper,
   minced*
¼ cup ~~green~~ onions, chopped
1½ tablespoons all-purpose flour
2 teaspoons sugar

¼ teaspoon salt
¼ teaspoon cornstarch
dash red pepper
2 eggs
~~1 cup heavy cream or half-and-half~~ Sour cream

▲ Combine first 8 ingredients, stirring well. Combine eggs and cream; add to the corn mixture. Spoon mixture into a 1-quart greased casserole. Place dish in a larger shallow pan and add water to depth of 1-inch to pan. Bake uncovered at 350° for 1 hour or until a knife inserted at side comes out clean.

CORN AND CARROT PUDDING

A delicious dish with turkey

8 servings

½ cup carrots, shredded
1½ cups creamed style corn
½ cup green pepper, chopped
1 teaspoon salt
2 tablespoons flour

2 tablespoons butter
1 tablespoon sugar
¼ teaspoon black pepper
1 cup scalded milk
3 eggs, well beaten

▲ Combine butter, flour, salt, pepper, sugar and milk. Heat and stir until smooth and thick. Add well beaten eggs and vegetables. Pour into buttered two-quart greased casserole dish and bake 30-45 minutes uncovered at 350° until lightly browned and still soft in the center. It will continue to cook some after removing from the oven.

Pass It On...Use extra care when cooking a custard-based dish. If overcooked, the pudding can "break" and become watery.

CURRIED EGGPLANT AND ZUCCHINI

6 servings

2 tablespoons olive oil
1 onion, chopped
2 cloves garlic, minced
1 teaspoon curry powder
¼ teaspoon red pepper
1 large eggplant, diced

1 medium zucchini, diced
3 fresh tomatoes, chopped
2 tablespoons parsley
salt
freshly ground pepper

▲ In a large skillet, heat oil and sauté onion and garlic until onion is limp. Add curry powder and pepper. Cook one minute. Stir in eggplant, zucchini, tomatoes and parsley. Stir well; lower heat and simmer 20 minutes covered. Stir occasionally. Season to taste with salt and pepper.

SOUTHERN BAKED CHEESE GRITS

Great for dinner buffets with baked ham and fried chicken

12 servings

1 cup unsalted boiling water
1½ cups quick cooking grits
3 eggs, beaten (use 2 for half
    recipe)
1 pound Cheddar cheese, grated

¾ cup butter
2 teaspoons salt
hot pepper sauce to taste
paprika to garnish (optional)

▲ Cook grits in water according to package directions. Remove from heat and add all other ingredients. Mix well. Adjust seasoning. Place in a two-quart oven-proof dish (one-quart for half recipe), uncovered, and bake in 350° oven for 1 hour (40 minutes for half recipe) until nicely golden on top.

Pass It On...*May be made a day ahead and frozen. If frozen, defrost in refrigerator before baking.*

MEXICAN HOMINY

A good accompaniment to a Mexican dinner

4 servings

2 (14½-ounce) cans of hominy,
drained
1 cup Monterey Jack cheese,
grated
1 onion, chopped and sautéd
1 clove garlic, minced

1 (8-ounce) carton sour cream,
thinned with milk
1 small can chopped green chilies
with juice
½ teaspoon cumin

▲ Mix above ingredients. Adjust seasoning to taste. Place ingredients in greased 1½-quart casserole. Bake at 350° for 30 minutes or until cheese bubbles.

Pass It On...You can't win if you don't play.

BARLEY AND MUSHROOM CASSEROLE

4 servings

Note: Can be fixed ahead and frozen.

4 tablespoons butter
1 cup pearl barley
1 large onion, chopped
1 cup mushrooms, coarsely
chopped

3 cups chicken, beef, or vegetable
broth
1 teaspoon salt, or to taste
¼ teaspoon pepper

▲ Preheat oven to 350°. Sauté barley in 2 tablespoons butter in skillet over medium heat for about 2 minutes or until lightly browned. Transfer to an ungreased 1½-quart casserole. Sauté onion in remaining 2 tablespoons butter for 4 to 8 minutes; add mushrooms and continue to sauté for 3 to 5 minutes. Add to casserole along with broth, salt, and pepper. Stir well. Cover and bake at 350° for about 1¼ hours or until barley is tender, stirring occasionally with fork. Once done, fluff with fork.

Pass It On...Life is not a cup to be measured, but a cup to be filled.

SHERRIED MUSHROOMS

4-5 servings

1 pound mushrooms, sliced
3 tablespoons sherry
1½ cups sour cream
¾ cup Parmesan cheese, grated

dash garlic powder
toast cups or pastry shells
parsley

▲ Sauté mushrooms in sherry. Add sour cream, Parmesan cheese and garlic powder. Serve in toast cups or pastry shells. Garnish with parsley for color.

Pass It On...*Never rinse fresh mushrooms. They absorb so much water that it hinders the cooking process. Instead, wipe mushrooms with a damp paper towel or use a mushroom brush.*

ONION CAULIFLOWER DELIGHT

8 servings

1 (10-ounce) package frozen
  cauliflower
2 (10-ounce) packages frozen
  onions in cream sauce

¾ cup sharp Cheddar cheese,
  grated
¼ cup almonds, slivered
1 tablespoon parsley, chopped

▲ Cut cauliflower into bite-size pieces. Prepare creamed onions according to packages. Add cauliflower, cheese, almonds and parsley to creamed onions. Put in a 1½-quart casserole. Bake, uncovered, at 350° for about 35 minutes or until bubbly and heated thoroughly. Garnish with more parsley, almonds or cheese.

Pass It On...*My husband thinks almost any leftover vegetable can be turned into a cream soup, and he's usually right. He just drains the vegetable and adds to stock such as chicken or beef broth, a small amount of cream and seasoning. Garnishing with mint or carrot curls makes the "leftover soup" seem like new.*

FANCY ONIONS

8-10 servings

2 pounds onions, small
½ cup raisins
¼ cup sugar
1 cup water

¼ cup vinegar
3 tablespoons tomato paste
3 tablespoons oil
salt and pepper to taste

▲ Mix all ingredients. Boil over low heat until onions are tender.

Pass It On...Cut onions into quarters if they are too large. Place onions in the freezer for a few minutes or cut the root end last to reduce tears.

CASSEROLE ONIONS

8 servings

6 large onions, sliced
¾ stick margarine
1 can cream of chicken soup
1 can milk

⅓ pound Cheddar or Swiss cheese,
    grated
1 loaf French bread, sliced
1 stick butter, melted

▲ Sauté onions in margarine and place in buttered 9x13-inch pan. Mix soup and milk; pour over onions. Sprinkle with grated cheese. Dip bread slices into melted butter. Place over top of casserole and bake 20 minutes at 350°.

Pass It On...I insert onions in the legs of pantyhose, knotting between each one. Hung in a cool, dry place, the onions will last a month or so. Also, eggs boiled in onion skins will turn a beautiful golden color. My European ancestors began this custom in our family, and we still eat the lovely boiled eggs each Easter morning.

BAKED VIDALIA ONION

A Southern treat

4 servings

4 Vidalia onions
4 ounces Parmesan cheese, grated

4 tablespoons butter

▲ Peel outer layer of onion and remove top stem. Cut into 4 sections only part way down. Wrap each onion in foil, leaving top open. Pour melted butter into onion; sprinkle with grated Parmesan cheese and close top of foil. Bake at 325° for 30-35 minutes until onion is soft and appears somewhat clear. Serve hot and season as desired.

Pass It On...Any sweet, mild onion may be used.

NANA'S ONIONS IN WINE SAUCE

8 servings

2 pounds tiny boiling onions
2 cups water
1 cup white wine
½ teaspoon salt
4 tablespoons butter
4 tablespoons flour

1 cup half-and-half
2 tablespoons parsley, chopped
dash of white pepper
3 tablespoons Parmesan cheese,
grated

▲ Pour boiling water over onions and let soak a few minutes for easier peeling. Peel away outer skin of onions. Put water, wine, salt and onions in a saucepan and bring to a boil. Reduce heat and simmer, uncovered, for 20 minutes. Drain, saving liquid. In a separate saucepan, melt butter. Stir in flour, then blend in half-and-half. Add 1 cup reserved onion liquid and cook, stirring constantly until thickened. Add parsley, pepper and onions. Pour into a one-quart casserole dish and sprinkle top with Parmesan cheese. Bake in a 375° oven for 25 minutes.

GRANNY POTATOES

1 medium potato and ½ apple per serving

Granny Smith apples
red new potatoes
rosemary

thyme
butter

▲ Slice first two ingredients thinly and place overlapping each other in a buttered baking pan. Sprinkle with rosemary and thyme. Dot with butter and bake at 375° about 30 minutes or until tender.

Pass It On...Replace one red potato with one sweet potato to the layer for color.

SAVORY MASHED POTATO CASSEROLE

10 servings

Note: Good to make ahead, allowing the flavors to blend.

4 pounds potatoes
1 (8-ounce) package cream cheese
1 cup sour cream
1 clove garlic, minced
2 teaspoons salt
1 dash pepper

¼ cup chives, chopped
paprika
butter
½ cup Parmesan cheese (optional topping)

▲ Peel potatoes. Cook in water until tender. Drain and mash. Mix next five ingredients into mashed potatoes. Beat at high speed until smooth and light. Place in lightly greased baking dish (10-cup). Add chives. Sprinkle with paprika and dot with butter. Sprinkle with Parmesan cheese if desired. Cover and refrigerate. Bake uncovered at 350° for 30 minutes until heated through.

Pass It On*...Before the senior prom, I invited my son and his date and several other couples for a Black and White Party. The guys wore their tuxedos and the girls also wore black and white. I decorated the table in black and white and served all black and white foods and drinks.*

POTATOES GRUYÈRE SOUFFLÉ

6-8 servings

3 cups potatoes (3-4 large baking potatoes), cooked and rinsed
¼ cup soft butter
2 ounces imported Gruyère cheese, grated
pinch of dried savory or thyme

2 teaspoons chives, minced
⅛ teaspoon pepper
1 teaspoon salt
1 cup heavy cream, whipped
3 eggs, yolks and whites separated

▲ Mix potatoes with next six ingredients. Beat egg yolks and fold into whipped cream. Beat egg whites until stiff but not dry. Fold potato mixture into egg yolk cream and then gently into egg white meringue. Place in ungreased 6-cup soufflé dish. Bake at 350° for 1 hour or until lightly browned.

Pass It On*...I rebake leftover potatoes by dipping them in water and then baking at 350° for about 20 minutes. Cutting a thin slice from each end of the potato speeds baking time when beginning with raw potatoes. Potatoes aren't good just for eating. I put raw potato slices in hot grease to clear it. More than once, I've added raw potato cut in pieces to remove salt and save oversalted soups or vegetables.*

SWEET-SOUR RED CABBAGE

4 servings

1 head red cabbage, about 2 pounds	*2 whole allspice*
4 slices bacon	*2 whole cloves*
4 tablespoons onion, chopped	*3 peppercorns*
2 apples	*½ cup raisins*
⅛ teaspoon caraway seeds	*½ cup vinegar*
2 bay leaves	*½ cup water*
	brown sugar

▲ Pull and discard the outer leaves from the head of cabbage. Cut into wedge-shaped sections. Remove the core, shred the cabbage and soak in cold water. Cook bacon over low heat in large fry pan until some fat is rendered out. Drain (keep bacon fat) and cool. Cut into small pieces. Sauté chopped onion in bacon fat until golden. Lift the cabbage from the water. Place in fry pan with the onion and let it simmer 10 minutes. Core apples and cut into very thin slices; add to fry pan. Add caraway seeds, bay leaves, whole allspice, whole cloves, peppercorns, raisins, vinegar and water. Stir. Cover pan and simmer for about one hour. Add boiling water during cooking, if necessary. Halfway through cooking, add chopped bacon and brown sugar, distributing over the top of the cabbage. If the water has not been absorbed when the cabbage is done, uncover the pan and cook gently until it is absorbed. Discard whole spices before serving.

Pass It On...*Serve with pot or pork roast, spare ribs or barbecue.*

ARMENIAN RICE

Great with near East dishes

4-6 servings

1½ cups converted white rice	*1½ teaspoons salt*
1 cup fine egg noodles	*3 cups boiling water*
6 tablespoons butter	

▲ Brown rice to golden color in butter. Add fine noodles; sauté until straw-colored; stir to avoid burning. Add salt and the boiling water. Cover and let simmer for almost 25 minutes or until all water is absorbed.

SPINACH ARTICHOKE CASSEROLE

10-12 servings

2 (10-ounce) packages chopped
  frozen spinach
1 pound fresh mushrooms
6 tablespoons butter
1 tablespoon flour

½ cup milk
½ teaspoon salt
⅛ teaspoon garlic powder
2 (13¾-ounce) cans artichoke
  hearts

Sour Cream Hollandaise:
1 cup sour cream
⅛ cup lemon juice

1¾ cups mayonnaise
paprika

▲ Cook spinach. Clean mushrooms and save 16 mushroom caps. Chop remaining caps and stems. Sauté pieces in 2 tablespoons butter. Sauté caps separately in another 2 tablespoons butter. To make cream sauce: Mix 2 tablespoons butter and flour. Cook until bubbly. Add milk gradually. Stir until smooth. Add seasonings, chopped mushrooms and spinach. Drain artichokes. Place in a two-quart casserole. Cover with spinach mixture. Blend sour cream, lemon juice and mayonnaise. Heat gently to make the Sour Cream Hollandaise. Spread over spinach mixture. Top with mushroom caps and bake, covered, at 375° for 25 minutes.

SPINACH WITH ARTICHOKES

12-14 servings

4 (10-ounce) packages frozen
  chopped spinach, cooked and
  drained
11 ounces cream cheese
5 tablespoons butter

juice of one lemon
salt, pepper and ground nutmeg to
  taste
2 cans quartered artichoke hearts,
  drained

▲ Cream butter and cream cheese together and put in bottom of a 9x13-inch glass baking dish. Combine rest of ingredients and put on top of cream cheese mixture. Cover with foil and bake at 350° for about 30 minutes.

Pass It On…As kids, my sister and I had to eat three bites of every food served, just to try it or to see if our tastes had changed even if we knew we hated it. My children now call it a no-thank-you helping. If they say, "No, thank you," they receive just enough for three bites and have to eat it all!

HAND-ME-DOWN BUTTERNUT SQUASH

Tastes like "light" sweet potatoes

4-6 servings

1 medium butternut squash
6 tablespoons butter, or more to
taste
honey

cinnamon
1 cup crushed graham cracker
crumbs mixed with 2
tablespoons melted butter

▲ Top of stove method: Peel squash, cut in half, remove seeds from cavity and cut into chunks. Boil squash in salted water until soft enough to mash. Drain well and mash until smooth (or use food processor). Add butter, honey, cinnamon, salt and pepper to taste. Pour mixture into greased or non-stick sprayed 8x8-inch pan. Spread graham cracker crumbs over top. Bake at 350° about 30 minutes or until warmed through. Microwave method: cut squash in half. Cook face down on waxed paper until soft. Cool. Scoop pulp out of shell and mash. Continue recipe at "add butter, honey, cinnamon, salt and pepper to taste."

Pass It On...At Thanksgiving dinner, our family draws names from a hat passed around the table. We then plan a fun gift (for Christmas Eve) to be accompanied by an original poem taped on top of the package. The inexpensive presents might be found around the house or purchased at a dime store. Regardless of the value, they must relate to the person's life or something unusual or funny that had happened during the year. On Christmas Eve, each person reads the poem, the funnier and crazier the better, and opens the gift. We enjoy this great way of reliving the year and relieving the pressure of opening real Christmas gifts, which we always do on Christmas morning.

SQUASH CASSEROLE

4-6 servings

6 medium green scallop squash
1 medium onion
16 saltine crackers
2 eggs

salt
pepper
sugar
butter

▲ Grind or finely chop squash, onion and crackers and mix together. Add eggs and seasonings to taste. Pour into greased casserole dish and dot with butter. Bake at 350° for 1 hour.

OLD FASHIONED SQUASH CASSEROLE

6 servings

3 pounds squash (yellow, zucchini,
*   or combination)*
1 small onion, chopped
½ teaspoon dried thyme leaves

1½ cups sharp Cheddar cheese,
*   grated*
¼ cup Parmesan cheese, grated
⅓ cup unseasoned bread crumbs
½ teaspoon black pepper

▲ Slice squash into rounds. Place in steamer or saucepan (with water) along with onions and thyme; cook until tender (about 10 minutes). Transfer cooked squash mixture to a greased two-quart casserole dish. Add Cheddar and Parmesan cheeses, bread crumbs and pepper. Stir lightly to combine. Top with additional Parmesan cheese if desired. Bake at 350° for 25 minutes until lightly browned.

Pass It On...For the 40 years my mother-in-law prepared Thanksgiving dinner and the 33 years I inherited it, we've written "The Shortest Thanksgiving Prayer" on the back of the place card. Before the meal, we read this prayer in unison: "Thou has given so much to us, give one thing more, a grateful heart. Amen." Along with the prayer came another tradition. If the place card was left with the hostess, the guest would always come back. Could this have been to save rewriting in addition to being a hospitable gesture, I wonder? Through the years, many people have taken the prayer to use at their Thanksgiving tables.

AUTUMN STIR-FRY

6 servings

1 tablespoon peanut oil
salt
2 cloves garlic, minced
1 teaspoon fresh ginger, minced
2 cups broccoli florets

1 red or yellow pepper, cut into
*   one-inch pieces*
1 sweet potato, peeled and
*   shredded*
2 cups savory cabbage
¼ cup roasted peanuts

▲ In a wok, heat oil. Sprinkle with salt. Add garlic and ginger; cook stirring constantly for two minutes. Add broccoli and stir-fry 3 minutes. Add pepper, sweet potato and cabbage. Stir-fry until vegetables are crisp, but tender. Serve sprinkled with peanuts.

SHERRIED SWEET POTATO CASSEROLE

Especially good for holiday dinner

8 servings

8 sweet potatoes or yams (or three
    18-ounce cans)
1 cup brown sugar
2 tablespoons cornstarch
½ teaspoon salt
½ teaspoon orange peel, shredded

2 cups orange juice
½ cup raisins
6 tablespoons butter or margarine
⅓ cup dry sherry
¼ cup nuts, chopped or ½ cup
    peanuts, chopped

▲ Boil or bake potatoes until just tender. Peel and cut lengthwise into ½ - 1-inch thick slices. Arrange in 9x13-inch pan. Sprinkle with salt. In saucepan, combine brown sugar, cornstarch, ½ teaspoon salt, orange peel, orange juice and raisins. Cook and stir over medium heat until thick and bubbly. Cook 1 minute longer. Add butter, sherry and nuts. Stir until butter is melted and pour over potatoes. Bake at 325° about 30 minutes or until potatoes are well glazed, basting occasionally.

TOMATO EGGPLANT CASSEROLE

6 servings

1 medium eggplant
3 tablespoons margarine
3 eggs, beaten
black pepper
1 teaspoon onion, chopped

½ teaspoon oregano
½ cup saltines, crumbled
6 sliced tomatoes
½ cup Cheddar cheese, grated

▲ Peel and dice eggplant; cook in salted water until tender, about 10 minutes. Drain and mash. Blend in margarine, eggs, pepper, onion, oregano and crackers. Turn into an oiled casserole. Cover with tomato slices; sprinkle with cheese and bake at 375°. Bake about 30 minutes or until top is browned.

Pass It On...*Use drained, canned whole tomatoes if fresh tomatoes are unavailable.*

TOMATO PARMESAN PIE

A delectable, colorful dish - especially good in the summer

6 as entree, 8 as vegetable

pastry for single 9-inch crust
1 egg white, beaten
¾ cup Parmesan cheese, grated
¾ cup green onions and tops,
    thinly sliced
2-3 firm tomatoes

flour, salt, and pepper
½ cup fresh mushrooms, sliced
2 tablespoons ripe olives, chopped
    or sliced
2 eggs and 1 egg yolk
1 cup half-and-half

▲ Preheat oven to 400°. Line a 9-inch glass pie pan with pastry, flute edges, place pie weights on crust and prebake for 10 minutes. Cool and brush with egg white. Sprinkle crust with 2 tablespoons Parmesan cheese and half of the onions. Slice tomatoes in thick slices (scant ½-inch). Roll in flour and put in the pastry in a single layer. This will take 6 or 7 slices. Sprinkle generously with salt, freshly ground black pepper, half the cheese, the rest of the onions, mushrooms and olives. Beat eggs with a fork only enough to mix the white and the yolk. Stir in the half-and-half. Pour over tomatoes, tilting pan to settle liquid to bottom. Sprinkle top with remaining cheese. Bake in 400° oven for 35 to 45 minutes, until pastry is browned and pie is set but still a little quivery in the center. Let cool 20 to 30 minutes before cutting. Serve warm. This may be cooled completely and reheated.

TOURLU

A wonderful way to use any summer vegetable

6 servings

1 small eggplant, cubed
2 large onions, largely diced
3 medium carrots, bias slant cut
2 celery stalks, bias slant cut
1 red or green pepper, largely
    diced
1-2 potatoes, cubed
1 pound fresh green beans
1 can pear-shaped tomatoes,
    quartered (or fresh tomatoes)

3-4 small zucchini, cubed
½ cup each olive oil and ketchup
2 tablespoons salt
1½ teaspoons sugar
¼ cup fresh basil, chopped or 1½
    teaspoons dried basil
¼ teaspoon pepper
chopped parsley for garnish
    (optional)

▲ Place all ingredients in a large casserole dish. Bake above ingredients for about 1 hour in 350° oven. Serve hot or at room temperature.

***Pass It On**...My mother always cheered our embarrassing moments by saying, "Ten years from now, this will be funny!"*

VEGETABLES PROVENCAL

A beautiful dish; enhances dinner party buffets

4-6 servings

½ cup olive oil
2-3 garlic cloves, minced
3 large baking potatoes
2 medium zucchini
9 plum tomatoes

8-12 ounces baby Swiss, Gruyère,
or Havarti cheese, grated
2 tablespoons dried parsley
½ teaspoon dried dill
salt and pepper to taste

▲ Preheat oven to 425°. Gently sauté the minced garlic in the olive oil until golden brown. Spray a 9x13-inch pan with a non-stick cooking spray. Slice potatoes, zucchini and tomatoes. Layer the bottom of the pan with half of the sliced potatoes, followed by half of the zucchini and half of the tomatoes. Top with half of the cheese. Sprinkle with 1 tablespoon parsley, ½ teaspoon basil and ¼ teaspoon dill. Layer the remaining vegetables in the same order, ending with the cheese. Sprinkle remaining herbs on top. Drizzle olive oil/garlic mixture evenly over the vegetables and bake, uncovered, at 425° for 45 minutes.

Pass It On...Fresh herbs can be substituted for the dried, just increase the amount to taste.

VEGETABLES MANDARIN

4-6 servings

1 cup carrots, thinly sliced
1 cup green beans, cut in 1-inch
*   pieces*
2 tablespoons salad oil
1 cup cauliflower, thinly sliced
½ cup green onion, thinly sliced

1 cup water
2 teaspoons chicken base granules
2 teaspoons cornstarch
dash garlic powder
½ cup almonds, whole

▲ Cook and stir carrots and beans with oil in skillet over medium heat for 2 minutes. Add cauliflower and onion; cook 1 minute. Add mixture of water, chicken base, cornstarch and garlic. Cook and stir until sauce is thickened. Vegetables should be crisp, but tender. If they need to cook longer, reduce heat and cover until desired doneness. Add almonds.

Pass It On...Place fresh vegetables in a large wooden bowl or basket for a nice touch in the kitchen.

SESAME ZUCCHINI

6 servings

4 or 6 zucchini, depending on size
¼ cup butter
¼ cup onion, finely chopped
½ clove garlic, finely chopped
½ cup cherry tomatoes, cut in half,
    or 1 small tomato, sliced thin

2 tablespoons toasted sesame seeds
¼ cup finely chopped parsley
salt
fresh ground pepper

▲ Wash and slice zucchini on the bias. Blanch with boiling water one minute. Drain. Melt butter, add onion and garlic; sauté until soft and golden (about 2 minutes). Add zucchini, cover and cook 2 minutes. Add tomatoes, cover and cook 1 minute. Season with salt and pepper. Add sesame seeds and parsley. Toss and serve.

HEARTY STUFFED ZUCCHINI

4-6 servings

2 large zucchini
1 cup light sour cream
¼ teaspoon garlic powder

¼ cup Monterey Jack cheese
2 tablespoons wheat germ

▲ Cut zucchini in half lengthwise. Cover in a glass baking dish and microwave on high 4 to 6 minutes or until tender. Make a ¼-inch deep hollow cut in each half (almost the entire length of squash). Mix cream and garlic powder. Spread evenly over zucchini. Sprinkle with cheese and wheat germ. Cook on high in microwave 1-2 minutes until cheese melts.

SHREDDED ZUCCHINI

4-6 servings

6 small zucchini
2 tablespoons butter
2 teaspoons water

⅓ cup sour cream
paprika
salt and white pepper

▲ Wash and dry zucchini. Grate on medium side of grater. Dry zucchini by twisting in a tea towel. Melt butter; add zucchini. Cook and stir at low heat for 5 minutes. Add sour cream and seasonings. Serve immediately.

Pass It On…Zucchini, like mushrooms, contains a great deal of water. Try tossing the zucchini with salt, placing in a colander, and allowing to drain for 30 minutes. Squeeze out any additional moisture.

OKRA PATTIES

8 servings

1 pound fresh okra, chopped ½ *cup water*
½ *cup chopped onion* *1 egg*
1 teaspoon salt ½ *cup cornmeal*
¼ *teaspoon pepper* *oil for frying*

▲ Combine okra, onion, salt, pepper, water and egg. Mix flour, baking powder and cornmeal. Add to okra mixture. Spoon into about ½-inch hot oil, flattening slightly with back of spoon to form pattie shape. Cook over medium heat until browned, turning once. Drain on paper towels.

OKRA GUMBO

4-6 servings

1 pound fresh okra *2 ears fresh corn*
1 medium onion *2-3 tablespoons oil*
1 (16-ounce) can diced tomatoes *salt and pepper*

▲ Wash okra and allow to thoroughly dry before removing stem end and cutting into one-inch pieces. Chop onion and cut corn kernels off the cob. Combine okra, onions and corn in medium skillet and sauté in oil about 5 minutes to seal okra and soften corn and onion. Add tomatoes, salt and pepper. Cook on medium heat until liquid has nearly evaporated, stirring occasionally.

Pass It On…Drying and sautéing the okra prevents the "gooeyness" usually associated with okra.

Desserts

Legendary Delta Chocolate Pie

4 sticks butter
3 cups sugar
3 squares unsweetened chocolate
4 teaspoons vanilla
6 eggs
2 half pints whip cream
slivered almonds or walnuts
grated chocolate

9" x 13"

4 oun
of an
1/4 cup
ed sugar
1/ teaspoon ic
1/4 cup whipped

ip creamcheese in m
y. Add Imperial 10 x P
and lemon extract
in whipped cream

Just a reminder —
Auction committee
meets Tuesday at 7:30 pm
Pass it on — Legendary
Delta Pie will be
served!

PRAL
Serves: 3 doz
Degree of di
eparation
/bak

Sparkling
juice
mix

PETITE BAKED ALASKAS

10 servings

Fudge Cake:

1½ cups flour, sifted
2 cups sugar
½ cup cocoa
1 teaspoon salt
1 teaspoon baking powder
1⅓ cups butter, room temperature

4 eggs
2 teaspoons vanilla
2 tablespoons corn syrup
1 cup chopped nuts, toasted
3 pints favorite ice cream

Meringue:

7 egg whites at room temperature
¼ teaspoon cream of tartar
¼ teaspoon salt

⅔ cup sugar
½ teaspoon vanilla

▲ For fudge cake: Sift the flour, sugar, cocoa, salt and baking powder into a mixing bowl. Add the butter, eggs, vanilla and corn syrup. Mix the ingredients thoroughly for about 2 minutes. Fold in nuts. Spread mixture into a greased 9x13-inch cake pan. Bake at 350° for 40-45 minutes. Cake will be moist. Cool cake, cut into 2-inch rounds and freeze. Set paper cupcake liners into cupcake pans and fill each liner with a scoop of ice cream. Freeze. For meringue (make just before assembly): Beat the egg whites until foamy; add in cream of tartar and salt. Continue beating until soft peaks form; add the sugar, 1 tablespoon at a time, and continue beating until the peaks are stiff and shiny.

To assemble: Place cake rounds on a baking sheet. Peel off the cupcake liners from the frozen ice cream, and set each ice cream mold onto the center of a cake round. Quickly cover the cake and ice cream with meringue, carefully masking where the cake and ice cream meet. Place in freezer until ready to bake. To bake: Preheat oven to 500°. Take the Alaskas directly from the freezer to the oven, and bake for 1 minute, or until the meringue is lightly browned. Serve immediately.

Pass It On...*Serve chocolate, butterscotch, strawberry or other appropriate sauce.*

PEACH COBBLER

Melt-in-your-mouth flavor with minimal effort

4-6 servings

½ cup butter or margarine
⅔ cup sugar
⅔ cup flour
⅔ cup milk

2 teaspoons baking powder
3 cups fresh peaches, sliced and
*   slightly sweetened*
⅛-¼ teaspoon nutmeg, optional

▲ Melt butter in a 2-quart baking dish (a 2-quart soufflé dish works well) in a 350° oven. The baking dish will be very hot. In a separate bowl, mix sugar, flour, milk and baking powder. Pour mixture over melted butter in the hot baking dish. Spoon sliced sweetened peaches over batter. Put back into 350° oven and bake 1 hour. Serve warm with vanilla ice cream.

POTS DE CRÈME

6 servings

¾ cup milk
1 (6-ounce) package semi-sweet
*   chocolate chips*
1 egg

2 tablespoons sugar
1 teaspoon vanilla
pinch of salt

▲ Heat the milk just to the boiling point. Place all the other ingredients in the blender and add the hot milk. Blend at low speed for 1 minute. Pour into 6 small containers and chill for several hours.

Pass It On...Recipe may be doubled, but it is easier to do one batch at a time. Be creative with containers, even find matching jelly jars.

ICE CREAM

1 gallon

3 eggs
1½ cups sugar
1 tablespoon vanilla
½ teaspoon salt

1 large can evaporated milk
½ gallon whole milk (or 1 quart
*   whole milk and 1 quart half-*
*   and-half cream)*

▲ Beat eggs, add sugar beating until thick. Add rest of ingredients. Freeze about halfway, then add fruit or candy of your choice, continue freezing until very thick.

Pass It On...My mother always made birthdays special by having a birthday chair. She decorated Dad's host chair with crepe paper ribbons and bows in the birthday child's favorite colors. It made dinner especially festive, and the birthday child felt like royalty!

SWEDISH CREAM WITH STRAWBERRIES

Luscious on the tongue

6 servings

2½ cups whipping cream
1 cup sugar
1 envelope unflavored gelatin

2 cups sour cream
1 teaspoon vanilla
1 quart ripe strawberries

▲ Mix cream, sugar and gelatin in a pan. Heat gently, stirring continually until gelatin is completely dissolved. Cool until slightly thickened. Fold in sour cream and vanilla; pour into a crystal serving bowl (or individual dessert dishes). Chill in the refrigerator until firm. Slice and sweeten strawberries. At serving time, top the jelled cream with the slightly sweetened berries.

Pass It On...*Try other fruits for a different, exquisite taste.*

YAKIMA VALLEY APPLE DESSERT

12-16 servings

Crust:
2 cups flour
¾ cup butter or margarine

½ cup sugar
¼ teaspoon almond flavoring

Filling:
1 cup sour cream
1 teaspoon cinnamon
¾ cup sugar

1 teaspoon almond flavoring
5-6 apples, peeled and sliced

Topping:
⅓ cup flour (more if needed)
⅓ cup brown sugar

¼ cup firm butter or margarine
1 teaspoon cinnamon

▲ Preheat oven to 325°. Mix crust ingredients completely. Press into 10-inch spring form pan and bake for 35 minutes. Increase oven temperature to 375°. Mix sour cream, cinnamon, sugar and almond flavoring. Add apples and pour filling into baked crust. Bake for 15 minutes at 375°, then reduce heat to 325° and bake 45 minutes longer. Remove from oven. Crumble all topping ingredients together and sprinkle over dessert. Increase oven temperature to 400° and bake for 10 minutes.

Pass It On...*On birthdays: Forty is the old age of youth. Fifty is the youth of old age.*

LIME MERINGUES

A delightful, delicate cool dessert after a seafood salad luncheon

6 servings

Meringue:

3 egg whites	*⅛ teaspoon salt*
¼ teaspoon cream of tartar	*¾ cup sugar*

Filling:

3 egg yolks	*1½ teaspoons grated lime rind*
¼ cup sugar	*1 cup heavy cream, whipped*
4 tablespoons fresh lime juice (2-3 limes)	*green food coloring*

▲ Beat egg whites until foamy; add cream of tartar and salt; beat until stiff, but not dry. Add sugar gradually (a tablespoon at a time), beating well after each addition. Beat until very stiff. Cover a baking sheet with heavy brown paper. Pile meringue into 6 mounds, about 3 inches in diameter. Make a 2-inch depression in center of each with a teaspoon. Bake in a slow oven at 275° for 1 hour. Cool shells, fill with lime filling. For a soft meringue shell, chill 6 to 24 hours. (Avoid making meringues when weather is hot and humid). For filling: Beat egg yolks until lemony yellow; add sugar and lime juice. Cook over boiling water (in double boiler), stirring constantly until thickened. Add lime rind. Remove from heat. Tint with a drop or two of green food coloring. Chill. Fold lime mixture into whipped cream. Fill meringue shells. Top with a sprig of mint, candied violet, or a strawberry or pansy.

Pass It On...*Cream will whip better using a chilled bowl and beaters. However, if the whipped cream doesn't thicken, add an egg white and chill completely. Then re-whip.*

HALF-BAKED CHOCOLATE MOUSSE

Delicate, but wonderfully chocolately

6-8 servings

*8 ounces semi-sweet baking
    chocolate
1 tablespoon instant coffee powder
¼ cup boiling water
8 eggs, separated*

*⅔ cup sugar
2½ teaspoons vanilla
⅛ teaspoon salt
1½ cups heavy cream
⅓ cup confectioners' sugar*

▲ Preheat oven to 350°. Butter a 9-inch glass pie plate and dust with fine, dry bread crumbs. Set aside. In a double boiler place chocolate; dissolve coffee in boiling water and pour over chocolate. Cover and let stand over very low heat, stirring occasionally with wire whisk. Remove from heat and continue to stir until smooth. Set aside to cool. Beat egg yolks until thick then gradually beat in sugar until mixture is thick and lemon-colored. Gradually beat in chocolate and add 1 teaspoon vanilla. Beat egg whites with salt until stiff but not dry. Stir ¼ of egg whites into chocolate mixture. Fold in remaining egg whites gently, until blended.

Fill pie plate with enough mousse mixture so it is level with edge (about half of mixture). Cover and refrigerate the remaining uncooked mousse. Bake 25 minutes, then turn off heat and leave in oven another 5 minutes. Remove and cool for 2 hours on wire rack. The mousse will sink in middle to form a pie shell (when shell is cooled, fill with uncooked mousse). Refrigerate 2-3 hours. Beat cream, remaining vanilla, and confectioners' sugar until stiff and spread over pie.

***Pass It On**...Craving chocolate? You may be low in magnesium. Try whole grains first, and the craving may go away.*

MAI TAI MOUSSE

A show-stopper in both looks and taste

10 servings

20 lady fingers, split
2 envelopes unflavored gelatin
½ cup pineapple juice from canned
   pineapple
5 eggs, separated
1 cup scalded milk
⅓ cup fresh lime juice (2-3 limes)

⅓ cup white rum
1 (20-ounce) can crushed
   pineapple, drained
1¼ cups sugar
1 cup heavy cream, whipped
½ cup macadamia nuts or walnuts,
   chopped

▲ Line sides and bottom of a 10-inch spring form pan with the split lady fingers. Soften gelatin in the pineapple juice. Beat egg yolks in the top of a double boiler; gradually stir in ¾ cup of sugar. Slowly blend in the scalded milk. Cook for about 5 minutes until mixture thickens. Add gelatin mixture, then lime juice and rum. Add drained pineapple. Chill until thickened, but not set. Beat egg whites until they form very soft peaks; continue beating and slowly add the remaining ½ cup of sugar. Carefully fold together pineapple custard mixture, whipped cream, and beaten egg whites. Pour into the spring form pan. Chill overnight or for several hours. May also be frozen for later use. To serve, remove pan rim and sprinkle with nuts.

Pass It On...Crème Fraîche is sometimes difficult to find. I make my own by whisking equal parts heavy cream and sour cream together. Cover loosely and leave on the kitchen counter overnight. Refrigerate for a few hours before serving over fresh fruit. It may also be added to sauces for richness as it will not separate when heated.

PEACHES BY JIMINEY

6 servings

Crust:

1¾ cups flour, sifted
2 tablespoons sugar
½ teaspoon salt

¼ teaspoon baking powder
½ cup butter

Filling:

4 to 6 fresh peaches, peeled and
halved (If fresh peaches are
not available, use canned
Freestone halves; drain well)

1 cup sugar
1 tablespoon cinnamon
2 egg yolks, beaten
1 cup heavy cream

▲ For crust: In food processor combine flour, sugar, salt and baking powder. Add butter, cut into slices and process until crumbly. Press evenly over bottom and halfway up sides of 8-inch square glass baking dish. Press firmly until mixture holds. For filling: Arrange peach halves cut side down, closely over mixture. Sprinkle mixture of sugar and cinnamon over peaches. Bake, uncovered, at 400° for 15 minutes. Mix egg yolks and cream; pour mixture over peaches and bake, uncovered, 30 minutes more. Cool about 30 minutes before serving warm. Can be served chilled.

Pass It On...With a food processor to make the crust, the recipe becomes quick and easy.

PUMPKIN PUDDING

8-10 servings

8 eggs
3 cups sugar
1 (16-ounce) can pumpkin
1 cup butter
1 cup white raisins
½ cup flour
1 package coconut

1 teaspoon cinnamon
½ teaspoon salt
½ teaspoon nutmeg
½ teaspoon allspice
3 tablespoons bourbon
1 cup half-and-half
1 cup pecans

▲ Combine eggs, sugar, butter, cream and pumpkin. Add flour, raisins and pecans. Add coconut, spices and bourbon. Cook at 250° for about 2 hours. Serve with dollop of unsweetened whipped cream on top.

Pass It On...Use orange whipped cream by combining ½ cup whipping cream, 1 tablespoon powdered sugar, ½ teaspoon grated orange peel and 1 tablespoon Grand Marnier.

IRISH BREAD PUDDING

10-12 servings

12 slices of white bread
1 cup sugar mixed with 1
tablespoon of cinnamon
raisins and/or chopped apple,
optional

8 eggs
1 cup sugar
4 cups milk

▲ Butter 9x13-inch baking dish. Cut crusts off bread and lightly butter both sides. Layer in dish: sugar mixture, bread, raisins or apples (if used), sugar mixture, bread, sugar mixture. Beat eggs, sugar and milk. Pour over bread and let soak in. Place dish in a larger dish containing 1 inch of hot water. Add more hot water until water level reaches halfway up side of pudding dish. Bake at 350° for 1 hour. Cool for 10 minutes before cutting and use caution when removing from oven - it's very hot.

Pass It On...In honor of our Irish boss, we decided to celebrate St. Patrick's Day. We decorated the office with green, played Irish music, and served Irish Stew, green salad, cloverleaf rolls, Irish Bread Pudding and lime green drinks. For fun, we played a rousing game of "Pin the Braugh on Erin."

LEMON OR LIME SHERBET

10-15 servings

1 (3-ounce) package lemon or lime
flavored gelatin
1 cup sugar
½ cup water
6-8 ice cubes

juice of 2-3 lemons or limes
depending on size and amount
of tang desired
grated rind of lemons or limes
2½ cups milk (2% or skim milk
may be used)

▲ Heat water and sugar until sugar is well dissolved. Add gelatin and dissolve. Add ice cubes to cool mixture. Add juice, grated peel and milk to gelatin-sugar mixture. Freezing instructions: Method 1 - Can be frozen in a plastic bowl in freezer. Stir frequently. Fluff up in food processor or blender when frozen. Freezing instructions: Method 2 - Follow manufacturer's directions. Works well in hand cranked machine. Keep the freezing unit in freezer prior to freezing sherbet.

TIRAMISU

12 servings

*1½ pints (buy 2 pints) Mascarpone
   cheese*
1 quart cream, whipped
½ cup sugar

2 packages lady fingers
6 cups espresso coffee
cocoa, unsweetened

▲ Mix Mascarpone cheese and sugar. Fold in whipped cream. Quickly dip or liberally sprinkle the lady fingers with 6 cups of instant espresso coffee and line glass serving dish with lady fingers on bottom (lady fingers will get soggy if there is too much coffee). Cover with whipped cream and Mascarpone cheese mixture. Repeat with layer of lady fingers and whipped cream mixture. Sprinkle with cocoa on top. Refrigerate at least 30 minutes before serving.

Pass It On...If lady fingers are not available, use angel food or sponge cake.

APRICOT WHIP WITH MADEIRA

6 servings

¾ pound dried apricots
¾ cup sugar
⅔ cup Madeira
2 egg whites

1 cup heavy cream, whipped
*¼ cup toasted almonds, sliced or
   slivered*

▲ Cover apricots with water (the water should just cover the fruit). Add sugar and cook down until apricots are tender and liquid has formed almost a glaze. Cool. Puree fruit, juice and Madeira. Beat egg whites until stiff and fold into apricot mixture along with ½ cup whipped cream. Pour into sherbet glasses. Top with remaining ½ cup whipped cream. Sprinkle with almonds.

Pass It On...Serve in balloon wine glasses for an elegant touch.

APRICOT GRANDE

4-6 servings

1 (17-ounce) can apricot halves
½ cup drained syrup

1 ounce Grand Marnier
2 ounces brandy

▲ Drain apricots, reserving ½ cup syrup. Coarsely chop apricots. Heat syrup and mix in apricot pieces. Add Grand Marnier and brandy. Ignite and pour over ice cream at table side.

RHUBARB TORTE

6-8 servings

Crust:
2 cups flour
2 tablespoons sugar

1 cup butter, softened

Filling:
6 egg yolks
2 cups sugar
4 tablespoons flour

1 cup half-and-half
6 cups rhubarb, cut in ½-inch
    pieces

Meringue:
6 egg whites

¾ cup sugar

▲ Mix crust ingredients together and pat into 9x13-inch pan. Bake at 350° for 10 minutes. Combine first 4 filling ingredients with electric mixer. Stir in rhubarb. Pour this over the baked crust. Bake at 350° for 45 minutes. Beat egg whites and sugar to make a stiff meringue. Spread this over baked torte immediately, as it comes from the oven. Seal edges. Bake at 350° for 15 minutes. Cut in squares and serve warm.

PRALINE SAUCE

6 cups

1 box light brown sugar
1 box dark brown sugar
¼ teaspoon salt
1 tablespoon vanilla

1½ cups milk
½ stick butter
1½ cups corn syrup
1 cup chopped pecans

▲ Mix all ingredients except pecans in a heavy saucepan. Bring to a boil, stirring constantly. Reduce heat and simmer for a few minutes. Add pecans and mix well. Serve warm over cheesecake, custard, ice cream, waffles or pancakes.

FRUITY ICE CREAM

6-8 servings

1½-2 pounds fruit, mashed
juice of 1 orange and 2 lemons
2 cups sugar

2½ cups water
1 pint whipping cream, whipped

▲ Boil sugar and water until sugar is dissolved. Cool, then add to mashed fruit and juices. Chill well. Fold in whipped cream. Pour into ice cream freezer and freeze until firm.

Pass It On…Especially good with strawberries, peaches or berries such as blueberries, raspberries or boysenberries.

CHOCOLATE FUDGE PUDDING CAKE

8 servings

Cake:

1 cup flour
¼ teaspoon salt
¾ cup sugar
2 teaspoons baking powder

½ cup milk
2 tablespoons butter, melted
½ square chocolate, melted
½ cup nut meats

Topping:

1 cup brown sugar
1 cup confectioners' sugar

4 teaspoons cocoa
¼ teaspoon salt

▲ Combine all cake ingredients together and mix. Pour batter into a buttered baking pan. Mix all topping ingredients and spread on top of batter. Very carefully, pour 1¾ cups boiling water over cake and topping. Bake 40 minutes in moderate oven. Serve with whipped cream and whole peach or pear may be served with it. The cake rises to top and sauce goes to the bottom of the pan.

Pass It On... *"As a new bride, I thought I'd treat my husband to this 'goodie'. Being a real novice in the kitchen, I used a pan with a removable bottom and it was an utter disaster! I spent the baking time catching the dripping sauce that ran out of the bottom of the pan and pouring it back over the batter!" - Kathleen Davis Nye, Delta Delta Delta National President (1968-72).*

Pass It On...*Split a bought angel food cake into three layers. Stack, spreading layers with your choice of canned pie filling. Top with whipped cream and berries. Example: lemon pie filling and blueberries or chocolate pie filling and strawberries.*

BEAR WALLOW MOUNTAIN CAKE

16 servings

4 cups unpeeled green apples,
chopped
2 eggs, beaten
1¼ cups sugar
¼ cup canola oil
2 cups all-purpose flour, sifted

2 teaspoons soda
2 teaspoons cinnamon
1 teaspoon salt
1 cup pecans, chopped
1 teaspoon vanilla

Caramel Sauce:
½ cup brown sugar
½ cup white sugar
½ cup heavy cream

½ cup butter or margarine
1 tablespoon flour
1 teaspoon vanilla

▲ Mix apples and sugar together; add eggs and oil. Sift dry ingredients; add to batter with nuts and vanilla. Bake 1 hour at 350° in a 9x13-inch pan. Top with caramel sauce. For caramel sauce: Mix all sauce ingredients in a small saucepan, and bring to boil over medium heat. Pour over cake. Serve warm.

Pass It On...If brown sugar has hardened, use a cheese grater to get the right amount, or put the hard brown sugar in a sealable plastic bag along with a slice of bread and seal. Sugar will be soft in several hours.

MOTHER'S APPLE CAKE

8-10 servings

Note: Requires 1-2 day refrigeration.

Cake:
2 cups sugar
1½ cups oil
2 eggs
3 cups apple, diced and peeled
3 cups flour

1½ teaspoons baking soda
1 teaspoon salt
1 cup pecans, chopped
1 cup coconut
2 teaspoons vanilla

Glaze:
1 cup confectioners' sugar

6 tablespoons lemon juice

▲ Heat sugar and oil together. Add remaining cake ingredients. Grease and flour tube or Bundt pan. Bake at 300° for 1½ hours. Let cool for 10 minutes before glazing with confectioners' sugar and lemon juice mixture. Refrigerate 1-2 days.

CARROT CAKE

16-20 servings

Cake:

1½ cups corn oil
2 cups sugar
3 eggs
2 cups flour, sifted
2 teaspoons cinnamon
2 teaspoons baking soda

2 teaspoons vanilla
1 teaspoon salt
2 cups carrots, shredded
1 cup walnuts, chopped
½ cup pineapple, crushed

Icing:

1 (3-ounce) package cream cheese
1 (1-pound) box powdered sugar
½ cup margarine or butter

⅛ cup pineapple, crushed
½ cup walnuts, chopped

▲ Combine all cake ingredients in a large bowl and mix until well-blended. Pour batter into a 9x13-inch greased pan. Bake at 350° for 1 hour. Cool, ice with cream cheese icing. For icing: Cream margarine, cream cheese, and powdered sugar until just slightly fluffy. Mix in pineapple and walnuts.

Pass It On...For a tropical theme party, I frost any sheet cake with blue colored icing for water. To make fine sand, I process regular chocolate covered candies in a blender or food processor. After covering one corner area with "sand," I add cut out palm trees from paper plates. White Lifesavers become innertubes while bear-shaped graham crackers lie on top "swimming in the water." Frosting glues them in place. A stick of gum mounted on top of two Lifesavers becomes a diving board. Inserting a toothpick through the gum holds it up. More bears sun on the sand beach lying out on tiny cut out napkin pieces. Sometimes I even add faces and swimsuits to the teddy bears using frosting and a toothpick. To complete the theme, I put the cake on a baking sheet covered with aluminum foil and blue cellophane. Fish cut outs can even be placed between the foil and cellophane.

LOW CHOLESTEROL CHOCOLATE CAKE

A healthy, delicious cake

9-12 servings

Cake:

1½ cups flour, sifted
4 tablespoons unsweetened cocoa
1 cup sugar
½ teaspoon salt
1 teaspoon soda

⅓ cup canola oil
1 egg white
1 cup skim milk, soured with 2
   tablespoons vinegar

Glaze:

2 tablespoons margarine
2 tablespoons cocoa

2 tablespoons water
confectioners' sugar

▲ Preheat oven to 350°. Place cake ingredients in bowl in order given. Beat well. Place in greased 9-inch square pan. Bake at 350° about 30 minutes. For glaze: Melt margarine in saucepan; add cocoa, water, and enough confectioners' sugar for desired consistency. Pour and spread on cooled cake.

Pass It On...I remember birthdays and special occasions when my mother wrapped coins in foil and inserted them into the cake or cupcakes. We had such fun seeing who got the most money.

Pass It On...When baking chocolate cakes, I dust the greased pans with cocoa instead of flour for more attractive and tastier concoctions. Also, I butter the vessel before melting chocolate in it — this also works for easy removal of molasses and corn syrup.

CHOCOLATE INTEMPERANCE CAKE

8-10 servings

Filling:
1½ pounds semi-sweet chocolate
½ cup strong coffee
3 eggs, separated

½ cup Kahlua or Tia Maria
  liqueur
2 tablespoons sugar
½ cup heavy cream

Cake:
1⅓ cups unsifted flour
1 teaspoon baking powder
½ teaspoon salt
⅔ cup butter

4 ounces baking chocolate
4 eggs
2 cups sugar
2 teaspoons vanilla

Chocolate Glaze:
½ pound semi-sweet chocolate

⅓ cup water

▲ For filling: Melt chocolate with coffee in a double boiler. Remove pan from heat when melted. Beat egg yolks until pale yellow and stir in chocolate. Gradually stir in liqueur. Cool. In separate bowl, beat egg whites, gradually adding sugar until whites are stiff. Whip cream, fold into cooled chocolate mixture, then fold in egg whites. Refrigerate until ready for use.

For cake: Sift flour with baking powder and salt. Melt butter and chocolate over hot water. Beat eggs well, gradually add sugar, beating well. Beat in chocolate and vanilla. Mix in flour. Grease and lightly flour two 9-inch cake pans and one jelly roll pan. Line the jelly roll pan with wax paper and grease the wax paper. Spread thin layer of batter in pans. Bake at 350° for 18-20 minutes. Cool cake rounds and remove from pans. Trim one round to fit the bottom of buttered 1½-quart soufflé dish. Cut strips of cake from jelly roll pan to line sides of a spring form pan. Pour cooled mousse into lined pan and trim second cake round to fit top. Chill 3-4 hours or overnight until firm. Unmold and cover with glaze. For glaze: Mix chocolate in water and stir until smooth. Spread over top and drizzle down sides. Chill again and serve in slender slices.

FRENCH COUNTRY CHOCOLATE CAKE

A very moist, dense cake

8-12 servings

4 ounces semi-sweet chocolate, melted
2 tablespoons rum or strong coffee
1 stick (¼ pound) butter
⅔ cup granulated sugar
3 eggs, separated

pinch salt
1 tablespoon granulated sugar
⅓ cup almonds, ground
¼ teaspoon almond extract
¾ cup sifted cake (or all-purpose) flour

Chocolate Glaze:

1 ounce semi-sweet baking chocolate
1 tablespoon dark rum

3 tablespoons sweet butter
½ pint heavy cream, whipped for garnish

▲ Cream butter and sugar together until fluffy. Beat in egg yolks. With rubber spatula, blend into butter and sugar mixture the melted chocolate, rum or coffee, almonds and extract. Beat egg whites, sprinkle in sugar and salt; beat until stiff. Stir in ¼ of egg whites to lighten mixture, gradually fold in the rest gently. Pour into greased 8-inch round pan, pushing batter to edge. Bake at middle level of oven at 325° for 25 minutes. Center should move slightly when shaken. Cool in pan 10 minutes. Invert cake onto rack. Cool 1 hour before glazing. For chocolate glaze: Melt chocolate over, not in, hot water. Beat in butter, 1 tablespoon at a time over cold water until the mixture is of spreading consistency; add rum. Pour over cooled cake. Serve in small wedges with a fluffy whipped cream on the side and a pansy, candied violet, etc. for garnish.

Pass It On*...Check each recipe: one cup sifted flour is slightly less than one cup flour, sifted. The difference may not seem like much, but it is!*

FOUR GENERATIONS COMPANY CAKE

Delicate as great grandmother's lace collar

8 servings

Cake batter:
½ cup butter, softened
½ cup sugar
4 egg yolks, well-beaten
4 tablespoons milk

¾ cup flour, sifted
1 teaspoon baking powder
½ teaspoon salt
1 teaspoon vanilla

Meringue topping:
4 egg whites
1 cup sugar

½ cup almonds or pecans, slivered

Filling:
½ pint heavy cream

sweetened strawberries, sliced

▲ For cake batter: Cream softened butter, add sugar, creaming until light; add egg yolks and milk. Sift flour with baking powder and salt; add to creamed mixture on low speed until smooth. Add vanilla and spread batter thinly in 2 well-greased 8 or 9-inch slip-bottom pans. For meringue: Beat the egg whites until smooth and glossy (soft-peak stage). Add sugar a tablespoon at a time, and beat to stiff-peak stage. Spread on top of batter in each pan and sprinkle with nuts. Bake at 325° for 20-30 minutes. Meringue should be a pretty beige color. Let cool. Turn layers out carefully, meringue-side up. Whip the cream (add a tablespoon of confectioners' sugar to stabilize) and spread on top of meringue on bottom layer. Add sliced strawberries. Place second layer, meringue side up also, on top of whipped cream.

Pass It On...*To cut baked meringue, use a knife coated with butter or margarine.*

CRANBERRY-ORANGE CAKE

A holiday favorite

16 servings

Cake:

2½ cups flour, sifted
1 cup sugar
½ teaspoon salt
¼ teaspoon soda
½ teaspoon baking powder
1 cup walnuts, chopped

1 cup whole fresh cranberries
1 cup dates, diced
grated rind of 2 oranges
2 eggs, beaten
1 cup buttermilk
¾ cup salad oil

Glaze:

¾ cup orange juice

¾ cup sugar

▲ Sift flour, 1 cup sugar, salt, baking powder and soda together. Stir in walnuts, cranberries, dates and orange rind. Combine eggs, buttermilk and oil; add to fruit mixture and blend well. Pour into well-greased and floured 10-inch tube cake pan. Bake 1 hour at 350°. Let stand in pan, bottom side down, until luke warm. Reheat if it cools too much. Remove cake to rack over large pan (cookie sheet with sides). Combine orange juice and ¾ cup sugar (can use 2 racks, so glaze can be poured over top and bottom until all is absorbed). Set in dish or plate; wrap in heavy foil. Refrigerate for 24 hours. Keep refrigerated. Serve with whipped cream. Cake will keep for 4-6 weeks. May be frozen.

Pass It On...Buy cranberries in season and freeze for use all year.

POPPY SEED CAKE

12-15 servings

1 box lemon cake mix with
   pudding
1 package instant lemon pudding
   mix

4 eggs
½ cup oil
1 cup water
¼ cup poppy seeds

▲ Mix all ingredients together for 4 minutes. Spray Bundt cake pan with non-stick aerosol, pour in ingredients. Bake at 350° for 40-50 minutes.

Pass It On...Prefer large eggs for baking. Using extra large eggs may cause cakes to fall when cooled.

LEMON CUSTARD CAKE

4-6 servings

3 tablespoons butter or margarine
1 cup sugar
3 eggs, separated
5 tablespoons flour
¼ teaspoon salt

1 cup milk
¼ cup fresh lemon juice
2 teaspoons lemon rind, freshly
grated

▲ Cream butter, add sugar gradually, mix until creamy. Add egg yolks beaten with a fork. Add flour and salt. Add milk, lemon juice and rind. Set aside. Beat egg whites until stiff but not dry. Fold into custard mixture. Pour into a greased 9x5-inch glass baking dish placed in a pan of hot water. Bake at 350° about 45 minutes to 1 hour. Can be refrigerated.

Pass It On...Can be made in custard cups. Garnish with whipped cream, sprigs of mint or raspberry sauce.

WILLIAMSBURG ORANGE-WINE CAKE

12-15 servings

½ cup butter, softened
1 cup sugar
2 eggs
1 teaspoon vanilla
2 tablespoons orange rind, freshly
grated
2 cups seedless golden raisins

1 cup walnuts, chopped
1½ cups flour
½ teaspoon salt
1 teaspoon baking soda
1 cup buttermilk
2 teaspoons cream sherry

Sherry Butter Cream Frosting:
½ cup butter, softened
3 ounces cream cheese, softened
2½ cups confectioners' sugar

4 teaspoons cream sherry
1 teaspoon vanilla

▲ Cream butter until light; gradually add sugar and cream; beat until fluffy. Add eggs, 1 at a time, beating well after each addition. Sift flour, baking soda and salt; add alternately with buttermilk, beginning and ending with flour. Beat well after final addition. Pour into well-greased 9x13-inch pan. Bake at 350° for 25 minutes. Cool cake and brush with 2 teaspoons cream sherry. Sherry Butter Cream Frosting: Mix all frosting ingredients together until smooth and of spreading consistency. Spread over top of cooled cake.

Pass It On...Dust raisins and other fruit with flour before adding to batter.

CREAM CHEESE POUND CAKE

16-18 servings

3 cups plain flour, sifted
3 cups sugar
¼ teaspoon salt
6 eggs

1½ cups (3 sticks) butter
8 ounces cream cheese
1 teaspoon vanilla

▲ Sift salt and flour together. Cream butter, sugar and softened cream cheese until fluffy. Add eggs, one at a time, beating well after each egg. On low speed slowly add flour and vanilla to above mixture until well blended. Bake in slow oven in greased and floured 10-inch tube pan (275° for 2 hours or 300° for 1½ hours).

Pass It On...If I bake a "sad cake," as my grandmother called it, I crumble the failed cake and make it a trifle with whipped cream, bananas, pineapple or other fruit. When using canned fruit, I rinse it with water for a fresher taste.

POUND CAKE

16-18 servings

3 sticks (1½ cups) butter
3 cups sugar
5 large eggs
3½ cups cake flour, unsifted

pinch salt
1 cup milk
1 tablespoon vanilla

▲ Cream butter and sugar until light and fluffy. Add eggs one at a time, beating well after each addition. Add vanilla. Alternately add flour and salt with milk, mixing until smooth. Pour into a greased and floured tube or Bundt pan. Start in a cold oven and bake at 325° for 1 hour and 20 minutes. Cool in pan for 20 minutes, then remove from pan and finish cooling. Place on serving plate and dust with powdered sugar, if desired.

CRIMSON PRIDE CAKE

1 (3 layer) cake

¼ pound white chocolate, coarsely chopped
½ cup boiling water
1 cup butter, softened
1¾ cups sugar
4 eggs, separated

½ teaspoon vanilla extract
½ teaspoon almond extract
2½ cups sifted cake flour
1 teaspoon baking soda
1 cup buttermilk
1 (21-ounce) can cherry pie filling

Fluffy Frosting:
1 cup light corn syrup
pinch of salt
2 egg whites

¼ cup sifted powdered sugar
1 teaspoon almond extract

▲ Combine chocolate and water, stirring until chocolate melts; set aside to cool. Cream butter. Slowly add sugar, beating at medium speed until mixture is light and fluffy. Add egg yolks, 1 at a time, beating well after each addition. Add white chocolate mixture and flavorings to butter and egg mixture. Sift flour and soda together. Add this to above mixture alternately with buttermilk, beginning and ending with flour mixture. Mix, but do not beat, after each addition. Beat egg whites (at room temperature) until stiff peaks form; fold into chocolate mixture.

Pour into 3 greased and floured 9-inch round cake pans. Bake at 350° for 25 minutes or until wooden pick inserted in center comes out clean. Cool in pan 10 minutes. Remove layers from pans and cool completely on wire racks. Place 1 cake layer on cake platter; spread with ⅔ cup cherry pie filling. Top with second cake layer and pie filling. Top with third cake layer. Frost sides and 1 inch of top edge with Fluffy Frosting, leaving an 8-inch circle on top of center of cake. Spread remaining pie filling on center of cake. For fluffy frosting: Combine corn syrup and salt in small sauce pan; bring to a boil over medium heat. Beat egg whites (at room temperature) at high speed of electric mixer until soft peaks form. Continue beating egg whites, and gradually add syrup mixture at a slow steady stream. Gradually add sugar, 1 tablespoon at a time, beating until frosting is thick enough to spread. Beat in almond extract.

Pass It On*...Especially festive on Valentine's Day. Make the opening on top layer in the shape of a heart to fill with cherry pie filling.*

CHOCOLATE CREAM TORTE

Beautiful, as well as delicious

12-15 servings

Meringue:

6 egg whites
½ teaspoon salt
½ teaspoon cream of tartar

1 teaspoon almond extract
1½ cups sugar
½ cup flaked coconut

Filling:

1 (6-ounce) package semi-sweet
   chocolate chips
1 cup miniature marshmallows

1 (5-ounce) can evaporated milk
1 cup whipping cream

▲ In large mixing bowl, beat egg whites, salt, cream of tartar and extract. Beat until soft peaks form, then gradually add sugar and beat until peaks are stiff. Fold in coconut. Spread mixture on greased parchment paper making 3 8-inch circles. Bake at 300° for 25-30 minutes. Melt chocolate chips and marshmallows in evaporated milk until melted and blend. Cool. Whip cream and fold into chocolate mixture. Spread on meringue. Layer meringue and chocolate until all three layers of meringue are used. Leave edges of meringues clear of chocolate. Chocolate mixture does not spread well, so pour it evenly over meringues. Decorate edges with coconut. Refrigerate. Slice at the table like pie.

***Pass It On**...Meringues can be made into small circles and kept in a container in a dry place for several weeks. For a quick dessert, fill with peppermint or coffee ice cream and top with hot fudge sauce.*

CHOCOLATE TRUFFLE TORTE

12-16 servings

Crust:

1½ cups chocolate wafers, finely crushed

6 tablespoons butter, melted

Filling:

3⅓ cups semi-sweet chocolate chips

½ cup unsalted butter

1½ teaspoons flour

1½ teaspoons sugar

1 teaspoon vanilla extract

6 egg yolks

6 egg whites

▲ Heat oven to 300°. Combine 6 tablespoons melted butter and wafer crumbs. Press into the bottom of a 10-inch spring form pan. Bake crust for 12-15 minutes, then cool slightly. Raise oven temperature to 425°. Melt chocolate chips with ½ cup butter in double boiler over hot water (or melt in microwave). Cool chocolate slightly. Beat egg yolks with flour, sugar and vanilla; mix with melted chocolate. In a separate bowl, beat egg whites until stiff peaks form. Fold about ¼ of the chocolate mixture into the egg whites, then gently fold this mixture into the remaining chocolate until no white streaks remain. Pour the mixture into the crust. Bake at 425° for 15-20 minutes. The torte will continue to set as it cools. When cooled, wrap and freeze. Thaw slightly before serving.

Pass It On...We have started a tradition in our home that will last forever, I hope! When report cards come, I prepare a special dinner. I set the formal dining room table with our best china, crystal and silver. The child with the best report card (or who has met his or her grade goal) sits at the head of this grand table, eats his or her favorite meal, and also wears a crown. The children love being treated like royalty and drinking apple juice from crystal wine goblets. The treat has made them feel so special that I've had to make another crown. So far, both my children have received straight A's every quarter since the family tradition began.

BECKY'S CHEESECAKE

16-20 servings

Crust:
2 cups graham cracker crumbs
⅓ cup sugar

½ teaspoon cinnamon
7 tablespoons butter, melted

Filling:
3 (8-ounce) packages cream
    cheese, softened
1½ cups sugar
6 eggs

16 ounces sour cream
2 tablespoons cornstarch
1 tablespoon lemon juice
2 teaspoons vanilla

Topping:
Any canned pie filling or fresh
    fruit, dipped in melted currant
    jelly (for a glaze)

▲ For crust: Mix above ingredients and press on the bottom and around the sides of a 12-inch spring form pan. Bake crust in 350° oven for 10 minutes. For filling: Beat cream cheese and sugar until smooth and fluffy. Add the rest of the ingredients; beat until smooth (do not overbeat the filling). Pour into cooled crust; bake 1 hour or until lightly browned around the edge. Turn off oven; leave in oven 30 minutes. Chill in refrigerator overnight. For topping: Top with any canned pie filling or fresh fruit (such as blueberries, strawberries or raspberries). Dip fruit in melted currant jelly for a glaze. Arrange on top of cheesecake.

Pass It On...For perfect, or nearly perfect cheesecakes: bring all ingredients to room temperature. Beat the cream cheese until about the consistency of sour cream. Heavily butter the springform pan. Spread the batter evenly in the pan with no mound in the center. Place a small pan of water in the oven with the cheesecake to prevent cracking and to provide moisture. Serve sliced if it still cracks.

PUMPKIN CHEESE CAKE

10-12 servings

Crust:

2½ cups graham cracker crumbs
½ cup sugar

⅔ cup margarine, melted

Filling:

3 (8-ounce) packages cream
*   cheese, softened*
1½ cups sugar
6 eggs

1½-2 teaspoons cinnamon
½ teaspoon nutmeg
8 ounces mashed pumpkin
*   (canned or fresh)*

Topping:

1 (8-ounce) carton sour cream
2 tablespoons sugar

dash of salt
2 teaspoons vanilla

▲ Combine crust ingredients and press into bottom and sides of a greased 10-inch springform pan. Bake at 375° for 5 minutes. Cool. Cream softened cream cheese and sugar. Add eggs, mixing after the addition of each egg. Blend in pumpkin and spices. Pour cheese and pumpkin mixture into cooled graham cracker crust-lined springform pan. Bake 1 hour and 10 minutes at 350° (or until set). Test by inserting a clean knife in the center of the cake - it should come out clean. Remove from oven. Mix sour cream, 2 tablespoons sugar, salt and 2 teaspoons vanilla. Spread on baked cheesecake. Return to oven for five minutes. Cool and refrigerate.

PECAN ROLL COOKIES

50 cookies

1 cup margarine, creamed with
    4 tablespoons confectioners'
    sugar
2 cups white flour

1 teaspoon vanilla
1 tablespoon cold water
2 cups broken pecans

▲ Mix above ingredients together. Flour hands and roll teaspoons of dough in date-like shapes. Put on greased cookie sheet and crease with a knife lengthwise. Bake at 275° for one hour. Roll in confectioners' sugar while still warm.

Pass It On... "A dedicated volunteer force is one of the best ways to meet the many challenges facing this country. Along with making a difference in the life of our country and in the lives of others, volunteers make a difference in their own lives as well." - Elizabeth Hanford Dole, President of the American Red Cross and former Secretary of the U.S. Department of Transporation (1982-1987), Chairman, Federal Trade Commission (1973-1979); attorney; wife of U.S. Senator Robert Dole (Kansas). Recipe also contributed by Ms. Dole.

BRIDE'S DELIGHT

12-16 servings

1 cup butter
1 egg plus 1 egg yolk
2 teaspoons almond extract
1½ cups sugar

2½ cups flour, sifted
½ teaspoon salt
½ cup almonds, sliced
1 egg white

▲ Cream butter, sugar, egg, egg yolk and almond extract until fluffy. Add flour and salt. Press into an 8- or 9-inch round cake pan. Mix egg white with 2 teaspoons water and brush over cakes. Sprinkle with sliced almonds and lightly with sugar. Bake at 325° for 25-35 minutes (it should not brown). Serve cut in wedges either alone or with strawberries and whipped cream topping.

CHOCOLATE HEART COOKIES

30 (2-inch) cookies

1 cup all-purpose flour, sifted
¾ cup unsweetened cocoa powder
¼ teaspoon salt
2 cups sugar

1 cup unsalted butter, melted
3 eggs
½ teaspoon vanilla

▲ Butter a 15x10x1-inch baking pan. Line the bottom with parchment or foil. In mixing bowl, combine sugar and butter. Stir in eggs and vanilla. Combine flour, cocoa, salt; add the butter mixture and stir until combined. Spread evenly into prepared pan. Bake in a 350° oven for 15 minutes, or until a toothpick inserted near the center comes out clean. Cool in pan on a wire rack. Cover and chill 3 to 24 hours. Turn the baking pan over onto a cutting board or countertop and release the chocolate layer. Remove the paper or foil. Cut the layer into heart shapes using cookie cutters or a knife.

Pass It On...Save scraps and serve as "broken hearts."

ITALIAN FRUIT COOKIES

60 squares

1 cup shortening
1 cup sugar
3 eggs
1 lemon rind, finely grated
1 teaspoon vanilla extract

2 cups all-purpose flour
⅛ teaspoon salt
1 teaspoon baking powder
½ cup white wine
3 cups fruit preserves

▲ Preheat oven to 350°. In a large mixing bowl, cream the shortening and sugar. Continue mixing and add the eggs, grated lemon rind and vanilla. Mix flour, salt and baking powder. Add flour mixture and wine alternately to sugar mixture. Dough will be soft and sticky. If it seems dry, add more wine. Grease a 15½x10½-inch baking sheet (the type with a rim on all four sides). Spread ¾ of the dough on the baking sheet. Spread preserves of choice on top of the dough. Tear off chunks of the remaining dough and roll between hands to form long strips. Add a little flour if it makes it easier to work with. Place the strips on top of the preserves, forming a lattice pattern. Bake at 350° for 40 minutes until dough is golden brown. Cool and then cut into squares. Serve in paper cupcake cups.

MACADAMIA NUT COOKIES

40 cookies

7 ounces granulated sugar
1½ ounces light brown sugar
6 ounces butter
2 small eggs
½ teaspoon vanilla extract
8½ ounces all-purpose flour

¼ teaspoon baking soda
4½ ounces Macadamia nuts,
  chopped
6 ounces chocolate chips
baking paper

▲ Cream the granulated sugar, brown sugar and butter until fluffy. Add in eggs and vanilla. Sift the flour with baking soda and incorporate into the batter together with the chocolate chips and nuts. Divide the dough into two equal pieces. Roll each piece into a rope about two inches thick. Cut each rope into about 24 equal pieces. Place the pieces on sheet pans lined with baking paper. Bake at 375° about 12 minutes.

40 CALORIE OATMEAL COOKIES

3 dozen cookies

¾ cup flour, sifted
¼ teaspoon baking soda
1 teaspoon cinnamon
1 teaspoon vanilla
1 tablespoon water
¼ cup canola oil or any vegetable
  oil

½ cup sugar
½ cup dark brown sugar
½ cup egg substitute
1½ cups 1-minute oatmeal
¼-½ cup raisins
¼ cup walnuts or pecans (optional)

▲ Blend sugars, vanilla and oil; add the egg. Sift cinnamon, baking soda and flour; stir into sugar mixture. Stir in the oatmeal, raisins and nuts. Spray cookie sheet with non-stick cooking spray and drop by teaspoonfuls onto cookie sheet. Bake for 10 minutes at 350°.

GRANDMA'S RAISIN COOKIES

6 dozen cookies

2 cups raisins
1 cup water
1 teaspoon baking soda
1 cup shortening
2 cups sugar
1 teaspoon vanilla

3 eggs, beaten
4 cups flour, sifted
1 teaspoon baking powder
1 teaspoon cinnamon
½ teaspoon nutmeg

▲ Add water to raisins in a sauce pan. Boil briskly for 5 minutes. Cool. Stir in baking soda and let stand. Cream shortening and sugar until light and fluffy. Add vanilla, eggs, cooked raisins and liquid. Add sifted dry ingredients. Drop by teaspoon onto greased baking sheet. Bake for 12-15 minutes in a 350° oven. Remove from pan at once.

Pass It On...When creaming butter or shortening and sugar for a dessert, the consistency should look like mayonnaise before other ingredients are added.

SUGAR COOKIES

3-4 dozen cookies

1 cup margarine
1½ cups sugar
2 eggs
3 cups flour

1 teaspoon baking powder
½ teaspoon salt
1 teaspoon vanilla

▲ Cream margarine and sugar; add eggs and vanilla. Beat well. Sift dry ingredients, blend into creamed mixture. Chill dough well. Roll out on lightly floured board, cut into your favorite shape. Place on baking sheet and sprinkle with sugar. Bake at 350° for 10 minutes.

Pass It On...My grandmother always had the cookie jar filled with these cookies. She even baked the scraps. The cookies were wonderful hot from the oven.

POTATO CHIP COOKIES

2-3 dozen

1 cup butter
½ cup sugar
½ cup pecans

1 teaspoon vanilla
½ cup potato chips
2 cups self-rising flour

▲ Mix butter, sugar, pecans and vanilla. Add crushed potato chips and flour. Form into small balls and place on ungreased cookie sheet. Press balls with bottom of a glass dipped in sugar. Bake at 350° for 8-10 minutes.

HOLIDAY DELIGHTS

Bet you can't eat just one!

9 dozen

1 cup brown sugar
½ cup margarine
4 eggs
3 teaspoons baking soda
3 tablespoons milk
¾ cup bourbon whiskey
3 cups flour
1 teaspoon nutmeg

1 teaspoon cinnamon
1 teaspoon allspice
1½ pounds chopped pecans
1 box raisins
1 pound candied pineapple
1 pound candied cherries
1 cup coconut

▲ Cream brown sugar and butter. Add eggs 1 at a time to creamed mixture. Combine flour, spices and soda. Alternately mix flour mixture and milk into creamed butter mixture. Mix pecans, fruit, coconut, whiskey and add to mixture. Drop by teaspoonful into mini-cupcake liners and bake in miniature muffin tins for 8-10 minutes at 300°. Be careful not to overbake! Store in tightly covered plastic container.

Pass It On…You may also lightly brush peach brandy over top of cookies to "season" them for the holidays!

SCOTCH SHORTBREAD

A traditional cookie of Scotland

8-12 portions

1¼ cups all-purpose flour
3 tablespoons cornstarch

¼ cup + 1 tablespoon sugar
½ cup butter, cut into chunks

▲ In a bowl, combine butter, flour, cornstarch and ¼ cup of the sugar. With fingers, rub mixture together until very crumbly with no large particles remaining. Press into firm ball with your hands. Place dough in an 8- or 9-inch cake pan with removable bottom. Press out firmly and evenly. Impress edges with fork tines, then prick surface evenly. Bake at 325° until pale golden brown, about 35-40 minutes. Remove from oven, cut with sharp knife into 8-12 wedges, and sprinkle with 1 tablespoon sugar. Let cool; remove pan sides; transfer to serving tray or airtight container.

Pass It On...Wonderful served with fresh berries.

BEL VIEW FARM APPLE SQUARES

16 bars

1 cup sifted all-purpose flour
1 teaspoon baking powder
¼ teaspoon salt
¼ teaspoon cinnamon
¼ cup butter or margarine
½ cup sugar
½ cup light brown sugar, firmly packed

1 egg
1 teaspoon vanilla
½ cup pared cooking apples, chopped
½ cup walnuts, chopped
2 teaspoons sugar
½ teaspoon cinnamon

▲ Preheat oven to 350°. Melt butter in medium sized saucepan over low heat. Remove from heat and beat in sugars, egg and vanilla with wooden spoon until smooth. Sift flour, baking powder, salt and ¼ teaspoon cinnamon together; add to butter mixture. Add apples and walnuts; stir until thoroughly combined. Batter will be very thick. Spread into 8x8x2-inch greased pan. Combine sugar and ½ teaspoon cinnamon. Sprinkle over batter. Bake for 25-30 minutes, or until top springs back when lightly pressed with fingertips. Cool; cut into squares.

Pass It On...Mary Ann invited some of her children's friends, including my daughter, for a cookie bake-off. After the kids ate a few, she drove the girls to deliver the rest to elderly friends, favorite teachers, etc.

RASPBERRY CHOCOLATE CHIP BARS

2 dozen bars

1 cup butter
1½ cups sugar
2 egg yolks
2½ cups flour
1 (10-ounce) jar raspberry
  preserves

1 cup semi-sweet chocolate chips
¼ teaspoon salt
4 egg whites
2 cups nuts, finely chopped

▲ Cream butter with egg yolks and ½ cup sugar. Add flour and knead with fingers. Pat batter out on a greased cookie sheet to about ⅜-inch thickness and bake 15-20 minutes at 350° until lightly browned. Remove from oven and spread with preserves and chocolate chips. Beat egg whites with salt until stiff. Fold in remaining cup of sugar and nuts. Gently spread on top of preserves and chocolate. Bake for about 25 minutes at 350°. Cut into squares or bars.

Pass It On...When my daughter was an infant, I craved the company of other new moms but felt inadequate to clean the house and entertain. So I sent out postcards to eight other women with babies to join the "Buggy Brigade." Each mom brought her own sack lunch, stroller and baby. We strolled several miles through the neighborhood and park, stopping to eat lunch and feed the little ones before heading back.

Pass It On...Try substituting bottled Key lime juice and grated lime zest for the lemon juice and zest in a favorite lemon bar recipe. Add a scant drop of green food coloring for a fresh look. Use a glaze of powdered sugar mixed with a little lime juice instead of the usual topping of sifted powdered sugar.

FOOTBALL HUDDLE BARS

3 dozen

1 cup sugar
1 cup butter, softened
¼ cup molasses
1 egg yolk
1 teaspoon vanilla
2 cups flour

1 (12-ounce) package semi-sweet
   chocolate chips
1 cup raisins
1 cup peanuts
⅓ cup peanut butter

▲ Preheat oven to 350°. Mix sugar, butter, molasses, egg yolk and vanilla. Stir in flour and 1 cup chocolate chips. Press dough into ungreased 13x9x2-inch pan and bake 25-30 minutes. Cool. Mix remaining chocolate chips, raisins, peanuts and peanut butter in a 2-quart saucepan. Heat over medium-low heat, stirring constantly, until chocolate chips are melted. Spread over crust in pan. Refrigerate at least 2 hours. Cut into bars.

Pass It On...Mom and Dad worried when my brothers and sisters and I moved to various parts of the state and began having kids, that the cousins wouldn't develop close relationships. When the oldest grandchild turned five, our parents began Camp Cousins. Using the lake cabin, they invited the three grandchildren to spend several days around July 4th with them, no moms or dads allowed. Today each three-year-old looks forward to his or her first summer at Camp, and Camp Cousins has grown to 16 grandchildren ages three through 19. Even the teens wouldn't miss. Grammy and Grandad bake dozens of cookies and prepare favorite foods for the freezer. The older grandkids pitch in and help with the little ones. Everyone has a great time swimming, playing games, singing and enjoying each other — at least that's what I'm told. Moms and dads still aren't allowed!

PUMPKIN SQUARES

Perfect served with ice cream or whipped cream

20-25 bars

Base:

1 cup flour
½ cup butter

½ cup oatmeal
½ cup dark brown sugar

Filling:

2 cups pumpkin
1 (13½-ounce) can evaporated
   milk
½ cup brown sugar
¾ cup sugar

2 eggs
½ teaspoon ginger
½ teaspoon salt
1 teaspoon cinnamon
¼ teaspoon cloves

Topping:

½ cup pecans
2 tablespoons butter

½ cup dark brown sugar

▲ For base: Mix flour, butter, oatmeal and ½ cup brown sugar; press into ungreased 9x13-inch pan. Bake at 350° for 15 minutes. For filling: Mix pumpkin, evaporated milk, ½ cup brown sugar, sugar, eggs, ginger, salt, cinnamon and cloves. Pour over crust. Bake at 350° for 20 minutes. For topping: Mix topping ingredients together and sprinkle on top. Bake 15-20 minutes, or until filling is set.

Pass It On*...My mother fixed everything for Thanksgiving dinner except the turkey. My grandmother traditionally did that. I can still remember the excitement of her arrival with the big turkey in a roaster wrapped in quilts to keep it warm during the trip to our house.*

SEATTLE BARS

24 bars

½ *cup butter or margarine*
1 *(12-ounce) package butterscotch*
  chips
½ *cup dark brown sugar*
2 *eggs*
1½ *cups flour*
2 *teaspoons baking powder*

½ *teaspoon salt*
2 *teaspoons vanilla*
1 *(12-ounce) package semi-sweet*
  chocolate chips
2 *cups mini marshmallows*
1 *cup chopped pecans*

▲ In medium saucepan, melt butter over medium heat. Add brown sugar and butterscotch chips and stir until melted. Remove from heat and let cool, then mix in vanilla and eggs. Combine flour, baking powder and salt. Add to butter mixture, mixing thoroughly. Stir in chocolate chips, marshmallows and pecans. Spread in a greased 9x13-inch baking pan. Bake at 350° for 25 minutes (do not over bake). Cool on rack and cut into squares.

Pass It On...Neither my father's nor my mother's family celebrated St. Nick's Day on December 6th when we were growing up, but the Ripp family does! Our Sarah's birthday is December 7th, and this kicks off our holiday season. With the house already decorated, on the day of the sixth we put an old wooden shoe and Sarah's stocking on her bed. Then we go out to dinner. When we return, Sarah finds the shoe filled with candy and fruit, a book about Christmas in her stocking and a St. Nick ornament to hang on the little tree in her room. My husband and I enjoy this tradition as much, if not more, than Sarah does because we know this is what childhood memories are made of. Sarah will always have her special St. Nick ornaments and the Christmas books she loves so much. We hope she will someday be able to share these with a child of her own. But most importantly, we know she'll always have the memory of this special family time just before her birthday.

NO-NAME BARS

2-3 dozen

Bottom Layer:
½ cup unsalted butter
¼ cup sugar
5 tablespoons cocoa
1 egg, beaten

1¾ cups graham cracker crumbs
½ cup chopped walnuts, almonds
*   or pecans*
1 cup coconut

Second Layer:
½ cup unsalted butter, melted
3 tablespoons milk

2 tablespoons instant vanilla
*   pudding mix*
2 cups powdered sugar

Frosting:
4 ounces chocolate chips
1 square baking chocolate

1 tablespoon butter

▲ For bottom layer: melt first 3 ingredients in top of double boiler; add egg and stir to cook and thicken. Remove from heat. Stir in crumbs, coconut and nuts. Press into ungreased 8-inch square pan. For second layer: Mix all ingredients well and spread over first layer. For frosting: melt all ingredients in double boiler and spread over bars. Chill until set. Cut into small pieces. Keep in refrigerator in covered container.

Pass It On…These bars are a well-known Pacific Northwest confection. They are named after Nanaimo, a city in British Columbia. Many years ago a neighbor gave me a plate of these cookies and the recipe when I arrived in Bellevue, Washington, as a transplant from California. What a lovely way to welcome a new neighbor with a local tradition.

"Alone we can accomplish little, but together we can make a difference." - Angela Hackett Driver, Delta Delta Delta National President (1988-92). Recipe was also contributed by Ms. Driver.

KAHLUA BROWNIES

16 brownies

½ *cup margarine*
2 *(1-ounce) squares unsweetened*
    baking chocolate
2 *eggs*
1 *cup sugar*

½ *teaspoon vanilla*
¾ *cup flour*
½ *teaspoon baking powder*
1 *cup walnuts, chopped*
3 *tablespoons Kahlua*

Kahlua Frosting:
1½ *tablespoons cocoa*
1½ *tablespoons Kahlua*
2 *teaspoons butter*

½ *teaspoon vanilla*
1½ *cups confectioners' sugar*

▲ Melt margarine and chocolate together. Set aside to cool. Beat eggs until light colored, then add sugar gradually. Add chocolate mixture to the egg mixture. Blend in vanilla. Stir in baking powder and flour. Fold in walnuts. Pour batter into a well-greased 8-inch square pan. Bake in a 350° oven for 25-30 minutes. After removing brownies from oven, brush with Kahlua while still warm. When cool, spread with Kahlua frosting. For Kahlua frosting: Combine all the ingredients and beat until fluffy. If frosting is too thick, add more Kahlua. If too thin, add additional confectioners' sugar.

Pass It On...Pile any fresh fruit in a baked pie or tart shell and cover with a fruit glacé for a fresh and pretty dessert. Make glacé by combining any fruit juice with sugar and cornstarch: 1½ cups juice, 1 cup sugar, 3 tablespoons cornstarch. Cook until thickened and clear. A little food coloring can be added for enhancement. Cool and pour over the mounded fruit. For a party make an assortment of fruit tarts for an impressive dessert tray.

REALLY RASPBERRY BROWNIES

24 brownies

Brownies:

1 cup unsalted butter, room
*   temperature*
1¼ cups sugar
½ cup brown sugar, firmly packed
4 large eggs
½ cup unsweetened cocoa
1 tablespoon Framboise brandy
*   (clear raspberry brandy)*

1 teaspoon vanilla extract
1¼ cups flour
¼ teaspoon salt
1½ pint basket fresh raspberries or
*   frozen, well drained*
*   raspberries*

Glaze:

4 ounces semi-sweet chocolate,
*   chopped*
2 tablespoons Framboise brandy

2 teaspoons hot water
powdered sugar

▲ Preheat oven to 325°. Grease 9x13-inch pan. Beat butter, sugar and brown sugar until fluffy. Add eggs, 1 at a time, beating well after each addition. Stir in cocoa, Framboise brandy, vanilla and salt. Gently mix in flour. Pour batter into pan. Sprinkle raspberries evenly over batter. Bake until tester comes out clean, about 30 minutes. Cool completely in pan on rack. For glaze: Combine chocolate, Framboise brandy and water in top of double boiler. Set over simmering water and stir until smooth. Cool slightly. Cut brownies into 3x2-inch bars. Sift powdered sugar over. Dip fork into glaze and drizzle glaze decoratively over brownies. Let stand until glaze sets, about 30 minutes. Can be prepared 8 hours ahead. Cover and store at room temperature.

TWO SISTERS' TEXAS TOFFEE

To share with friends

1 pound

1 (4½-ounce) chocolate bar
½ cup nuts, chopped very fine
1 tablespoon corn syrup
1 cup sugar

1 cup lightly salted butter
3 tablespoons warm water
1 teaspoon vanilla
cooking thermometer

▲ Cook corn syrup, sugar, butter and water until the cooking thermometer reaches 300°. Immediately remove from heat. Add vanilla and stir. Turn into a buttered 10x10-inch pan. Sprinkle with shredded chocolate and chopped nuts. Press with fork. Let toffee set in a cool place until hard, approximately 1 hour. Crack toffee into small pieces. Store in an air tight container.

Pass It On*...One Christmas when my children were young, I decided not to put their names on any presents. I had been frustrated to have them always guess what was inside weeks early. Every Christmas I devised a new system so I could identify the packages, but the children could not. My three adult children still request a "secret code" for their gifts. Through the years I've differentiated packages by: kind of paper used, number of pieces of adhesive tape on packages, kind of ribbon or bows, numbers (a total of birth dates or social security numbers) or key words or phrases.*

CHOCOLATE TRUFFLES

2 dozen truffles

½ cup undiluted evaporated milk
¼ cup sugar
2 cups milk chocolate morsels
  (11½-ounce package)

½-1 teaspoon almond extract
1 cup toasted almonds, finely
  chopped

▲ Combine evaporated milk and sugar in small heavy saucepan. Cook over medium heat until mixture comes to a full boil. Boil 3 minutes, stirring constantly. Remove from heat. Stir in morsels and almond extract until morsels melt and mixture is smooth. Chill 45 minutes. Shape into 1-inch balls. Roll in almonds and chill until ready to serve. Set in candy paper cups if desired. Store in refrigerator in air tight container.

Pass It On*...Replace almond extract with vanilla or maple extract, or a liqueur such as Frangelico, Crème de Menthe, Chambord or Grand Marnier.*

QUICK AND EASY MICROWAVE PRALINES

3 dozen

2 cups pecan halves
1 cup sugar
1 cup brown sugar, firmly packed

¾ cup evaporated milk
2 tablespoons butter
⅛ teaspoon salt

▲ Mix all ingredients in a 4-cup glass bowl. Microwave on high for 12 minutes, stirring every 3 minutes. Beat mixture vigorously with wooden spoon until tacky. Drop by teaspoonfuls onto buttered wax paper. Cool until firm.

Pass It On...*Keep nuts in refrigerator or freezer to retain freshness. Lightly toast before adding to a recipe.*

ALMOND CHEESE PIE

An Italian flavor that's not too sweet

8 servings

Crust:

1½ cups graham cracker crumbs
½ cup sugar

6 tablespoons (¾ stick) butter,
   melted

Filling:

2½ cups (1½ pounds) ricotta
   cheese (highest quality)
¾ cup sugar
1 cup toasted, ground almonds
½ cup semi-sweet chocolate chips

¾ cup fresh whipping cream
1 teaspoon almond extract
½ cup slivered almonds, lightly
   toasted
shaved chocolate for garnish

▲ Preheat oven to 350°. Combine crust ingredients in a 9-inch pie pan. Press firmly and evenly on bottom and sides. Bake 10 minutes. Toast and grind almonds. Chill chocolate well and grind in food processor or blender. Beat ricotta cheese and ¾ cup sugar. Stir in nuts and chocolate. Cool. Partially whip cream, add almond extract, and beat until cream holds peaks, fold into cheese mixture. Spoon into graham cracker shell. Garnish with slivered almonds and shaved chocolate. Refrigerate for at least 6 hours.

LEGENDARY DELTA CHOCOLATE PIE

Divinely silky texture and flavor

10-12 servings

Crust:

18 graham crackers, crumbled
  (1½ cups)

½ cup butter, melted

Filling:

1½ cups butter (no substitutes)

2¼ cups sugar

3 squares unsweetened chocolate,
  melted

3 teaspoons vanilla

6 eggs

1 pint whipped cream

pecans or almonds for top of
  whipped cream

▲ Combine crust ingredients and press into two 9-inch pans. Let set. With electric mixer, beat butter until fluffy, add sugar, and continue to beat. Add melted chocolate and vanilla; continue to beat. Add eggs one at a time, beating 3 minutes after each. Pour over crust, chill and top with whipped cream. Sprinkle with nuts and finely shaved sweet chocolate. Chill thoroughly.

Pass It On...To honor her parents, my friend Jo and her brothers rented a trolley and took their parents on a trip down memory lane, picking up old friends at appropriate locations in the city where they picked up high school friends. Then they toured past the high school and childhood homes. College friends joined the group at a favorite university hangout. Off they went to visit the Tri Delta and Beta houses where they'd lived during college. The trolley picked up more friends from adult years at the neighborhood lake bandstand. The day ended at church for dessert and a time of sharing favorite memories.

THE BEST SOUTHERN PECAN PIE

8-10 servings

unbaked 9-inch pie shell
½ cup butter
½ cup dark brown sugar
¾ cup white corn syrup
¼ cup pure maple syrup

3 eggs, slightly beaten
1 teaspoon vanilla
2 cups pecans
1 cup heavy cream, whipped

▲ Preheat oven to 350°. Cream butter well, then add sugar slowly, creaming together well. If it curdles, don't worry. Slowly stir in syrups, eggs, vanilla and 1 cup of pecans. Pour into uncooked shell. Top with rest of nuts (laying the perfect halves in a pattern over the top, starting with the outside edges and working in circles to the center) and bake at 350° for 55 minutes. Cool. To serve, cut in small wedges and top with a dollop of whipped cream.

Pass It On...To celebrate Mardi Gras, my friends decorate with the traditional colors of green, gold and purple. Cari sprinkles gold coins and inexpensive plastic bead necklaces about the table top. She includes milk punch, Grillades, Southern Baked Grits and The Best Southern Pecan Pie on her menu.

FRESH RHUBARB PIE

8 servings

pastry for two-crust 9-inch pie
1⅓-1⅔ cups sugar
⅓ cup all-purpose flour
½ teaspoon grated orange peel

4 cups cut-up fresh rhubarb, sliced
2 tablespoons butter or margarine
milk

▲ Heat oven to 375°. Stir together sugar, flour and orange peel. Cut rhubarb into ½-inch pieces. Turn half the rhubarb into pastry-lined pie pan; sprinkle with half the sugar mixture. Repeat with remaining sugar and rhubarb; dot with butter. Cover with top crust or make a pretty lattice crust. Seal and flute. Brush the pastry with milk, and if desired, sprinkle with additional sugar. To prevent overbrowning, cover edge of pie with foil. Bake for 25 minutes. Remove foil; bake 25 minutes more. If additional browning is desired, raise oven temperature to 425° and check every 5 to 10 minutes. Serve warm or cool.

Pass It On: A juicy fruit pie is more likely to bubble over when topped by lattice than when the juices are held in by a top crust (be sure to build up a high pastry edge).

FRESH STRAWBERRY PIE

8 servings

1 baked 9-inch pie shell
1 quart strawberries
1 cup sugar
3 tablespoons cornstarch
2 tablespoons white corn syrup

1 cup water
pinch of salt
2 tablespoons strawberry gelatin
  (dry)
1 cup whipping cream

▲ Stem, wash and slice berries (reserve tips to use on top). Place in baked pie shell. Cook the sugar, cornstarch, corn syrup, water and salt until clear. Cool slightly and add 2 tablespoons strawberry gelatin (dry). Pour over berries in pie shell, cool and top with whipped cream.

WALNUT-CARAMEL PIE

8-10 servings

2½ cups sugar
1¼ cups water
3 tablespoons light corn syrup
1½ cups whipping cream, heated

1 cup butter
1½ pounds walnuts
1 egg
pastry for two-crust pie

▲ Combine sugar, water and corn syrup in large heavy saucepan. Cover and bring to boil over medium heat. Boil 1 to 2 minutes. Remove lid and continue boiling until mixture is a rich caramel color. Remove from heat and immediately add heated cream. Stir with a wooden spoon. Add butter and stir until butter and cream are incorporated. If mixture forms lumps, place over low heat for a few minutes. Stir in walnuts. Cool, then chill before pouring into pie shell. Roll out bottom crust and place in 10-inch pie pan and fill with chilled nut mixture, mounding in the middle. Fit top crust over filling and refrigerate for 1 hour. Beat egg and brush over surface. Cut hole in middle of top crust and remove (to expose filling). Bake at 425° for 10 minutes. Reduce heat to 350° and bake 25 minutes. Cool slightly before serving. Best served slightly warm.

NORA'S HOT WATER PIE CRUST

3 double crusts or 6 single crusts

4 sticks margarine
6 cups flour

½ cup water at rolling boiling
point

▲ Put margarine in bowl and cut into chunks. Pour boiling water over margarine and stir until it gets soft. Stir in 6 cups flour. Mixture will be soft. Store in refrigerator. Use as needed at room temperature. Roll out on well-floured pastry cloth.

***Pass It On**...When I was a little girl, I loved watching my grandmother roll out pie crust, always hoping she'd have scraps. She'd combine those scraps, roll them out, sprinkle with sugar and cinnamon, twist, and bake at 350° until brown. If she had enough, she'd bake the pieces in irregular squares minus the sugar and cinnamon, and we'd enjoy strawberries and whipped cream on top.*

***Pass It On**...My grandmother taught me an easy way to handle pie crust pastry. She rolled the pastry between two sheets of waxed paper, then put it in the freezer for 3 or 4 minutes. After the pastry stiffened, she removed the top sheet of waxed paper and inverted the pastry into the pie pan. After carefully positioning the pastry, she then removed the other sheet of paper. So easy — and leaves no messy clean up!!*

Pass it on

Pansy, symbol of friendship

PHONE MEMO

TO	Mary Estelle
FROM	Martha
OF	

DATE 3-1-90 TIME

AREA CODE

NO.

EXT.

MESSAGE: please send instructions for your "Garbage Can Cookout" — want to do it on 3-15

SIGNED

PHONED	CALL BACK	RETURNED CALL	WANTS TO SEE YOU	WILL CALL AGAIN	WAS IN

Dear Chris,
Thank you for the wonderfully decadent Fudge Sauce you gave me for Christmas. It was gone in a jiffy so it's great that you passed along the recipe as well!

the Rogers

TABLE SETTINGS

▲ To add color to the table, pour candies (foil wrapped chocolates, red hots, jelly beans, candy corn, mints, etc.) into crystal goblets.

▲ Traditionally my family has made placemats and table runners using Christmas cards from the previous year. Each family member takes turns selecting one card at a time for his or her placemat. Cards are then trimmed and arranged on the sticky side of plain or patterned contact paper which has been cut to placemat or table runner size. (It works better to arrange the collage first before actually sticking the cards on.) Each person writes his or her name and the date on the placemat. Once the cards have been secured, a sheet of clear contact paper is cut to size and put over the cards. Not only are the placemats colorful and practical, they also can be easily made by children for grandparents, teachers, etc. We make a different "set" every year!

▲ On a serving table, group crystal or silver bowls containing herbs or potted flowers. Plant the flowers in the garden the following day.

▲ Gather baskets of all shapes and sizes. Set serving dishes inside. Garnish with ribbon or greenery.

▲ Make an "egg tree" by sticking a white spray-painted branch into a clear vase filled with jelly beans. Place the vase on artificial grass. Hang eggs from the branches or glue on small Easter items.

▲ At holiday dinners, we personalize ornaments with the guests' names and use as placecards or napkin holders. The visitor then takes home a memento of the occasion.

▲ To set the mood, I place a candle in front of each plate using a different candle holder or a different color or size of candle. At other times, I gather various types of candlesticks for the center of the table. (To prolong the life of candles, put them in the freezer for a few hours before lighting them. They will drip less.)

▲ To add a touch of nostalgia and fun at our last family gathering, my cousin placed photos of the guests at their plates and scattered family pictures in the middle of the table. She used the same idea later as a graduation party theme, replacing the faces of paper dolls with first grade pictures of the graduates.

▲ Depending upon the holiday or season, one of my friends scatters candy or strings of berries or popcorn on the table. She adds different color napkins that match and places them in clear glasses.

▲ For a quick, easy and inexpensive centerpiece, keep an artificial evergreen wreath on hand. Place the wreath on the table. In the center, put any color candle under a hurricane glass globe. Trim the wreath with flowers, fruits, vegetables, bows or ornaments appropriate to the season.

▲ To include school colors on the table at a high school or college reunion, inflate balloons in the appropriate colors and tie to balloon sticks. Put styrofoam or florist's clay in the bottom of a basket. Line the basket with colored napkins or tissue. Stick the balloons at various levels. Against the basket, prop a stuffed animal representing the school's mascot. For better table eye contact, use long sticks or fill balloons with helium.

▲ Arrange a mixture of clear bottles on a mirror. For impact, use different heights and sizes. For a coke party, use coke bottles. For a coffee, choose different coffee cups and mugs. For an elegant luncheon, mix silver and crystal bud vases. Serve cookies, sandwiches or other finger foods from mirrors to complete the effect. (Note: Mirror squares can be purchased in various sizes at wallcovering stores. Glue felt on the backs or glue the squares on boxes).

▲ Last spring, a college friend invited us for a brunch. We raved over her beautiful and expensive (we thought) centerpiece. Nanette finally confessed she had simply taken a large grapevine basket and added greenery and wild flowers from their farm. Napkins the color of the Indian Paintbrush flowers provided a special touch.

▲ Display antique or fashion dolls on draped lace, velvet or satin fabric for a feminine table decoration.

▲ For a baby shower serving table, purchase a medium to large stuffed toy. Add inexpensive baby items such as a pacifier, bottle, bib, rattle, etc. Surprise the mother and father-to-be by letting them take the centerpiece home as a gift.

GARBAGE CAN COOKOUT

40 servings

1 new 20 gallon metal garbage can
18-inch foil
 empty aluminum cans
 cement blocks
40 potatoes, scrubbed
10 pounds carrots, peeled
9 pounds whole onions, peeled

7 heads of cabbage, washed
12 pounds smoked sausage
40 ears of sweet corn, shucked
 (optional)
2 bottles liquid margarine with 2
 tablespoons salt added

▲ Place foil-lined metal garbage can on cement blocks and build a fire under the can. Place alumnium soda cans filled with water on the bottom of the can. Add water until cans are covered. Place grill or wire netting over cans. Allow fire to become very hot (steam will start to rise). Layer the vegetables beginning with potatoes, carrots, onions, corn and cabbage on the wire netting. Place one potato on top. Cover and cook about 45 minutes. Check the potato on top; if done, add sausage, cover and cook another 20 minutes. When done, remove ingredients to separate containers. Cut vegetables into serving sizes and squirt with liquid margarine and salt mixture.

Pass It On...On April 16, my mother would throw an Income Tax Party. Now, when I throw my own Income Tax Party, I use tax forms as placemats and whatever odds-and-ends I might have left over. I look for quotations dealing with taxes; for example, Arthur Godfrey said, "I'm proud to pay taxes in the United States - the only thing is, I could be just as proud for half the money." I write the sayings out on signs (similar to candidate signs) and place them along the front walk and around the backyard. Fill a jar with pennies at the table where people get name tags and ask them to guess the number of pennies. The person who guesses closest wins the jar. Serve cake for dessert with a sign posted by the table saying "Let them eat cake." I try to throw the party outside so that pop, beer and wine can be kept cool in wheelbarrows and dinner can be cooked, believe it or not, in a garbage can. Everyone always has a great time and somehow forgets about the "sting" of April 15.

APRICOT CHUTNEY

Makes one quart

Note: Keeps indefinitely in the refrigerator.

½ pound dried apricots, cut in
  pieces
¾ cup dark raisins
1 (16-ounce) can of crushed
  pineapple and juice
½ cup wine vinegar
1 pound dark brown sugar

1 teaspoon salt
½ teaspoon each ground spice:
  ginger, allspice, turmeric,
  cinnamon
¼ teaspoon each: cayenne pepper,
  black pepper
1 cup water

▲ Mix all ingredients together and bring to a boil. Reduce heat and simmer about 30 minutes, stirring frequently so it will not stick to the pan and burn - add water if necessary. Cool, place in jars, and refrigerate.

Pass It On...*Serve with curried entrees or scrambled eggs.*

CRANBERRY CHUTNEY

Makes 7 cups

1 (16-ounce) package cranberries
2 cups sugar
1 cup water
1 cup fresh squeezed orange juice,
  plus peeling of one orange,
  chopped

1 cup seedless raisins
1 cup celery, chopped
1 cup apple, chopped
1 cup pecan meats, broken
1 tablespoon grated orange peel
1 teaspoon ground ginger (dry)

▲ Combine cranberries, sugar and water. Cook over low heat for 15 minutes, stir often. Remove from burner, add remaining ingredients, cover and chill for 24 hours.

LEMON CURD

Makes 1 cup

Note: Refrigerates for up to two weeks.

½ cup butter
zest from 2 large lemons
½ cup lemon juice

1½ cups sugar
3 whole eggs
3 egg yolks

▲ In double boiler, melt butter; add lemon juice and zest. Add sugar slowly and heat until dissolved. Beat whole eggs and yolks in a separate bowl. Remove lemon mixture from heat and cool to lukewarm. Add beaten eggs slowly to lemon mixture and return double boiler to heat. Cook and stir for about 20 minutes. Use to fill tart shells, between cake layers or as a spread for muffins.

Pass It On..."Zest" *is the colored rind of citrus fruit. Use only the colored part since the white pith tastes very bitter.*

GRAMMIE'S GRANOLA

A great Christmas gift

Makes 6 cups

3 cups quick-cooking oatmeal (not instant)
½ cup wheat germ
½ cup almonds and/or pecans, slivered or chopped (best with both)
½ cup coconut

¼ cup sunflower seeds, unsalted
¼ cup sesame seeds
⅓ cup dark brown sugar
½ teaspoon salt
2½ teaspoons vanilla
¼ cup canola oil
½ cup dark or golden raisins

▲ Mix all ingredients (except raisins) in 9x13-inch baking pan. Bake, uncovered at 250° for 1 hour stirring every 15 to 20 minutes. Bake until toasted. Add raisins. Cool and store in airtight container.

Pass It On...Serve with vanilla yogurt, plain milk, or sprinkled on fruit or ice cream. Increase or delete nuts, seeds, or coconut according to tastes or allergies.

NO SALT HERB BLEND

Use in place of salt to season

5 teaspoons onion powder
2½ teaspoons garlic powder
2½ teaspoons sweet Hungarian
   paprika

2½ teaspoons dry mustard
1¼ teaspoons thyme
½ teaspoon ground white pepper
¼ teaspoon celery seed

▲ Mix well and place in clean, dry container with a perforated insert for easy dispensing.

Pass It On...Craving salt might mean too much stress. Drink a glass of water. Try some slow, deep breaths. Then travel mentally to a favorite location and relax for a few minutes.

HERB POT FOR PASTA

▲ Plant the following herbs in a 12-inch pot to use for pasta sauces and dishes: Put one basil plant in the middle of the pot. Around the edge, plant one thyme plant, one sweet marjoram plant, one parsley and one Greek oregano. Put in a sunny location. Snip off the flavorful leaves for summer sauces, salad dressing and herb butters.

Pass It On...Other good herbs to plant are chives, rosemary, tarragon, sage, dill and mint. Use for seasoning meats, pasta, chicken, seafood, eggs, bread, rolls and butter.

VINEGARS

A wonderful gift packaged in pretty containers

▲ Place a mixture of mint, dill, basil, chive blossoms, tarragon and/or thyme in a clean and sterilized jar. Heat white distilled vinegar nearly to boiling and pour over herbs. Cover with plastic wrap and then the lid (a metal lid directly on jar will react with vinegar). Set aside and let steep three weeks. Taste and if strong enough, discard herbs and strain through coffee filter into a clean jar or bottle. Cork and label.

Pass It On...Make fruit vinegars by adding fruit liqueurs (such as raspberry or pear) to distilled white vinegar to taste. Seal in clean jars or bottles. Vinegar also cleans the residue in vases.

HERB BUTTER

Servings vary

1 cup butter
2 teaspoons lemon juice
2-3 cloves garlic
1 teaspoon white pepper

1-2 tablespoons dried herbs or 1½
cups fresh herbs (parsley,
basil, rosemary, tarragon, etc.)

▲ Put all ingredients in blender or food processor and blend well. Put in mold and refrigerate. Use flavored butter on meats, seafood, chicken, vegetables, rolls, etc.

Pass It On...*Keep cut herbs in fresh water in the refrigerator.*

JALAPEÑO JELLY

Makes 8½ pints

¾ cup ground red peppers
½ cup ground jalapeños, seeded
1½ cups apple cider vinegar
6½ cups sugar

1 bottle Certo
½ pint jars
paraffin

▲ Seed and grind peppers. Add pepper juice to vinegar. In heavy, large pan, bring to boil all ingredients, stirring occasionally. Let boil about 10 minutes. Remove from heat. Add Certo. Bring to boil again. Take off heat immediately. Let set for a while - stir occasionally so peppers won't settle at the bottom. Pour into ½ pint jars. Pour paraffin on top.

COCKTAIL NUTS

A sure hit for football games, tailgates or anytime

20 servings

1 pound raw peanuts, shelled
1 cup sugar

½ cup beer

▲ Combine all ingredients in a frying pan and cook over low heat until all liquid is absorbed. Place on cookie sheets with sides and bake at 300° for 30 minutes, until sugar has caramelized. Stir occasionally. Cool and serve. Store in air tight tin in a cool place.

CINNAMON PECANS

Great for parties or gifts

Makes 2 cups

2 cups pecan halves

Syrup:
1 cup sugar   **5 tablespoons water**
¼ teaspoon salt   **1½ teaspoons vanilla**
1 tablespoon cinnamon

▲ Preheat oven to 250°. Place pecan halves in a shallow pan and warm in the oven. While warming the pecans, make the syrup. Combine syrup ingredients and bring contents to a soft ball stage. Remove nuts from the oven and add to the syrup. Beat constantly until nuts have absorbed all the syrup. Pour onto a sheet of waxed paper until cooled. Store in an air tight container in a cool place.

Pass It On...One year, my friend Allison, invited our group to wear hats to our monthly bridge party—no baseball caps allowed. She gave prizes for the best hat, most outlandish, most feathers, biggest veil and most fruit. The grand winner was the person looking most like his or her hat.

SPICED CANDIED PECANS

8 (2-ounce) servings

1 egg white, room temperature   **1 teaspoon salt**
1 tablespoon water   **1 teaspoon cinnamon**
1 cup sugar   **1 pound pecan halves**

▲ Preheat oven to 300°. Beat egg white and water until frothy, but not stiff. In a bowl, sift sugar, salt and cinnamon. Pour pecans into egg whites. Stir until well-coated and moist. Add sugar mixture. Mix pecans until well-coated. Spread evenly on ungreased cookie sheet. Bake in a 300° oven for 30 minutes, stirring every 10-15 minutes. Cool and separate. Store in air tight tin in a cool place.

Pass It On...Christmas ornaments make wonderful stocking gifts for children. Put the year on each ornament, and by the time the child sets up housekeeping, he or she will have a nice collection of holiday decorations. It's amazing how mom and dad can't remember which ornament goes to whom, but the recipients can!

SPICED PECANS

Makes 1 cup

2 tablespoons canola oil   *1 tablespoon chili powder*
1 tablespoon Worcestershire sauce   *1 cup pecan halves*

▲ Place oil in skillet over medium heat. Add seasonings, then stir in pecans. Cook, stirring constantly, until pecans are toasted.

SARA'S CURRIED PICKLES

3-4 cups

Note: Best eaten after about two weeks.

3 pounds cucumbers   *1½ teaspoons celery seed*
1⅔ cups white vinegar   *1 cup water*
1 cup sugar   *2 tablespoons salt*
1½ teaspoons curry   *canning jars*
2 tablespoons mustard seed

▲ Wash and slice cucumbers into ¼-inch rounds. Combine the remaining ingredients and boil. Add cucumbers, bring just to a boil. Spoon into jars, attach lids. Refrigerate.

REFRIGERATOR PICKLES WITH ONIONS

7 cups

Note: Requires at least 24 hours refrigeration. Stores up to one month.

6 cups cucumbers, thinly sliced   *½ teaspoon salt*
2 cups onions, thinly sliced   *½ teaspoon mustard seed*
1½ cups sugar   *½ teaspoon celery seed*
1½ cups vinegar   *½ teaspoon ground turmeric*

▲ In a glass bowl, alternately layer sliced cucumbers and onions. In a medium saucepan combine sugar, vinegar, salt, mustard seed, celery seed and ground turmeric; bring to a boil, stirring just until sugar is dissolved. Pour vinegar mixture on top of cucumber/onion mixture. Cool slightly. Cover tightly and refrigerate at least 24 hours before serving.

Pass It On...*Place these in a French or Mason canning jar if possible. A fresh looking and tasty recipe with sandwiches.*

SWEET AND SOUR DILLIES

1 large jar

Note: Requires overnight refrigeration.

*1 (32-ounce) jar unsliced dill
    pickles*
2 cups sugar

1 cup vinegar
2 sticks cinnamon

▲ Drain, rinse and slice pickles lengthwise. Combine sugar, vinegar and cinnamon in a small sauce pan. Bring to a boil. Return pickle slices to the jar and pour hot liquid over them. Refrigerate overnight. Keeps indefinitely.

SPICY PEACH POTPOURRI

½ cup Star Anise
½ cup dried orange peel
1 cup dried peach slices
¼ cup cinnamon chips
⅜ cup whole allspice
⅜ cup whole cloves

¼ cup whole coriander
¼ cup cut ginger root
⅜ cup sandalwood chips
¼ cup revacersi leaves
10-15 drops peach oil
10-15 drops cinnamon oil

▲ Mix all ingredients together and store in covered container for 2-3 days to maximize aromas.

Pass It On...Last minute evening drop-in guests and no time to clean the house? I turn my lights down low, burn lots of candles and add a fragrant potpourri scent. Everyone thinks my home is delightful, and no one sees the dust. Just once, my husband inadvertently switched on the bright lights revealing the real situation. Now I add to my list, place tape over the light switch.

CRANBERRY-RASPBERRY RELISH

One quart

Note: Keeps about two weeks.

*1 pound fresh cranberries, finely
    chopped*
*2 Granny Smith apples, peeled,
    cored, and finely chopped*
1 cup sugar

½ cup sweet orange marmalade
*1 (10-ounce) package frozen
    raspberries, thawed and
    drained*
1 teaspoon lemon or lime juice

▲ Chop cranberries, then apples in food processor. Combine with rest of ingredients. Cover and refrigerate.

Pass It On...Great with turkey or game birds.

PUPPY CHOW

A great snack for children and a hit at potlucks

15-20 servings

1 (12-ounce) package chocolate chips
⅓ cup creamy peanut butter

1 (12-ounce) box Crispix cereal
2 cups confectioners' sugar

▲ Melt chocolate chips and peanut butter. Pour over Crispix. Stir gently until all are coated. Dump in large plastic bag with confectioners' sugar and shake until pieces are coated. Strain to remove excess confectioners' sugar.

Pass It On...January in Colorado can be a very cold month. People don't drop in much, so it can get lonely for a stay-at-home mom...unless she has a Soap Opera and Bon Bon Party. Sixteen moms and 18 little ones chose to pass up an afternoon of soaps for this one. Each guest arrived in a soap opera or soap opera watching costume (sweats, robes and curlers, even soap star impersonators). We feasted on candy, snacks, popcorn and potato chips. We played games, keeping track of scores with grocery coupons. When the kids got grouchy, we called it a day...but a fun one!

DECADENT FUDGE SAUCE

Great over fruit and for dipping

Makes 3½ cups

¼ pound butter
4 ounces unsweetened chocolate
3 cups sugar

½ teaspoon salt
1⅔ cups evaporated milk
2 teaspoons vanilla

▲ Melt butter and chocolate in top of double boiler. Gradually add sugar and salt. Stir in evaporated milk a small amount at a time. Heat thoroughly and add vanilla. Store in covered jar in refrigerator. Serve warm over ice cream, cake or as fondue for fruit.

Pass It On...I have a hard time remembering what foods I've served to which guests, so I keep a party notebook, recording the party day, guests, food, allergies and any details of interest such as theme, decorations and entertainment. That way I don't repeat, but I have a source of tried and true ideas.

JEZEBEL SAUCE

A wonderful gift and a great accompaniment with wheat crackers

Two pints

1 (12-ounce) jar apple jelly
1 (12-ounce) jar pineapple
preserves

2½ ounces horseradish
½ ounce dry mustard (small can)

▲ Mix all ingredients over low heat. Pour into jars for gifts.

Pass It On...*A wonderful gift and great accompaniment with wheat crackers and as a meat sauce.*

FOOTBALL TID-BITS

Fantastic for football gatherings

15-20 servings

1 package dry ranch dressing
1 teaspoon garlic powder
1 teaspoon dill

1 teaspoon lemon pepper
1 cup light vegetable oil
24 ounces of oyster crackers

▲ Mix ingredients together and add crackers. In a large storage bag, seal and toss the ingredients until they are well mixed.

Pass It On...*I keep my greeting cards in a large accordion file, each section clearly marked: birthday (family), birthday (humorous), birthday (belated), sympathy, anniversary, etc. I also jot down special sayings from cards I've received and add them to the appropriate pocket. Buying boxes of cards, cards on sale or just buying cards when I find ones I like and filing them this way always gives me a ready supply for any occasion.*

GIFT CUPBOARD

How to come up with something at a moment's notice

▲ Keep a "gift cupboard" in an out-of-the-way closet or drawer. Buy gifts, particularly on sale, with no one special in mind. Then when a gift occasion occurs, check the gift cupboard. Versatile items to keep on hand include:

▲ Small silver or brass picture frames (great for new babies, weddings, birthday or any occasion for both men and women)

▲ Neutral towel sets

▲ Stationery, notecards and address books

▲ Personal care items (hand lotions, bubble bath, bath gel, soaps, etc.)

▲ Bookmarks that can be inserted in a card

▲ "Coffee table" books

▲ Unisex baby gifts (books, shoes, socks and bibs)

▲ Baskets (can be lined with pretty fabric or an odd napkin), fill with almost anything such as a mug and coffee or tea, spices, homemade goodies, pretty soaps or a book (even one you've read and want to pass on)

▲ Potpourri (Pick fresh pansies. Dry and press. Add on top of purchased potpourri for a lovely, colorful present.)

▲ Small clay or ceramic pots (Plant basil or mint inside for a welcomed hostess gift.)

▲ Roll of quarters (appropriate for college students, hospital patients and their families or travelers)

▲ Mylar balloons (Save and add helium and ribbon to make a bouquet.)

▲ Greeting cards (Keep an assortment. Buy a cute card when you see it or even recycle special cards with a new date.)

▲ For a little girl, use a hairbow to seal a bag of cookies or candy.

▲ For children's gifts, pack cookies, candy or granola in an inexpensive toy - sand pail, bathtub boat, plastic tea set, baseball cap, dump truck, etc.

FOR THE BASIC KITCHEN
So you're moving to your first apartment or house...

hot pads

trivets

dish towels

apron

3 saucepans with lids (1-quart, 2- quart, 3-quart)

Dutch oven (4 to 5-quart)

skillet with lid (10-inch)

2 baking sheets (also called cookie sheets)

broiler pan with rack (in a pinch, rack can be used for cooling breads, cakes, etc.)

2 round baking pans (9-inch)

muffin tin (12-cup) or 2 muffin tins (6-cup)

square baking dish (8-inch)

rectangle baking dish (13x9x2-inch)

pie plate (9-inch)

casserole (1 or 1½-quart, 2-quart and 3-quart)

dry measuring cup set (¼, ⅓, ½ and 1-cup)

liquid measure (1-cup, 4-cup)

measuring spoons

stainless or glass mixing bowl set

rubber spatula, wire whisk, 3 wooden mixing spoons, slotted spoon, cutting board, can opener (preferably electric), bottle opener, cork screw, vegetable peeler, cheese grater, metal spatula, ladle, set of tongs, long-handled meat fork and ruler

4 knives (utility, chef's, serrated bread and slicing) and knife sharpener

colander, sifter and timer

tea kettle

pitcher

canisters

hand held electric mixer

coffee maker

salt and pepper shakers

FOR THE WELL-EQUIPPED KITCHEN

So now you want to make cooking more enjoyable...

pizza pan

pepper mill

garlic press

meat mallet

pie server

ice cream scoop

cookie or biscuit cutters (a flour-dusted glass will work)

egg separator

liquid measures (2-cup)

3 strainers (graduated sizes)

basting brush

instant-read thermometer

stockpot (8 to 10-quart)

non-stick skillet (10-inch) and skillet (6 to 8-inch)

baking pan (13x9x2-inch)

2 square baking pans (9-inch)

rolling pin, pastry blender and potato masher

double boiler

Bundt pan (12-cup)

2 loaf pans

2 wire cooking racks

6-8 custard cups

toaster or toaster oven

blender or electric, heavy-duty stand mixer

electric skillet

electric knife

cookie jar

kitchen shears

popcorn popper

metal apple corer

FOR THE GOURMET KITCHEN

So you're ready to try more challenging recipes...

springform pan

miniature muffin pans

tube pan (10-inch)

tart pan

large dough bowl

oven thermometer

candy and meat thermometer

bulb baster

liquid measure (2-quart)

pastry bag and assorted tips

cheesecloth

vegetable steamer

jellyroll pan

baking dish (11x7x1½-inches)

soufflé dish (2-quart)

egg poacher

funnel

spice grater

set of scales

set of metal or wooden skewers

citrus juicer

wok

coffee grinder

food processor

cake carrier

pie carrier

ice cream freezer

parchment paper

fancy gelatin mold

PASS IT ON...BY AIR, LAND OR SEA

The tricks of the traveling and packing trade

▲ Make a list of everything you plan to pack at least one week before the trip, so you have time to have everything cleaned and at its best.

▲ Pack everything for one day in a plastic bag that seals and pack all lingerie in shoes.

▲ Roll sweaters and other knits to prevent creases and conserve space.

▲ Pack hanging clothes on hangers in plastic cleaning bags.

▲ Put hose in a separate bag or pouch to avoid snags.

▲ Keep neckties from wrinkling by placing them in the center of a magazine and packing it flat.

▲ Spray tissue paper with your favorite scent and fold clothes and paper together. Clothes don't wrinkle and they smell good.

▲ Mix clothing from all parties in bags so that in case a bag is lost or misrouted, all travelers have some familiar clothing.

▲ Plastic bubble sheets between clothes layers prevent wrinkles and protect breakable purchases on the return trip.

▲ Plastic sandwich bags protect breakable or pressurized containers like perfume bottles, shaving cream and mouthwashes.

▲ Assemble a travel drawer of sample size toothpaste, shampoo, hairspray, etc., or keep a travel kit packed.

▲ Include a small travel alarm clock, just in case.

▲ In a pinch, sew on a button with dental floss.

▲ If planning to shop extensively, line the bottom to the suitcase or bag with brown wrapping paper for mailing items home. Tuck in tape and scissors. Pack a soft suitcase so that mementos have a handy return pack.

▲ Take a 75 or 100 watt lightbulb to make working or reading easier since most hotel room lamps use no more than 60 watt bulbs.

▲ Include in a well-stocked purse: a small tape measure, duct tape (for repairing luggage, mailing packages, etc.), $1 bills, quarters, small calculator, aspirin, clear fingernail polish and stamped postcards (for jotting notes to friends when waiting)

▲ When sending a child to camp: pack by the day, in sealable plastic bags or not, include a pre-wash stain remover, mail a letter early so it awaits the child's arrival, provide self-addressed, stamped postcards or envelopes with stationery and offer your child a 50 cent or dollar premium for their use.

RECIPE FOR A HAPPY HOME

4 cups of love (blends well with anything)

2 cups of loyalty (can improve flavor of any situation)

3 cups of forgiveness (recipe won't work without this ingredient)

5 tablespoons of hope (recipe can't blend without it)

2 teaspoons of tenderness (makes recipe easier to swallow)

4 quarts of faith (cannot fail - if this ingredient is included)

1 pound of laughter (when sprinkled lightly over everything, this adds a final, wonderful touch)

▲ Mix love and loyalty with faith and then blend with tenderness and forgiveness. Add hope, sprinkled abundantly with laughter, and bake in the sunshine. Recipe is more successful if served daily with generous helpings for everyone. "You can enjoy cooking if you season the food with warm love."

Pass It On... *"Our golden word to me is not giving up but a giving out, enthusiastically, and receiving in return some of the richest blessings that life can bestow." - Sarah Ida Shaw Martin, founder of Delta Delta Delta.*

CONVERSIONS AND EQUIVALENTS

U.S. Weights and Measures
1 pinch = less than 1/8 teaspoon (dry)
3 teaspoons = 1 tablespoon = 1/2 ounce (liquid and dry)
4 tablespoons = 2 liquid ounces = 1/4 cup
5 1/3 tablespoons = 1/3 cup
16 tablespoons = 8 ounces = 1 cup = 1/2 pound
32 tablespoons = 16 ounces = 2 cups = 1 pound
64 tablespoons = 32 ounces = 1 quart = 2 pounds
1 cup = 8 ounces = 1/2 pint
2 cups = 16 ounces = 1 pint
4 cups = 32 ounces = 2 pints = 1 quart
16 cups = 128 ounces = 4 quarts = 1 gallon

Approximate Equivalents
1 quart = about 1 liter
8 tablespoons = 4 ounces = 1/2 cup = 1 stick butter
1 cup all-purpose presifted flour = 5 ounces
1 cup granulated sugar = 8 ounces
1 cup brown sugar = 6 ounces
1 cup confectioners' sugar = 4 1/2 ounces
Spaghetti - 8 ounces = 4 cups cooked
Popcorn - 1/4 cup = 5 cups popped
Bread - 1 slice = 3/4 cup soft or 1/4 cup fine dry bread crumbs
Graham crackers - 14 squares = 1 cup finely crushed
Apples - 1 medium = 1 cup sliced
Bananas - 1 medium = 1/3 cup mashed
Lemons - 1 medium = 3 tablespoons juice, 2 teaspoons shredded peel
Limes - 1 medium = 2 tablespoons juice, 1 1/2 teaspoon shredded peel
Peaches, pears - 1 medium = 1/2 cup sliced
Strawberries - 4 cups whole = 4 cups sliced
*Carrots, without tops - 1 pound (6-8 medium) = 3 cups shredded or
    2 1/2 cups chopped*
Celery - 1 medium bunch = 4 1/2 cups chopped
Mushrooms - 1 pound (6 cups) = 2 cups cooked
Onions - 1 medium = 1/2 cup chopped
Potatoes - 1 medium = 2/3 cup cubed or 1/2 cup mashed
Almonds - 1 pound in shell = 1 1/4 cups shelled
Pecans - 1 pound in shell - 2 cups shelled
Walnuts - 1 pound in shell = 1 1/2 cups shelled
Cheese - 4 ounces = 1 cup shredded
Whipping cream - 1 cup = 2 cups whipped
Boneless meat - 1 pound raw = 2 cups cooked
Cooked meat - 1 pound = 3 cups chopped

EMERGENCY SUBSTITUTIONS

1 cup cake flour = 1 cup minus 2 tablespoons all-purpose flour

1 tablespoon cornstarch (for thickening) = 2 tablespoons all-purpose flour

1 teaspoon baking powder = ¼ teaspoon baking soda plus ½ cup buttermilk or sour milk

1 package active dry yeast = 1 cake compressed yeast

1 cup granulated sugar = 1 cup packed brown sugar or 2 cups sifted powdered sugar

1 cup honey = 1¼ cups granulated sugar plus ¼ cup liquid

1 cup corn syrup = 1 cup granulated sugar plus ¼ cup liquid

1 square (1 ounce) unsweetened chocolate = 3 tablespoons unsweetened cocoa powder plus 1 tablespoon butter or margarine

1 cup whipping cream, whipped = 2 cups whipped dessert topping

1 cup whole milk = ½ cup evaporated milk plus ½ cup water or 1 cup reconstituted nonfat dry milk (plus 2 teaspoons butter or margarine, if desired)

1 cup light cream = 2 tablespoons butter plus 1 cup minus 2 tablespoons milk

2 cups tomato sauce = ¾ cup tomato paste plus 1 cup water

1 cup tomato juice = ½ cup tomato sauce plus ½ cup water

1 clove garlic - ⅛ teaspoon garlic powder or minced dried garlic

1 small onion = 1 teaspoon onion powder or 1 tablespoon minced dried onion, rehydrated

1 teaspoon dry mustard = 1 tablespoon prepared mustard

1 teaspoon finely shredded lemon peel = ½ teaspoon lemon extract

1 cup sour milk = 1 cup milk + 1 teaspoon vinegar (let stand for ½ hour)

CONTRIBUTORS

Cris Franklin Abbott
Marne Mills Adams
Sarah Engelken Adams
June Rickard Aldridge
Sara Alenduff
Amy Alexander
Barbara Moore Allan
Shirley Perry Allen
Joyce Ahlers Allen
Holly Allen
Joann Deecroft Allredge
Cathy White Altenbern
Mary Estelle Kanning Amberg
Pat Kraft Ammon
Jen Anderson
Beth Billett Anderson
Ann Anderson
Deanne Beede Anson
Jinx Shinn Archambeault
Priscilla Armstrong
Rebeka Arrington
Marilyn "Lynn" Cropper Asprooth
Mary Wakeman Assily
Austin Alumnae Chapter
Marianne Austin-McDermon
Linda Backes
Mary Boyle Bahr
Charmaine Petrich Bailey
Pam Guffey Baker
Rose Hess Baldacci
Pam Guffey Balser
Alice Persons Bangs
Norma Hedderjohn Bannerman
Janet Barber
Linda Barker
Meta Barkman
Cathy Crawford Barnette
Siri Barsen
Barbara Bauhof Barth
Bartlesville Alumnae Chapter
Janet Mayer Bates
Mary Katherine Argondizzo Bauer
Diane Bauerle
Layne Bautista
Jean Rockwell Beach
Carolyn Read Beall
Laura Bell
Elinor Vinson Benefield
Adel Denton Bennett
Cindy Fuhr Berger

Claire Brinley Berner
Tricia Bernhardt
Cindy Orme Bertram
Audrey Pederson Bethel
Barbara Bevan
Linda Ramsey Biggott
Joy Carlisle Bixby
Susan McDonald Black
Jennifer Bland
Marlene Blaue
Holly L. Mazurek Bleicken
Fran Potter Bliss
Anne Piddington Boggiano
Mary Gray Bolin
Janice Wootten Bond
Kris Bonner
Kerry Bordeaux
Susan Borland
Mariam Born
Kris Confare Bottne
Corrine Wright Boulanger
Mable Grimes Bradley
Sandra Brandes
Frances King Breazeale
Martha Rice Brewer
Erin Donahue Brinkman
Sharon Parker Brose
Broward County/Ft. Lauderdale
    Alumnae Chapter
Lynne Cellio Brown
Sally Brown
Kay Highbaugh Brown
Ann Lee Bruen
Donna Grimland Bruno
Jacquie Larson Buckert
Barbara Peterson Bull
Holly Hirmon Bullard
Laurel Buntin
Kristen Distelzweig Burda
Dorothy Ulrici Burger
Joyce Tuecke Burkhart
Sandy Burmester
Margie Burnett
Amy Burton
Penny Brooks Bynum
Cynthia Byrne
Susan Sperry Cage
Suzanne Raymond Cahoon
Clarice Caldwell
Donna Cocca Callahan

Karrie Camp
Catherine Campbell
Marlene Hansen Campbell
Ava Curry Campbell
Gwen Suner Carey
Joyce Snodgrass Carleton
Christine Carlson
Barbara Koch Carlson
A. Eileen Carmouche
Marie Chinnici Carpenter
Ruth Pavlicek Carroll
Jackie Zittle Carter
Shari Carter
Barbara Castano
Jocelyn Cenna
Jane Chadbourne
Ginny Taylor Channell
Lindsay Tucker Chapman
Sheryl Gwen Chesivior
Chloe Childers
L. Elizabeth Lint Claflin
Nina Harris Clark
Lucille Clark
Robin Clawson
Jil Longway Click
Shirley Beistel Climo
Jody Cochran
Sally Hendrix Coleman
Jean Hopper Collins
Beda Atwood Collins
Colorado Springs Alumnae Chapter
Sunny Conly
Arlene Wayt Cook
Fay Freeman Cook
Cari Cook
Andrea Fuller Cooper
Susan Copsey
Ann Corbett
Christine L. Cragin
Jan Greer Crawford
Tina Kulbeth Creel
Carolyn Parks Cremer
Jody May Cromwell
Elizabeth Oakes Crowder
Cletha Cruchelow
Kathryn Culpepper
Mary Cummins
Rachel Cunningham
Dawn M. Cunningham
Nancy Martin Currell
Cynthia D'Ambrosio
Elizabeth Bowne Dame

Joanne Strietelmeier Daniel
Dr. Mona Hirschi Daniels
Ann Dannehl
Sally Murphy Davis
Deborah Smoak Davis
Cynthia Meurlot Deadrick
Meade A. Deklotz
Wendi Delatte
Kelly Demmel
Donna Easton DeNiro
Janice Zilar Dennen
Ann McCaslin DeRosear
Marilyn Jensen Desgranges
Suzanne Salbach Deubner
Margaret Nelson Dewey
Carol Fuson Dilatush
Jeannette Cassady Dittman
Jean Dodds
Elizabeth Hanford Dole
Cari Dooley
Colleen Dorsman
Marjorie Myers Doud
Pat Brown Dougherty
Alberta Downey
Nicci Leser Downs
Ann Lawson Drees
Judith Lee Driskell
Angela Hackett Driver
Dione DuBois
Nancy DeLong Dugas
Milton Duke
Linda Lewis Dumas
Helen Eckes-Roth
Linda Anderson Edmiston
Edmond Alumnae Chapter
Martha Wallace Edmunds
Sally Anderson Edwards
Elizbeth Wallace Empen
Normita Ellis Error
Margie Perez Esquibel
Molly Evangelesti
Rebecca Jones Evans
Ann Fairchild
Laura Faison
Mary K. Farrington-Lorch
Fayetteville Alumnae Chapter
Mary Scott Felix
Nicole Fenz
Ann Ferner
Connie Curpen Fey
Amy Fields
Mary Lou Axcell Finch

Beth Barnes Finley
Evelyn Wells Fisher
Lucy Puckett Fisher
Mary Yocum Fisk
Helen Acroyd Fleck
Mary Edith Fluckey Fletcher
Penelope Coiner Fletcher
Doris Lunde Flurer
Leslie Foley
Eleanor Kothe Forney
Martha Fortenberry
Eugenia Buckley Franco
Sheri Rhineberger Frantzis
Edna Fredel
Phyllis Fruitt
Joan Emhardt Fulton
Anne Snipes Garabedian
Nancy Ammentorp Garell
Carol Sibley Garner
Robin Garretson
Linda Pauley Gartner
Ann Gautier
Peggy Geib
Joan Hock Geiger
Janice Waidley Gemmell
Janelle Gerber
Liz Kendall Gifford
Pricilla Papel Gilbert
Letty Ann Ginn
Julie Gitlin
Rosemary Broadie Goings
Patricia McMahon Goodrich
Kitty Godman Gordy
Betty Spring Gorman
Debye Grady
Margaret A. Gray
Mary Hensler Grayson
Capitola Roberts Green
Sharon Green
Catherine Alznauer Greenblum
Gail Greene
Eileen Rougeou Gremillion
Ruth Gue
Mimi McGarey Guercio
Elaine Diehm Guilfoyle
Marion Kahman Gurnee
Karen Gustafson
Janet Tierney Guy
Chris Hepburn Guzzardo
Carrie Lee Von Haase
Shari Lewis Hacker
Jane Rothgeb Hackett
Cassandra Ashcraft Hackett

Marilyn Halamandaris
Marilyn Halbrook
Grace Hall
Helen Hawks Hall
Margaret Paddock Haller
Harriette Hamilton-Rothe
Melissa Hamman
Betty Joyce Hand
Eleanor Handorf
Pat Hansee
Cele Hansen
Patricia Cyr Hansen
Cathy Thompson Hanson
Jody Sparks Hantel
Midge Beasley Harbour
Elise Barnes Hardy
Dana Hillstedt Harmon
Lee Ann Lackland Harmon
Peg Hart Harrison
Helen Hartford
Kelly Christiansen Hassall
Judy Hathaway
Hattiesburg Alumnae Chapter
Donna Reid Hayes
Debbie Landmann Hayes
Nancy Andrew Hayes
Gene Chambers Hayes
Barbara Zimmer Hazelrigg
Marilyn Blotter Hazenfield
Lisa LaLande Heath
Virginia Buehren Heidrich
Kelly Witt Heins
Anne Leigh Hellbusch
Kristin Heller
Roberta Gehman Heller
Jean Helsby
Joyce HildeBrandt Henderson
Cele Hensen
Janet Lillard Henthorn
Diane Beth Herkness
Helen Chapman Herzog
Pam Herring Hicks
Margaret Gothard Hicks
Barbara Burgess Hildreth
Mary Walters Hilliard
Kathy Robinson Hillman
Bettye Schaubeger Hinson
Hillary Lynn Hodges
Kathryn A. Hodgkiss
Maryon Hoffman
Teresa Richardson Hogan
Joan Holmberg-Jackson
Janalee Smith Holmes

Cynthia Pettibone Hope
Marilyn Hrubes
Jeanette Harley Huber
Katy Huehl
Kim Huffman
Melody Huffman
Dixie Thronton Humphry
Suzanne Kellogg Hunter
Karen Cordill Hunter
Chrys Grafrath Hyde
Joan Bence Hyde
Mary Fletcher Iglinsky
Polly Coles Ikel
Lesley Iritani
Rosalyn Blach Jackson
Lisa James
Dorothy Jarmoska
Susan Sobolov Jaynes
Evamae Beemer Jensen
Candy Rougeou Johnson
Mary Ann Schroll Johnson
Dorothy Johnson-Smith
Ann Johnston
Brenda Ramsey Jones
Susie Jones
Marilyn Jones
Carol Cooper Jones
Laura Van Santen Jones
Peggy Newell Jordan
Sherry Hildreth Jorgenson
Linda Trojan Juba
Irma Swickard Judkins
Annichen Bohn Kassell
Debbie Keckeisen
Mary Ann Keesecker
Melissa Keisling
Lili Rambossek Keller
Ruth Keller
Patti Kennedy
Ann White Kennedy
Susanne Klaus Kennedy
Patricia Smith Keresey
Barry Kiick
Ruth McDowell Kinnard
Linda Luedemann Kiolbassa
Susan Kingsbury
Kingwood-Humble Alumnae Chapter
Ruth Troutman Kinser
Penny Kopp Kirchhoff
Carol Kirsheman
Jamie London Knorr
Marie Levie Knowlton
Ruth Pearcy Knox

Elaine Hanna Koisch
Mary Kooglee
Lynne Kopp
Mary Burdic Kratville
Heather O'Brien Krombholz
Patty Krueger
Marge Kruger
Christie Krugler
Arlette Marow Kuehl
Genevieve Hartley Kuraner
Chris Ladisch
Lafayette Alumnae Chapter
Delia Scott Lamb
Renee Lane
LeAnne Lange
LaVerne Lankford
Susan Parker Lauer
Marilyn Wahl Launspach
Barbara Laveaga
Karen Sue Watson Lawhead
Marge Lawler
Connie Curtis Laws
Jane Fearheiley Lawson
Dede McClelland Leigh
Mary Lois Akers Leonard
Susan Vaughn Lessen
Lynn Lessen
Kathy Hearn Leuelling
Robin Levatino
Paula Lewis
Jan Lindgren
Barbara Fortenbacher Lindrup
Mary Anderson Linkous
Sheila Linn
Angela Amorous Lodin
Carole Dickinson Logan
Evelyn Lomneth
Lori Longnecker
Shirley Libby Love
Judith Lowe
Louise Thayer Ludwig
Margaret Frank Ludwig
Patricia Jackson Lukens
Lufkin Alumnae Chapter
Cheryl Walton Macey
Cathy Eicher MacInnes
Jean Alspach Mack
Linda MacKay
Marilyn Newton Madison
Marjorie Hayes Maehler
Charlotte Denz Mahon
Katie Makarias
Jane Teree Maloney

Anne Marcus
Mary Jo Marshall
Jann Driver Martelli
Cindy Sommer Martens
Karen Martin
Joan Rose Martin
Jan Stone Massey
Ann Timson Mateer
Susan Mathews
Vickie Brown Matinkus
Pam Matthews
Joanne Matthews
Janet Berkman Maxon
Max's Opera Cafe/Sacramento
    Alumnae Chapter
Ann Maxwell
Ellen McCabe
Melanie Mahnken McCabe
Sue McCann
Anne Loughridge McClanahan
Carol McCloud
Cathy McClain McCrann
Marianne Austin McDermon
Ila Fern (Hoppe) McDougal
Maggee Gerlicher McElroy
Pam McEvoy
Nini McGahie
Beverly Hill McGeary
Mari LuMoon McGinnis
Kay Mackie McGrath
Lynda Burt McHutchison
Nancy McIntosh
Cheryl McIntosh
Camilla Buckley McKinney
Joann McMackin
Barbara Baske McRitchie
Margaret Tyler Meadows
Dody Mean
Betty A. Melton
Debbie Hillmer Mersfelder
Maribeth Messineo
Shirley Michael
Marcia Strong Middents
Florence Wilson Miles
Shelley Hubbard Millage
Jo Houdeshel Miller
Jane Coffman Miller
Tracee Price Mills
Joyce R. Mills
Marian Minogue
Helen Neissier de Modensi
Elizabeth E. Moeller
Sue Monroe

Kimberly Clagett Moore
Bebe Murrell Moore
Julie Sadilek Moore
Bobbi Olney Moore
Alice Burros Moore
Meridith Nye Moran
Danette Harmon Morgan
Donna Lou Archibald Morgan
Helen Jackson Morgan
Linda Olson Morgandale
Leslie Henshaw Morris
Burtine Beal Morse
Dorothy Morten
Judith Harris Moss
Beth Bickham Mouton
Laurie Mueller
Beverly Apple Mulkey
Susie Murnan
Sue Murnanh
Joanne C. Murphy
Pat Murray
Katy Goldtrap Myles
Lucille Clark Myron
Nacogdoches Alumnae Chapter
Debra Miskimen Naughton
Lisa Naylor
Frances Emmit Neil
Bernice Carlson Newberg
Maryann Newenhouse
Yvonne Gardner Newhouse
Ginny Nicklas
Carolyn Sattelmeier Noonan
Bebe Nurrell Noore
Kathryn Nolte North
Cheryl Keating Nugent
Dana O'Neill
Kathleen Davis Nye
Constance Bennett Oakes
Ellen Ofa
Doris Oh
Janice Oimeon
Patricia Engholm Olin
Sally Oloizia
Doris Olt
Omaha Alumnae Chapter
Janet Scannell Osborne
Mary Ellen Robinson Overman
Grace Annear Overton
Christi Owens
Mabel Laurence Paddleford
Annie Laurie Parkhurst
Gael Neugebauer Parks
Marlene Lungren Parrish

Karen Metzger Parry
Cynthia Quay Paynter
Peabody Hotel - Orlando
Sonja Pellow
Mary Carolyn Pendleton
Zoe Gore Perrin
Betty Littleton Persons
Jeanne Johnston Phillips
Kristen Kronemyer Pieper
Fannie Vick Pierce-Reiter
Nancy Foster Piper
Plano Alumnae Chapter
Peggy Broehl Plattner
Dorothy Pohnl
Betty Pollack
Kim Samuel Powers
Anne Rich Pratt
Sue Price
Ruth Dubuque Price
Carolyn Cramer Pritchett
Nancy Pritzel
Jane Pearcy Pruce
Ruth McDonald Prust
Elizabeth Harbison Rall
Pam Rayburn
Cathleen Synder Raymer
Marth Reavis-Swanson
Ruth Beach Reed
Nina Spearman Reese
Jennifer Dentinger Reevis
Sharon Reinhardt
Louise Reiss
Marriott's Desert Springs Resort
Jane Noyes Rhoades
Betsey Weston Rice
Martha Marrow Rice
Kathe Surles Riggs
Eve Woods Riley
Jane Chaffee Ripp
Mary Pat Hoff Ritenour
Vicki Roark
Patsy Reece Robb
Tracey Renee Robb
Kristi Staph Roberge
Donna Machemehl Robertson
Mary MacLeod Robinson
Diana Dixon Rotert
Lydia (Toni) Howard Rucker
Linda Ruiz
Mary Ellen Ryniker
Julia J. Salsman
San Antonio Alumnae Chapter
Beth Manilla Sandora

Nancy Fees Savoy
Su-Su Hackett Sawyer
Cecile Scanlon
Aletha Pitts Scarangella
Jan Schilling
Kay Gray Schirtzinger
Sallie Pope Schleder
Maria Schneider
Annette Hinkle Schnepf
Jeanne Northrup Schoedinger
Claudia Schott
Rosemary Carlstedt Schulz
Greta Schumacher
Joyce Clements Schumann
Jane J. Schwartz-Dinius
Marlene Wilcoxon Segin
Vickie Niewbaum Selzer
Anna Claire Seymour
Lynda Shaff
Diane Sharpe
Sara Frances Ferrell Shay
Priscilla Walker Shea
Mary Ellen Shea
Julie Sherburne
Genie Davis Sherman
Sara Chester Shoemaker
Shreveport Alumnae Chapter
Marilyn Morthland Shroyer
Joanne Shutrump
Anne Rivers Siddons
Barbara Walden Sileo
Sandye Thomasson Silvera
Lynn Bell Simmons
Wendy Pinos Simonovich
Krista Simurdak
Phyllis Johnson Sio
Harriet Franks Skeen
Julie Harkins Skillern
Jill Skinner
Nancy Smith
Kelly Liane Smith
Kim Smith Snowdon
Sallie Snyder
Kay Collins Snyder
Kay Snyder
Lisa Sauter Sommers
Sara Burwash Soracco
Mary Jane Souweine
Sherry Grisham Spears
Deborah Petrillo Spencer
Margaret Garlinghouse Sperry
Parie Stafford
Julie Stahl

Muriel Stanley
Anne-Marie Macpeak Staples
Joyce Tharp Starr
Barbara Mannoni Stave
Linda Stavropoulos
Mary-Clare Kalustian Stegmann
Sue Stenehjem
Robin Chapman Stewart
Christina Stimac
Barbara R. Stone
Ruth Zulauf Storey
Jennifer Peterson Streit
Jo Hudgens Suekoff
Alice Suhadolniks
Jessie Kerr Suitor
Ruth Sullins
Susan Mary Sullivan
Margaret B. Swanson
Mary Ann Swanton
Becky Sweat
Jill Talley
Carol Tarala
Laura Taylor
Donell Phillips Teaff
Tracy Teich
Martha Teppen
Patricia Thomas Terhune
Theta Gamma Chapter
Theta Sigma Chapter
Amy Frieze Thigpen
Kay Kuster Thomas
Carolyn Tolliver Thomas
Bari Lynn Lewis Thompson
Priscilla Fountain Thompson
Cathy Thompson-Hanson
Emily Cate Tidwell
Deb Oswald Tierney
Janet Tierney
Lynn Anne Molling Titus
Janet Tomesek
Bette Tompkins
Mary Noel Kenney Tompkins
Barbara Martin Topf
Carol Bliss Torrence
Ruth McClure Tout
Margaret Moore Towle
Betty Treffer
Pat Powers Trelease
Patty Trick
Sally Stone Trotter
Jean Tucker

Melinda Atkins Turner
Jennifer Maria Turner
Julia E. Tuthill
Carolyn Marshall Ulrich
Jayne Folks Underwood
Jacqueline Knoll Unger
Kathryn Childs Urbon
Chrissi Vaughn
Carol Ann Verhake
Julia Yanquell Viera
Waco Alumnae Chapter
Debbie Priebe Waggoner
Jane Roeser Wagner
Delia Cramer Walker
Katie Walker
Sis Wallace
Martha Adkins Wallbaum
Ona Finney Walls
Carmen Walters
Patricia Kutter Wampner
Mary Ward
Kathleen Potter Ward
Virgie Lueders Ward
Margaret H. Waters
Rosemary Pharr Collins Watts
Kathy Weatherholt
Judy Nelson Webb
Catherine A. Dickson Weber
Maxine Smith Weinman
Jean Berger Welch
Donna Axum Whitworth
Sybil Norton Wiegman
Judy Kruse Wilhelm
Constance L. Williams
Martha Toler Williams
Kim Wilson
Carolyn Wilson
Susan Pankin Wisseman
Barbara Wohlhueter
Susan Beaver Wommack
Marion Bassett Wootlen
Corrine Wright
Nan Yeager
Mary Foster York
Sarah English Young
Dorothy Jackson Young
Susan L. Ytterberg
Joan Zaglool
Barbara Hopkins Zakaryan
Karen A. Zecy
Peggy Ryan Zimmerman

INDEX

C

S

Notes ————————————————————————————————

Delta Delta Delta
P.O. Box 5987
Arlington, TX 76005-5987

Please send _____ copy(ies)   @ $17.95 each $ _____
                     Postage and handling @   3.00 each   _____
          Texas residents add sales tax@   1.40 each   _____
                                              Total   _____

Name _____

Address _____

City _____ State _____ Zip _____

Make checks payable to Delta Delta Delta

- -

Delta Delta Delta
P.O. Box 5987
Arlington, TX 76005-5987

Please send _____ copy(ies)   @ $17.95 each $ _____
                     Postage and handling @   3.00 each   _____
          Texas residents add sales tax@   1.40 each   _____
                                              Total   _____

Name _____

Address _____

City _____ State _____ Zip _____

Make checks payable to Delta Delta Delta

- -

Delta Delta Delta
P.O. Box 5987
Arlington, TX 76005-5987

Please send _____ copy(ies)   @ $17.95 each $ _____
                     Postage and handling @   3.00 each   _____
          Texas residents add sales tax@   1.40 each   _____
                                              Total   _____

Name _____

Address _____

City _____ State _____ Zip _____

Make checks payable to Delta Delta Delta